SMALL BUSINESS MARKETING MANAGEMENT

Ian Chaston and Terry Mangles

palgrave

First published 2002 by
PALGRAVE
Houndmills, Basingstoke, Hampshire RG21 6XS and
175 Fifth Avenue, New York, N. Y. 10010
Companies and representatives throughout the world

PALGRAVE is the new global academic imprint of
St. Martin's Press LLC Scholarly and Reference Division and
Palgrave Publishers Ltd (formerly Macmillan Press Ltd).

ISBN 0–333–99030–7 hardback
ISBN 0–333–98075–1 paperback

This book is printed on paper suitable for recycling and made from fully managed and sustained forest sources.

Cataloguing in Publication Data

A catalogue record for this book is available from the British Library.

A catalogue record for this book is available from the Library of Congress.

10   9   8   7   6   5   4   3   2   1
11   10   09   08   07   06   05   04   03   02

Printed and bound in Great Britain by
Creative Print & Design (Wales), Ebbw Vale

CONTENTS

PREFACE

A characteristic of Western world economies in the latter part of the 20th century was the decline in the number of large firms and the increasing importance of the Small and Medium Size Enterprise (SME) sector as the predominant source of employment. In recognition of the importance of small firms as a source of jobs, in the 1980s both governments and educational providers began to focus attention on the inclusion of small business management in university degree programmes and on expanding the provision of management training schemes for owner/managers.

In the case of marketing management, the initial response of course providers to an increased demand for university courses and management training schemes was to present small business marketing as being very similar to the practices utilised by large firms. The perspective of many academics and management trainers was that small firms, in the same way as large firms, should adopt a highly structured, strategic marketing orientation. As researchers in both Europe and North America began to study actual management practices in SME sector firms, however, it soon emerged that questions existed about the relevance of classicist marketing theories for optimising management processes in small firms. At the extreme, some academics argued that successful SME sector marketing is an intuitive approach rooted in the exploitation of social networks to acquire and retain customers. They proposed, therefore, that there was little point in exposing owner/managers to any of the formalised business paradigms that can be found in standard marketing texts.

The perspective of the authors of this textbook is that the actual marketing processes within small firms are located on a point somewhere between the two extremes of classicist strategic marketing theory and the intuitive, social network approach to marketing management. This opinion has evolved from extensive experience gained through activities such as research, delivering university degree programmes, developing Government-funded training programmes and working with owner/managers seeking to enhance business performance. With both owner/managers and students, the authors have adopted a perspective which says that although it is necessary to accept the preference for an intuitive, unstructured approach to marketing in the SME sector, benefits can accrue from complementing this managerial philosophy by applying more formalised processes to enhance day-to-day marketing operations within the small firms sector. Hence the purpose of this text is to demonstrate how formalised marketing theories and less formalised actual marketing practice can be combined to improve small firm market performance. The target audience for the text is undergraduate and postgraduate students participating in a small business marketing course and individuals employed in the SME sector.

Chapter 1 introduces classicist marketing, examines the relevance of such theories to the SME sector, examines the role of entrepreneurship and discusses the implications of transactional versus relationship marketing in the context of the small firm. A recognised constraint on the SME sector is the ability of firms to access and process information. Chapter 2 examines the implications of this constraint, reviews the information situation in start-up versus existing firms, discusses the role of accounting systems in the provision of data and introduces some basic principles of market research.

The scale of operations in most small firms is such that the survival of these organisations is often determined by events external to the firm, over which the owner/manager has no control. Chapter 3 reviews the nature of these external threats and introduces the concept of market system mapping as a path to identifying which environmental variables pose the greatest source of risk in terms of influencing the future destiny of the business. One approach to responding to market threats is to draw upon the resource-based view of the firm to identify internal competencies that can support successful marketing actions. Chapter 4 presents a competency model, examines how internal capabilities can influence performance and reviews the competencies that are required to underpin alternative strategic options.

By utilising knowledge of both markets and internal competencies, the small firm can evolve positioning options and identify potential sources of competitive advantage. Chapter 5 reviews the selection of an optimal market positioning. The chapter also examines how the move to 1:1 marketing by large firms and the advent of the Internet represent growing threats to the small firm strategy of avoiding competition by occupying a specialist market niche.

An ongoing debate in the academic literature is whether formalised, structured marketing planning has any relevance to small firms. Chapter 6 examines facets of this debate and presents the view that planning in small firms should not be directed towards the production of a detailed written report. Instead the activity should be perceived as an important route through to embedding organisational learning into the firm. A case example is provided to demonstrate the process of learning through planning, or 'marketing plearning'.

Chapter 7 examines the alternative options associated with innovation as the basis for executing new product and new market opportunity strategies.

The new product development process is reviewed in relation to the role of innovation to support strategy, the factors influencing new product success and the mechanisms for maximising the speed with which new products can be brought to market. Chapter 8 examines how promotional activities can influence customer behaviour, discusses how the resources available to small firms restrict promotional mix options and reviews the implications of the Internet as a promotional system alternative. This chapter also examines the role of networks to enhance SME sector promotional activities. Chapter 9 covers the topics of pricing and distribution management. Pricing is examined in relation to the influence of customer attitudes, sectoral conditions and the organisational circumstances confronting the firm. Pricing strategies and how the advent of the Internet can impact pricing decisions are discussed. Distribution is reviewed in relation to the limited channel power of small firms and also how this variable can be managed to provide the basis for a source of competitive advantage. The role of distribution networks is also examined.

As small firms grow, they will need to acquire greater capabilities in the area of information management. Chapter 10 examines why classicist views about marketing information systems are rarely relevant in the SME sector. An information management contingency theory is presented. The impact of the Internet on information management is discussed and a model presented on the evolution of real-time data management systems in SME sector firms.

The fastest area of SME sector growth is that of small service firms. Chapter 11 reviews the unique characteristics of service businesses, and materials are presented on exploiting service quality management as a source of differential advantage. Small firms often use entry into overseas markets as a strategy to sustain sales growth. Chapter 12 examines the relevance of classicist international marketing theory in relation to SME sector firms. Materials are presented on the role of networks and the factors that can influence success in overseas markets.

Throughout this book, the view is adopted that although successful marketing is dependent upon access to data, resource constraints and managerial skills limit the effectiveness of small firms to access and exploit information as a mechanism through which to optimise marketing decision-making. Materials are presented both on sources of data and on the application of information to enhance owner/manager understanding of how events external to the firm can impact on performance. To underline further the importance of exploiting low cost data sources, the text is accompanied by a free computer-based simulation which permits the reader to gain experience in the use of internal operational data as the basis for enhancing the effective management of customer needs. Please see back cover.

PHILOSOPHY AND PROCESS

LEARNING OBJECTIVES

After studying this chapter you should be able to understand:

1. the marketing concept;
2. the processes associated with mass marketing and rational planning models;
3. the role of relationship marketing in certain market scenarios;
4. the emergence of the concept of entrepreneurial marketing;
5. the strategic implications of merging transactional versus relationship marketing with conventional versus entrepreneurial marketing.

CHAPTER SUMMARY

Marketing is concerned with understanding and satisfying customer need. The original theories of marketing were evolved and developed by major US mass marketing, consumer goods brands in the 1950s and 60s. These companies applied rational planning models known collectively as a classicist management approach. Observations of service sector and industrial market firms in the 1970s and 80s suggested that classicist marketing may be inapplicable in certain market situations. An alternative philosophy to serve such markets more effectively is relationship marketing, where the primary focus is on building long-term customer loyalty. This can be contrasted with the approach of mass marketing firms which are orientated towards managing transactions.

Studies of small firms also reveal the inapplicability of classicist mass marketing theory and have led to the emergence of the alternative philosophy known as entrepreneurial marketing. Not all small firms are entrepreneurial however, because in sectors such as retailing and hotels, many are engaged in managing conventional business operations. Combining the philosophies of transactional versus relationship marketing and conventional versus entrepreneurial marketing permits the evolution of a hybrid marketing philosophy. Within such a hybrid model small firms may exhibit the attributes associated with transactional/conventional, relationship/conventional, entrepreneurial/conventional or entrepreneurial/relationship marketing orientations.

INTRODUCTION

All firms, no matter their size, are dependant for their long-term survival upon customers purchasing a sufficient volume of products or services at a price which causes total revenue to exceed operating costs. Achievement of this goal is usually made much easier if the firm fully comprehends the specific needs of customers and can make available products or services which deliver a greater level of satisfaction than equivalent offerings from competitors. The activities associated with understanding and satisfying customer needs constitute the basic elements of the managerial function known as marketing.

The foundation stones upon which many of the current theories of marketing management are based are those evolved by US corporations in the period following the end of the Second World War. Companies such as Procter & Gamble and Coca Cola demonstrated that by exploiting the benefits of mass production and then investing heavily in activities to build customer awareness of the benefits offered by their products, it was possible successfully to dominate markets. Their managerial philosophy of achieving a high market share for a standard product became known as 'mass marketing'.

Richard Tedlow (1990), a business historian at Harvard Business School, has analysed the life history of a number of well known US companies in the automobile, electrical goods, retailing and soft drinks sectors. From his research on company behaviour both before and after the Second World War, he has formulated some generic guidelines concerning effective strategies for establishing successful mass market brands. These include the following four desirable aims:

1. exploit the economies of scale associated with mass production to generate high absolute profits by selling large volumes of low margin goods;
2. re-invest generated profits in high levels of promotional activity as a mechanism through which to shape and mould market demand;
3. create a vertical system in which raw materials are sourced, production operations managed and products delivered to the final consumer. This vertical system usually involves integration within the firm of some steps (for example, the Ford motor company owning both car assembly and component manufacturing plants) accompanied by contractual relationships for other elements within the distribution system (for example, the

move by Coca Cola to reduce costs by supplying concentrate syrups to bottling companies who managed production and distribution in a specified market area);

4. having achieved market dominance through being the first company to exploit a strategy of high volume/low unit prices, create economies of scale barriers to ward off attacks from competitors.

During the 1950s and 60s, management practices within large American corporations tended to be based upon paradigms evolved by academics working in business schools such as Harvard, Stanford and MIT. Many of these academics were influenced by the writings of Alfred Sloan. This individual, who was responsible for rescuing General Motors during the 1920s recession, was of the opinion that the secret of successful management is grounded in the concept of applying rational planning to achieve the single minded goal of maximising profits. To assist in the formalisation of this theory, Sloan and his supporters from within the academic community, such as Chandler and Ansoff, drew upon the conceptual rules of business established by the economist Adam Smith (author of *The Wealth of Nations*) and the militaristic principles of the Greek and Roman empires. Described as a classicist approach to business, the principles of rational planning models as a path by which to optimise organisational performance have subsequently become the foundation stone upon which the syllabi of many business schools around the world have been constructed (Whittington 1993).

Unsurprisingly early writings on marketing management theory followed the theme of rational planning models, and early texts contained recommendations about the advantages associated with the strategic marketing planning process of the type shown in Figure 1.1. The entry point into the model

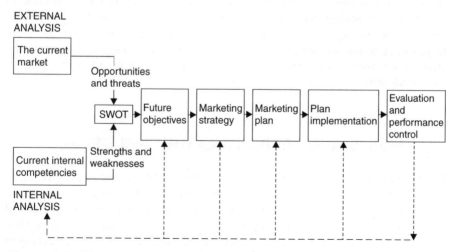

Figure 1.1 The classic marketing strategy planning process

described there is to execute a detailed study of both the internal and external environments confronting the organisation. This knowledge then permits definition of future performance goals, the strategy through which to achieve these goals, and the elements of the plan necessary for underpinning the adopted strategy. Delivery of the plan is achieved by utilising the '4 Ps' of Product, Price, Promotion and Place. Concurrent with implementation of the plan is the creation of a feedback and control system which provides the manager with the knowledge necessary to monitor effectively actual versus planned performance.

Even today, the rational planning approach is still recommended by leading academics as an effective approach to managing the marketing process. It also remains popular within many of the world's largest fast moving consumer goods (FMCGs) companies. It is necessary, however, to register the fact that over the last twenty years critics of the concept have emerged. One of its most vocal opponents has been Henry Mintzberg. He supports the school of thought which believes there is a need to place greater emphasis on observing actual management practices when seeking to evolve new theoretical paradigms. By drawing upon observations of real-world management behaviour, Mintzberg (1989) has questioned the basic premiss of classicist management theory which considers strategy formation to be a controlled, conscious process undertaken by man acting as a rational, economic thinker. He, and other individuals such as Cyert, March and Simon, believe rational, economic man is a figment of mythology rarely found outside of textbooks. Their perspective on the manager depicts an individual who is reluctant to embark on unlimited searches for information and instead is more likely to form an opinion on the basis of the first satisfactory option that is presented for consideration. These academics would also argue that as members of an organisation, managers survive by being willing to accept compromise in return for achieving acceptance of an opinion. Known as the processual approach to management, the ideas of this school of theorists downgrade the importance of rational analysis and instead perceive management as creating strategies through selecting those routines which, within the organisation, can be identified as contributing to success.

MANAGEMENT RESEARCH AND THE SMALL FIRM

In the 1970s, factors such as the impact of inflation, employers being forced to support the rising costs of social legislation aimed at the protection of workers' rights, and the growing success in world markets of Pacific Rim firms, all combined to influence the declining role of large corporations within economies across both Western Europe and North America. This reduction in the importance of the large corporation in Western economies was caused by events such as firms shedding labour (for example, in the European coal and steel industry), moves to automate labour intensive manufacturing process (for example, the introduction of robots into the car industry), some firms going bankrupt (for example, Pan Am), others moving production operations to nations in the developing world (for example, Texas Instruments) and others being taken over by Pacific Rim companies (for example, the UK computer firm ICL). One outcome of these events was a major reduction in the number of people being employed by large corporations. Further job losses also occurred in countries such as the UK, as politicians moved to reduce the proportion of GNP expended on the public sector and improve public sector productivity through the return of sectors such as telecommunications and utilities to the private sector.

By the 1980s, in many Western nations, many people faced the stark choice either of being unemployed or of starting their own business. In the UK, the trend towards self employment was hailed by politicians such as Margaret Thatcher as the advent of a new world which they labelled as the emergence of the 'enterprise economy'. Subsequently with *perestroika* acting as a catalyst which led to the fall of communism in Eastern Europe, as Government found it impossible to support the ongoing existence of large state run industries such as steel and shipbuilding, there also large numbers of people were forced to turn to self employment.

The outcome of both the restructuring of industry in the Western world and political reforms in the Eastern bloc is that by the 1990s, small firms became an increasingly important element of industrial economies in both Europe and North America. Recognition of this trend by academics has resulted in increased attention being given to acquiring an understanding of management practices within the Small and Medium Size Enterprise (SME) sector and the evolution of theories concerning the survival and growth of the smaller firm. A factor influencing this interest was that governments, having recognised the important job creation role of the SME sector, began to allocate large sums of money to create a diverse range of support services and financial aid packages. Concurrently as part of the processes associated with evaluating the effectiveness of such schemes, the Government also encouraged the academic community to undertake project assessment research.

There now exists an extensive body of academic literature concerning the factors influencing the performance of small firms. Gibb and Davies (1990) have suggested that these writings can be classified under the four major headings of entrepreneurial personality, organisational development, functional management skills and sectoral economics.

1. The *entrepreneurial personality* school, by building on McClelland and Winters' (1969) achievement model, seeks to link the personal characteristics of the owner/manager with the performance of the company. Kets de Vries (1977) and Gupta (1984) were able to show a correlation between

owner/manager personality and strategic decision making. Unfortunately although various studies have evolved typologies for classifying the entrepreneur, there appears to be conflicting evidence about the capability to clearly link these models to the observed performance of the business (Brockhaus 1982).

2. A common element in the *organisational development* school approach is to examine the relationship between the goals of the entrepreneur and the objectives of the organisation (Steinmetz 1969). In many instances, the discussion of relationships assumes the need for a move from an entrepreneurial to a 'professional' management style and is often characterised by recommended actions depending upon the firm's current position on an organisational 'stages of growth' model (Greiner 1972). However, given the subsequent debate on the needs of larger organisations to move in the opposite direction and become more entrepreneurial (Slevin and Covin 1990), some doubts must exist about whether the growth model philosophy should be offered as a normative theory through which to guide the activities of SME sector owner/managers.

3. The *functional management* school emphasises the need for the smaller firm to adopt a more formalised approach to activities such as strategic planning, marketing, finance and the installation of effective control systems (Brock and Evans 1989). Although this rational decision making approach has received extensive coverage in the literature, there is still only limited evidence to support the view that clear links exist between the acquisition of these competencies and the subsequent growth rate of the firm (Carland *et al.* 1989).

4. *Sectoral economics* studies usually seek to identify factors of influence within an industrial system as the basis for predicting potential for growth. They have been able to demonstrate clear relationships between the performance of original equipment manufacturers (OEMs) and growth rates of small business sub-contractors in sectors such as the car, computer and consumer electronics industries (Storey *et al.* 1987). Overall, however, these studies do not appear to provide the basis for a generalised predictive model for the management of SME sector organisations (Doctor *et al.* 1989).

MARKETING AND THE SMALL FIRM

In the case of research concerning the influence of marketing on the performance of small firms, early studies tended to focus on assessing the degree to which the SME sector was utilising large firm practices such as applying the strategic planning orientation models of the type shown in Figure 1.1. Most of these studies examined the somewhat broader issue of the relevance of classicist planning theory within the small firms sector. The common objective of many such studies has been to determine whether a relationship exists between the use of formal plans and the performance of the firm. Unfortunately the outcomes from this field of research are somewhat inconclusive. Whilst some researchers have concluded that development of a formal plan will improve performance, other studies have been unable to demonstrate such a conclusive relationship. One possible reason for this situation is the tendency of some researchers to use 'big business' language in their survey tools which are not understood by the small firm respondent. Bamburger (1980) in commenting upon this methodological issue advises that instead of basing research around phrases found in the strategic management literature, a more meaningful result can be achieved by examining broader frameworks of business behaviour. Similarly Gibb and Scott (1985) suggest that an approach which investigates the personal commitment and vision of the owner/manager is more likely to capture meaningful data on the utilisation of strategic management concepts within the SME sector.

Another factor influencing data on the adoption of a planning orientated approach to management is the variation in personality styles which exist within the SME sector. In an attempt to resolve this debate, Chell *et al.* (1991) have argued that as there is a need to distinguish between the small business owner/manager and the small business entrepreneur. This can be achieved by adopting a taxonomy of classifying owner/managers into four categories: Entrepreneur, Quasi-Entrepreneur, Administrator and Caretaker. Furthermore these authors feel that instead of just seeking to identify psychological characteristics, it is also necessary to determine how identified traits manifest themselves as modes of behaviour in particular circumstances. What has proved virtually impossible to validate, however, is the degree to which individuals exhibiting these different personality types perceive that utilisation of a formal business plan can contribute to enhancing the future performance of their firms.

By the mid-1980s, researchers such as Carson (1985) had adopted the Mintzberg philosophy of moving away from a positivist style of hypothesis testing and instead observing actual management practices. The results of such work stimulated the development of a somewhat different perspective on what might constitute effective marketing practices within the smaller firm. A basic tenet of this orientation is that observed marketing practices within small firms are a reflection of the fact that they face specific operational constraints which set them apart from larger organisations. Birley (1982) suggested that these constraints include (i) goals not based on analysis of opportunity, but determined by the actions which appeal to the owner/manager, and (ii) a lack of resources and/or knowledge which preclude decision making based on the classicist strategic marketing approach of analysing markets, selecting a long term growth strategy and optimally managing a detailed business plan. Carson *et al.* (1995) subsequently proposed that the lack of general management expertise and the limited number of customers will also influence the marketing processes employed by smaller firms.

7

This observation of actual management practice within the SME sector was a key stimulus to heightening the level of research activity concerned with the process of entrepreneurial marketing. This interest led to the formation by the American Marketing Association of the Marketing & Entrepreneurship Special Interest Group. Its annual conference proceedings are published under the direction of Professor Gerald Hills at the University of Illinois in Chicago. In an article summarising research to date, Hills and LaForge (1992) argue that four key factors of successful entrepreneurship – organisation creation, innovation, uniqueness, and growth – all have a special relevance to the precise nature of the marketing management process within entrepreneurial organisations. In this review article, the authors also support the continuing validity of Miller's (1983) earlier definition that any measurement of entrepreneurial style should encompasses the elements of risk taking, innovation and proactiveness.

Omura *et al.* (1994) by analysing scenarios in relation to the Schumpeterian Market Conditions and Kirznerian Market Discovery Dimensions concluded that traditional marketing is only applicable in situations where demand is stable and perceived customer needs are clearly understood. In the 'Omura Grid', entrepreneurial marketing is seen as a different process, most likely to prevail in those circumstances where the market is in disequilibrium and customers have needs which are not being fulfilled by existing suppliers. A similar conclusion is reached by Gardner (1991) who proposed that the influence of unsatisfied market need frequently results in entrepreneurial firms breaking with convention and exploiting opportunity through the provision of a new, innovative benefit solution.

It is necessary to recognise, however, that although entrepreneurial marketing may be a more prevalent style within the small business sector, crafters of management theory should recognise the views of Nevin (1994). He believes that in certain circumstances (for example, in a highly transactional, standard goods market in which customers are not interested in new, radically innovative products), some SME sector firms might find that the utilisation of a classic '4 Ps' approach to marketing is an effective path through which to deliver customer satisfaction. A possible example of this latter type of scenario can occur at the bottom end of the domestic replacement window market, where a number of small installation companies often offer the same product and the customer purchase decision is primarily determined by lowest available price.

EXAMPLE: BEATING THE BIGGER PLAYERS

Large consumer branded goods companies expend millions over many years to establish successful brands. Their approach is typically that of year-on-year careful analysis of the prevailing market conditions with modifications introduced to the marketing mix when it appears that another large brand might pose a competitive threat. One of the drawbacks of using a classicist strategic marketing approach to undertake an assessment of future scenarios, however, is the risk that the firm may overlook an emerging trend which initially appears to offer a limited incremental sales opportunity. Furthermore it is often the case that within large companies, even after a new trend has been identified, these organisations are unable to react with sufficient speed to be a 'first mover' within a market sector.

The ponderous, reasoned behaviour of large firms does, however, mean that small firms can sometimes launch a very successful market challenge. One such example is provided by Web Fuel, which was launched as the first breath mint available on the World Wide Web. Donna Slavitt and Amy Katz, two New York entrepreneurs, dreamed up the idea. The product aims to exploit two trends; firstly, that in the US breath freshener mints, as a confectionery category, are growing much faster than candy or gum and mints. Secondly, mints are the popular confectionery product amongst people surfing the Internet (www.webfuel.com). To add to the power of their idea, Web Fuel also uses 'in-tin advertising'. Advertisements inside the lids communicate the Web addresses for companies such as Amazon.com and generate over 15% of Web Fuel's revenues.

The tin is retailed at $2.95, somewhat pricier than the competition. The two entrepreneurs feel their product is more than a mint because they offer fresh breath, a dedicated online community of users who visit the site via a chat room and an in-tin Web guide (Poniewozik 1998).

THE RELATIONSHIP MARKETING DEBATE

As questions were being raised concerning classicist strategic planning versus entrepreneurial marketing in the small firms sector, studies of the marketing processes employed by large firms in both industrial and service sector markets were causing the emergence of a new school of thought which examines how firms can orchestrate internal resources and policies to create and sustain customer loyalty. Collectively this new orientation, which has both American (Berry 1983) and Nordic (Gummesson 1987) roots, is known as Relationship Marketing. Supporters of the 'new marketing' argue that in order to survive in highly competitive, rapidly changing markets, firms must move away from managing transactions and instead focus on building long term customer relationships (Webster 1992).

Not unsurprisingly, as with any new paradigm, relationship marketing attracted researchers from across various management disciplines who have articulated somewhat different perspectives on the use of the concept by organisations. One stream of research (Berry 1983) examined the concept in the context of service marketing. A second stream was concerned with inter-organisational exchange relationships encompassing buyer-seller relationships, resource dependency theory and social exchange theory (e.g. Håkansson 1982). The issue of developing effective and efficient channel relationships provided a third stream of research (for example, Buzzell and Ortmeyer 1995). Research on the role of relationships in value chains within the subject discipline of strategic management generated a fourth stream (for example, Norman and Ramirez 1993). Finally a fifth stream was that concerned with the impact which information technology has on relationships within and between organisations (for example, Scott Morgan 1991).

In an attempt to clarify and reconcile the various views which have been expressed within the literature, Coviello *et al.* (1997) have developed a classification system based upon a synthesis of both the American and European schools of marketing thought across the areas of service, interaction, channels and networking research. They concluded that there are two themes and within these, twelve dimensions in all. Under the theme of *relational exchange* they feel there are the following seven dimensions:

1. focus of the exchange
2. parties involved in the exchange
3. communication patterns between parties
4. types of contact between parties
5. duration of the exchange
6. formality of the exchange
7. balance of power within the exchange

The following five dimensions are those which Coviello *et al.* associate with the theme of *management activities and processes*:

1. managerial intent
2. managerial decision making focus
3. types of marketing investment made
4. the organisational level at which marketing decisions are implemented
5. managerial planning time frame

Some advocates of relationship marketing have suggested that traditional concepts based on the approach of focussing resources on the '4 Ps', which may have been appropriate in North American consumer branded goods markets of the 1950s and 60s, are no longer relevant in today's world. Gronroos (1994), for example, proposes that 'The usefulness of the 4 Ps as a general theory for practical purposes is, to say the least, highly questionable.' A somewhat less extreme position, however, has been proposed by Anderson and Narus (1991) who feel firms should adopt a segmentation philosophy ranging from building strong relationships with key customers through to utilising the traditional '4 Ps' approach for those customers seeking a standardised, generic product proposition. Their recommendation is that firms should balance customer orientation towards closer relationships against the cost/ benefit implications of sustaining relationships when selecting the most appropriate strategy to suit prevailing market conditions.

AN ALTERNATIVE MODEL OF MARKETING PHILOSOPHIES

A potential hazard with emerging theories of management is that polarisation of opinions may cause academics to reject alternative perspectives and at the extreme, begin to claim firms can only succeed by adopting their prescriptive solution. Fortunately the small business owner/manager is usually able to identify which espoused theories tend to exhibit an 'emperor's new clothes syndrome' and are capable of adopting those concepts which are best suited to managing prevailing market circumstances. Furthermore observation of such individuals would suggest that they often create effective hybrid management practices which are based on selecting, from various available theories, those elements of management practice most likely to contribute to enhancing the overall performance of their organisation.

In the case of relationship marketing, Jackson (1985) argued that the philosophy may not be relevant to all situations. To her, transactional marketing is probably more appropriate in those cases where the customer has a short time horizon and switching suppliers is a low cost activity. Thus a small computer manufacturer seeking a standard specification microchip can purchase this item from a number of manufacturers. In this case the purchase decision will be heavily influenced by which supplier is offering what are perceived as the best terms and conditions at the time of order placement. In contrast, where the customer has a long time horizon and the costs of switching are high, then the purchase decision will involve a careful search for a supplier who is prepared to invest time and money to build a strong, lasting relationship with the customer. An example of this latter type of situation would be a small engineering firm seeking to purchase the latest, state of the art, computer numerically controlled (CNC) machine tools. The company would carefully review the alternative project bid specification documents and make a commitment to the supplier who appears to work in closest partnership with the firm.

If one accepts Jackson's perspective, then the debate between transactional versus relationship marketing is one of choice; in other words, in virtually every industrial and/or service sector situation there are price oriented customers who respond well to a transactional marketing philosophy, whereas

11

there are other purchasers with whom a strong long-term relationship can be created. The objective for the small firm under these circumstances is to select the marketing philosophy which is most suited to the organisation's internal capabilities and/or the nature of the product proposition to be offered to the market.

The same proposal regarding internal capability and nature of product offering can be made in the context of an entrepreneurial versus a non-entrepreneurial marketing orientation. In accepting the emerging view that entrepreneurial marketing is a characteristic of the smaller firm, however, it is important not to fall into the trap of assuming that all small firms are entrepreneurial and all large firms are traditional transactionalists who use the classicist '4 Ps' marketing management model. For as Drucker (1985) has noted, some large firms utilise a strategic philosophy grounded in the delivery of superior satisfaction by continually seeking to exploit new, innovative product opportunities (for example, 3M Corporation, the founders of the Post-It market). Drucker posits that the reason researchers tend to associate entrepreneurial behaviour with the smaller firm is that this latter type of organisation is both structurally and culturally more able to respond rapidly to changing market opportunities. As Drucker points out, however, once an emerging opportunity is more clearly understood, existing large firms can then be expected to respond by launching new products capable of exploiting the new customer trend (for example, IBM's entry into the PC market following recognition of the success being enjoyed by Apple Corporation). It can be argued that some small firms are best suited to manufacturing standardised goods at a competitive price. Other firms are extremely competent at managing 'leading edge' technology and clearly this skill can best be exploited by adopting an entrepreneurial orientation of regularly launching new, innovative products. If one accepts the perspective that both transactional versus relationship and entrepreneurial versus conservative marketing are not mutually exclusive concepts, then this permits consideration of hybrid management models. The latter approach seems eminently more likely to be of greater benefit to the evolution of new theories of marketing than the trait of exhibiting an unchanging allegiance to a single, purist philosophy. Acceptance of alternative views of the world then permits the suggestion that all four of the following approaches to marketing are equally valid choices:

1. transactional-conservative style small firms which operate in markets where the customer is seeking standard specification goods or services at a competitive price and has little interest in building a close relationship with suppliers (for example, double glazing firms bidding on local government replacement window contracts).
2. relationship-conservative style small firms which operate in markets where the customer is seeking standard specification goods or services

but is willing to work closely with suppliers to optimise quality and/or obtain mutual benefits from creating an effective purchase and delivery system (for example, engineering firms supplying components to OEMs who operate JIT/TQM manufacturing philosophies).

3. transactional-entrepreneurial style small firms which operate in markets where customers are seeking innovative products or services which can be procured without forming a close relationship with suppliers (for example, software houses using direct mail to market low-cost, customised spreadsheet packages which solve sector specific management accounting problems).

4. relationship-entrepreneurial style small firms which operate in markets where customers work in partnership with suppliers to develop innovative new products or services (for example, producers of low volume, customised microprocessors utilised by specialist machine tool manufacturers).

One way of presenting these alternative marketing positions is to assume there are two dimensions influencing marketing strategy: closeness to customer and level of entrepreneurial activity. By using these two dimensions, it is possible to create a matrix of the type shown in Figure 1.2 to visualise the four alternative marketing styles that might offer alternative strategic choices to a firm.

The possible existence of alternative hybrid marketing styles stimulated initiation of a research project (Chaston 1998) to examine whether differences in style can be measured and whether style influences the overall performance of the firm. Miller (1983) has proposed that entrepreneurial style encompasses the elements of risk taking, innovation and proactiveness. Covin and Slevin (1988) applied this definition to evolve and validate a tool which uses statements of managerial process to measure the degree to which respondent

CLOSENESS WITH CUSTOMER

T Y P E O F	Innovative product	(3) Transactional- entrepreneurial marketing style	(4) Relationship- entrepreneurial marketing style
P R O D U C T	Standard product	(1) Transactional- conservative marketing style	(2) Relationship- conservative marketing style
		Low	High

Figure 1.2   Alternative marketing styles

13

firms exhibit an entrepreneurial style. Although a review of the literature provided a number of different descriptions of the characteristics exhibited by relationship orientated organisations, no appropriate scale appears to exist which can be used as research tool. Anderson and Narus (1991) have suggested that marketing strategy can be considered as a continuum ranging from transactional through to a relationship orientation. By adopting the same research design as in the Covin/Slevin study, it is also possible to determine a firm's position on a strategic continuum by seeking owner/managers' level of agreement with descriptive statements concerning management of customer relations.

SME sector UK manufacturing firms were asked to respond to statements concerning entrepreneurial and relationship marketing styles. Firms were classified into the four styles identified above according to whether their entrepreneurial and relationship scores were above or below the mean value for these two indices. Summary statistics for the performance of the four marketing styles are shown in Table 1.1. It can been seen from these data that the transactional-entrepreneurial firms have the highest overall sales growth rate, relationship-entrepreneurial and relationship-conservative firms have slightly lower, but similar, growth rates and conservative-transactional firms have the lowest growth rate.

The results of this study appear to support the possible existence of four different marketing styles which reflect a merger of the concepts of relationship and entrepreneurial marketing. In terms of commenting upon which is the most appropriate style for small UK manufacturing firms, on the basis of the significantly lower average sales revenue reported for transactional-conservative style firms, it does appear that this is the least appealing strategic option. This is in contrast with transactional-entrepreneurial, relationship-conservative or relationship-entrepreneurial marketing styles, all of which, on average, achieve higher revenue growth.

The results of the study should not, however, be used to make prescriptive recommendations about which is the best marketing style for a small firm to adopt. It is clearly very necessary to recognise that market circumstances and/ or the orientation of the owner/manager will influence this decision. For example a firm may operate in a market where customers are essentially transactionally orientated and/or the benefits of moving closer to customer

Table 1.1 Summary statistics by style of management

Style	Number of firms	Mean sales growth % p.a.
Transactional-entrepreneurial	22	5.71
Relationship-entrepreneurial	31	5.06
Relationship-conservative	23	5.09
Transactional-conservative	28	3.59

are greatly outweighed by the costs a firm would encounter in implementing such actions. Alternatively if the personal aspiration of the owner/manager is to develop radically innovative new product, then building extremely close links with customers might limit the firm's ability to become a leading edge supplier of technology because the pace of innovation might be constrained by the conservative nature of the average customer in their industrial sector.

EXAMPLE: A RELATIONSHIP-ENTREPRENEURIAL, ORIENTATION

Cross and Smith (1995) have provided a useful example of how by exploiting the opportunities presented by e-commerce, a small firm can successfully adopt an entrepreneurial approach to building stronger relationships with customers. PrePRESS Solutions Inc is $50 million player in the US $2.3 billion industry of image setting manufacturers. When in the late 1980s pre-press publishing capabilities began to migrate to less expensive computer platforms (from mini-computers to desktop systems), PrePRESS augmented their direct sales force with a catalogue business catering to new buyers looking for lower cost computer hardware and software. When fax-on-demand began to appear in the market, the company adopted this technology to communicate lengthy technical specifications to their customers. Then in April 1995, PrePRESS opened their first commercial website which took the innovative step of carrying both sector and company specific information. Contained within an ever evolving site are features such as an on-screen newspaper updated daily, the Cafe Moire chat site, a convention centre covering major trade shows in the industry, a free reference library, the PrePRESS online superstore and a print shop where users can download tips and tools for improving their pre-press processes.

FEATURES OF ALTERNATIVE MARKETING PHILOSOPHIES

The very different natures of the alternative marketing philosophies' styles highlighted in Figure 1.2 suggest that the following operational orientations will be needed to drive the marketing process within these four types of small firm:

1. *Transactional-conservative orientated small firms*
   Price/quality/value product combination superior to that of competition
   Standardised products
   Excellence in managing production and distribution logistics

Information system designed to rapidly identify manufacturing and/or logistic errors
2. *Relationship-conservative orientated small firms*
   Product/service combination which delivers complete customer-specific solution
   Product solution based on standard specification for industrial sector
   Obsession with finding even more effective solutions to customer problems
   Information systems which rapidly identify errors in solution provision
   Culture of all employees committed to working closely with counterparts within the customer organisation
3. *Transactional-entrepreneurial orientated small firms*
   Product offering outstanding superior performance versus competition
   Orientation towards even more innovation and extending the performance boundaries of existing products
   Excellence in entrepreneurial activity by all members of the workforce
   Culture of employees always challenging current methods of operation
4. *Relationship-entrepreneurial orientated small firms*
   Product contributes to ensuring customer output delivers superior performance relative to their competitors
   Orientation towards assisting customer achieve even more innovation and extending the boundaries of their existing products
   Excellence in joint entrepreneurial activity between employees and their counterparts in the customer organisation
   Culture of employees always working with their counterparts in the customer organisation to jointly challenge current operations within both organisations

At the end of the 1980s, marketing as a management discipline in the Western world entered a period where disagreements emerged between some academics seeking to defend their views about the applicability of the transactional, relationship, conservative and entrepreneurial marketing styles. Thankfully after a period of debate, the wiser heads amongst both academics and marketing practitioners prevailed. Their conclusion was that the identification of different marketing styles should not be perceived as an indication of significant errors having been made by earlier researchers. Instead the identified variances in organisational behaviour should be taken as evidence of the diversity of managerial practices that exist in the real world. As a consequence it is now accepted that variation across areas such as markets, customer behaviours, process technologies and organisational competencies are indications of the need for small firm marketing management theory to move away from a single, purist managerial concept towards a multi-faceted approach in which strategic decisions are influenced by whether the organisation has adopted a transactional or relationship and/or conservative or entrepreneurial orientation to manage the customer satisfaction process.

The concept of alternative marketing styles should not however, be interpreted as a recommendation that small firm owner/managers should reject all aspects of classicist strategic marketing thinking. In highly transactional markets, where customers seek standardised goods (such as groceries) then possibly many of the basic principles of marketing as originally developed by the large, multinational branded goods companies will probably remain relevant for the foreseeable future. Instead what is being proposed is the philosophy of adopting a more flexible approach to the management of the marketing process, whereby the small firm first determines the nature of customer need and then selects a marketing style most suited to prevailing circumstances. Thus, for example, if it is apparent that customer satisfaction can best be achieved through a new, innovative benefit solution, then perhaps an entrepreneurial marketing orientation would be the most effective route by which to generate sales revenue. Alternatively if customers exhibit a homogenous need for a standard product then possibly classicist strategic marketing centred around promotion and price may be the best approach.

DISCUSSION QUESTIONS

1. Review the processes associated with managing a mass marketing operation. Where possible illustrate the analysis with real life examples of known brands.
2. What are the factors which have caused small firms to become the dominant source of employment in many Western nation economies in the last 25 years? Which are the factors believed to influence the market performance of small firms?
3. Why is classicist mass marketing considered as an inappropriate management philosophy for most small firms? What alternative marketing philosophies might be considered as more appropriate for assisting small firms effectively to manage their marketing operations?

REFERENCES

Anderson, J.C. and Narus, J.A. (1991), 'Partnering as a focused market strategy', *California Management Review*, Spring, pp. 95–113.

Bamburger, I. (1980), 'Development and growth of firms', unpublished paper, University of Rennes.

Berry, L.L. (1983), 'Relationship marketing', in Berry, L.L., Shostack, G.L. and Upah, G.D. (eds), *Emerging Perspectives on Service Marketing*, American Marketing Association, Chicago, pp. 25–8.

Birley, S. (1982), 'Corporate strategy and the small firm', *Journal of General Management*, Vol. 8, No. 2, pp. 82–6.

Brock, W.A. and Evans, D.A. (1989), 'Small business economics', *Small Business Economics*, Vol. 1, No. 1, pp. 7–21.

Brockhaus, R.H. (1982), 'Psychology of the entrepreneur', in Kent, C.A., Sexton, D.L. and Vesper, K.H. (eds), *Encyclopedia of Entrepreneurship*, Prentice Hall, Englewood Cliffs.

Buzzell, R.D. and Ortmeyer, G. (1995), 'Channel partnerships streamline distribution', *Sloan Management Review*, Spring, pp. 85–96.

Carland, J.W., Carland, J.C. and Abbey, C. (1989), 'An assessment of the psychological determinants of planning in small business', *International Small Business Journal*, Vol. 7, No. 4, pp. 23–33.

Carson, D.J. (1985), 'The evolution of marketing in small firms', *European Journal of Marketing*, Vol. 19, No. 5, pp. 7–16.

Carson, D.J., Cromie, S., Mcgowan, P. and Hill, J. (1995), *Marketing and Entrepreneurship in SMEs*, Prentice Hall, London.

Chaston, I. (1998), 'Evolving "new marketing philosophies" by merging existing concepts: application of process within small high-technology firms', *Journal of Marketing Management*, Vol. 14, No. 4, pp. 32–46.

Chell, E., Haworth, J. and Bearley, S. (1991), *The Entrepreneurial Personality*, Routledge, London.

Coviello, N.E., Brodie, R.J. and Munro, H.J. (1997), 'Understanding contemporary marketing: development of a classification system', *Journal of Marketing Management*, Vol. 13, No. 6, pp. 501–22.

Covin, J.G. and Slevin, D.P. (1988), 'The influence of organisational structure on the utility of an entrepreneurial top management style', *Journal of Management Studies*, Vol. 25, pp. 217–37.

Cross, R. And Smith, J. (1995), 'Internet marketing that works for customers', *Direct Marketing*, Vol. 58, No. 4, pp. 22–5.

Doctor, J., van der Haorst, R. and Stokman, C. (1989), 'Innovation processes in small and medium-sized companies', *Entrepreneurship and Regional Development*, Vol. 1, No. 1, pp. 35–53.

Drucker, P.F. (1985), *Innovation and Entrepreneurship*, Butterworth-Heinemann, Oxford.

Gardner, D. (1991), 'Exploring the marketing/entrepreneurship interface', in Hills, G.E. and LaForge, R.W. (eds), *Research at the Marketing/Entrepreneurship Interface*, Joint UIC/AMA Conference, University of Illinois at Chicago, pp. 43–52.

Gibb, A.A. and Davies, L. (1990), 'In pursuit of a framework for the development of growth models of the small business', *International Small Business Journal*, Vol. 9, No. 1, pp. 15–31.

Gibb, A.A. and Scott, M. (1985), 'Strategic awareness, personal commitment and the process of planning in the small business', *Journal of Management Studies*, Vol. 22, No. 6, pp. 597–629.

Greiner, L. (1972), 'Evolution and revolution as organisations grow', *Harvard Business Review*, July-August, pp. 37–46.

Gronroos, C. (1994), 'From marketing mix to relationship marketing', *Journal of Academic Marketing Science*, Vol. 23, No. 4, pp. 252–4.

Gummesson, E. (1987), 'The new marketing – developing long-term interactive relationships', *Long Range Planning*, Vol. 20, No. 4, pp. 10–20.

Gupta, A.K. (1984), 'Contingency linkages between strategy and general manager characteristics: a conceptual examination', *Academy of Management Review*, Vol. 9, No. 3, pp. 399–412.

Håkansson, H. (1982), *International Marketing and Purchasing of Industrial Goods: An Interaction Approach*, J. Wiley, Chichester.

Hills, G.E. and LaForge, R.W. (1992), 'Research at the marketing interface to advance entrepreneurship theory', *Entrepreneurship Theory and Practice*, Spring, pp. 33–59.

Jackson, B.B. (1985), *Winning and Keeping Industrial Customers: The Dynamics of Customer Relationships*, Levington Books, Levington.

Kets de Vries, M. (1977), 'An entrepreneurial personality: a person at the crossroads', *General Management Studies*, Vol. 14, No. 1, pp. 41–53.

McClelland, D.C. and Winters, D.G. (1969), *Motivating Economic Achievement*, Free Press, New York.

Miller, D. (1983), 'The correlates of entrepreneurship in three types of firm', *Management Science*, Vol. 29, pp. 770–91.

Mintzberg, H. (1989), 'Strategy formation: schools of thought', in Fredickson, J. (ed.), *Perspectives on Strategic Management*, Ballinger, San Francisco.

Nevin, J.R. (1994), 'Relationship marketing and distribution channels: exploring fundamental issues', *Journal of Academic Marketing Science*, Vol. 23, No. 4, pp. 334–7.

Norman, R. and Ramirez, R. (1993), 'From value chain to value constellation: designing interactive strategy', *Harvard Business Review*, July-August, pp. 65–77.

Omura, G., Rogers, R.J. and Schmidt, J.B. (1994), 'Entrepreneurship as a market satisfying mechanism in a free market system', in Hills, G.E. and Mohan-Neill, S.T. (eds), *Research at the Marketing/Entrepreneurship Interface*, University of Illinois at Chicago, Chicago, pp. 161–71.

Poniewozik, J. (1998), 'It's not just a breath mint', *Fortune*, 17 August, pp. 40–1.

Scott Morgan, M.S. (1991), *The Corporation of the 1990s: Information, Technologies and Organisational Transformation*, Oxford University Press, Oxford.

Slevin, D.P. and Covin, J.G. (1990), 'Juggling entrepreneurial style and organisational structure – how to get your act together', *Sloan Management Review*, Winter, pp. 43–53.

Steinmetz, L. (1969), 'Critical stages of small business growth', *Business Horizons*, February, pp. 12–19.

Storey, D.J., Keasey, K., Watson, R. and Wynarczyk, P. (1987), *The Performance of Small Firms*, Croom Helm, London.

Tedlow, R.S. (1990), *New and Improved: The Story of Mass Marketing in America*, Heinemann, Oxford.

Webster, F.E. (1992), 'The changing role of marketing in the corporation', *Journal of Marketing*, Vol. 56, October, pp. 1–17.

Whittington, R. (1993), *What Is Strategy and Does It Matter?*, Thomson Business Press, London.

2 INFORMATION MANAGEMENT

LEARNING OBJECTIVES

After studying this chapter you should be able to understand:

1. the benefits of using information to assist decision-making;
2. the factors influencing the limited utilisation of market research by small firms;
3. the information that can be accessed by studying the basic trading records of the small firm;
4. the increasing volume of data associated with scaling up of business operations and the entry of the small firm into the world of online trading;
5. how to compare and contrast secondary versus primary research;
6. the benefits of information auditing;
7. the various techniques available for generating market research data.

CHAPTER SUMMARY

Market research is the systematic acquisition and analysis of data. The process is perceived as critical in large firms but many small firms lack the skills to undertake effective execution of this key activity. Even at start-up, many small firms could benefit from acquiring additional knowledge about market opportunities and internal operating costs. These data become even more critical in the ongoing operation of existing small firms.

Many small firms fail to appreciate that even the most basic systems such as their accounting records can provide invaluable insights about customer behaviour. As the small firm expands and management accounting systems are created, the wealth of such data sources is further enriched. Further data enrichment can occur as small firms move into web-based trading and the automation of back-office administration systems.

Market research can be divided into secondary (or desk) research and primary (or field) research. The former draws upon existing information sources, whereas primary research is concerned with generating new information. Primary data can be in a qualitative or a quantitative form. Techniques for generating data include observation, interviews and surveys.

INTRODUCTION

A characteristic of large companies is the heavy reliance placed upon the acquisition and analysis of vast quantities of data during the development of marketing plans and assessing actual performance against forecast. These activities are usually known as market research which is a process defined by Kotler (1994) as *the systematic design, collection, analysis and reporting of data and findings relevant to a specific marketing situation facing the company.*

In the case of a supermarket chain, for example, considering entry into a new town, extensive primary research (the generation of new data through activities such as observation and surveys) will be undertaken on issues such as sociodemographics of the population, traffic flows, pedestrian travel patterns, possible store location and the behaviour of competitors. These data will then be complemented by examining information on previous store openings in other towns to draw upon the lessons to assist in determining the forecasted performance for the new venture. Similarly major branded goods companies seeking to develop and launch a new or improved product will spend months researching the commercial viability of the concept prior to market launch. The research will include an assessment of existing data on market size, customer buying behaviour and the marketing activities of the competition. Potential market response to the new or improved product will be evaluated through activities such as focus groups, surveys and in-home placement tests. In many consumer goods markets, the new or improved product may also be placed into a test market to obtain a reading on actual sales performance prior to the final decision being reached on whether the item should be launched.

In large companies, even in the case of products that have been marketed for many years, during the preparation of the annual marketing plan the company will undertake a detailed review of existing research studies on overall market trends, customer behaviour and competition. These data will often be complemented by new research to update the brand group's understanding of recent market trends. The new research studies can include activities such as holding focus groups with customers, executing large scale mail surveys to measure customer usage and attitudes and initiating telephone surveys to measure awareness levels of the brand's current advertising campaign.

SMALL BUSINESS STARTUPS

Enter the phrase 'small business planning' into an Internet search engine and one will be advised of a myriad of sources offering guidance about undertaking this activity. Most of these sources will emphasise that development of a plan based on careful market research is the wisest course of action when considering the launch of a new small business venture. Typically the would-be entrepreneur is advised to research issues such as market size, number of customers, needs of customers, average customer expenditure and nature of the competition.

Where the startup business involves significant bank borrowing or the raising of equity capital, it is very probable that the financial community will require evidence that market research has been undertaken during the development of the proposed business plan. Furthermore it is probable that applications for funding will be unsuccessful where such data cannot be made available. The majority of small business startups, however, are one-person businesses that either require minimal external borrowing, or the entrepreneurs are able to fund the projects themselves. When one studies actual practices amongst this latter group, it is very apparent that most individuals ignore the well meaning proposals communicated by online advice sources about the need for careful market research prior to the launch of a new business idea.

To understand why minimal attention is given to using market research in the development of a startup business plan, it is useful to realise that there is a wide diversity of people who decide to launch new, one-person businesses. They include individuals working in a large firm who wish to gain greater control over their own destiny, (thus most new restaurants are started by chefs who work for other firms, acquire understanding of the commercial aspects of the catering business and then open their own outlet), people who have been made redundant or live in an area where there are few employment opportunities, people moving to an area where there are few jobs (for example, opening a guest house by the sea) and those pursuing a hobby which they want to evolve into a commercial proposition.

In many cases the business idea is not about delivering a new proposition to potential customers. Instead it only involves offering the same product or service that is already available from other existing businesses in the same locality. Under these circumstances, the new entrepreneur typically assumes that as other businesses are able to survive, then there is probably room in the market for another firm. Little or no research is undertaken, the business just opens with the hope customers can be attracted. In some cases this proves to be the case and in others, it emerges that the market is already over supplied and the new business is forced to close.

Small business experts might observe these events and suggest failure could have been avoided if market research had been undertaken prior to the business launch. It must be recognised, however, that in many markets where one is offering the same proposition as existing firms, it is both difficult and/or extremely costly to undertake research that can provide a forecast of certain success. For example, it might be proposed that somebody opening a new hairdressing salon should research whether existing businesses are successful. Unfortunately most such businesses are sole traders who do not have to publish their accounts. Additionally it is extremely unlikely that these owner/managers would be willing to respond to a survey asking them to share data about the financial performance of their business with a potential competitor. Under these circumstances probably all our new entrepreneur can hope to achieve is that by spending time observing existing salons, he or she may gain a perception of success and hope this limited evidence is an adequate indication that all will go well when they launch their enterprise.

In the case of individuals moving from a large company to the small business sector, the nature of their market research is rarely formalised in terms of undertaking a project to quantitatively assess factors such as market size, competition, and soon. More typically they have observed a failure of their employer to meet the specialist needs of a certain group of customers and determine that this represents an opportunity to launch their own business. In these cases, especially where they are frustrated by their current work environment, their motivation is often that of a strong desire to gain control over their future destiny. Under these circumstances they are often willing to take an 'intuitive business gamble'. However because they have usually accumulated extensive experience of a business sector whilst being employed by a large firm, this type of business startup is frequently quite successful.

For example, many small firms that operate as agents or distributors for other companies are often started by an individual who has previously worked as a sales representative for a large national or multinational company. One sector that exemplifies this scenario is the food industry. Sales representatives for large food manufacturers calling on retail outlets often encounter requests for speciality products that neither their company nor other large firms can supply. It is often the case that they know the only supply source for the requested goods is small firms, possibly located outside the country, who lack any form of sales representation within the market sector. Once the decision has been made to leave the large firm, then it is relatively easy for the individual to make contact with a number of these small firms, and offer to act as their agent or distributor. Because of their strong personal links with potential customers in the market, they are able to rapidly establish a successful new business.

EXAMPLE: INTUITIVE ENTREPRENEURS OR GAMBLERS?

Although Western governments spend millions delivering advice and training programmes on how to start small businesses, available statistics tend to indicate that only a minority of individuals take advantage of these schemes. As a result it seems reasonable to assume many potential small business owners are unaware that they should undertake market research before launching their new enterprise. The reality is that despite the fact many small business experts would consider this omission a major error of judgement, numerous new businesses are started every day and some even become very large trading entities. When one examines such cases, it often emerges that the owner has intuitively identified an opportunity and in the face of warnings from others about the inherent risks of what they are planning to do, just goes ahead and starts trading.

One such example is provided by Schneider's Popcorn Parties of Saskatoon, Canada (McClune 1995). The sister of the company's president had the idea of selling popcorn and food seasonings using the home party concept popularised by companies such as Tupperware. With no evidence or data about actual market potential, Colleen and Darrell Schneider started hiring agents to organise popcorn parties. Within five years the company, which sells popcorn and 17 companion flavours, achieved an annual turnover of $3 million.

Another example is provided by an American, Pete Slosberg, who wanted to enjoy the types of 'real ale' beers which he had drunk whilst visiting the UK. Finding that these seemed unavailable in the US, he started brewing his own beer. It then seemed like a good idea to turn his hobby into a business. So he launched Pete's Brewing, a microbrewery based in New York. Within ten years sales went from nothing to over $11 million.

A further example of intuitively identifying an unsatisfied market need and moving before anybody else recognised the opportunity is provided by John Erickson, the founder of Senior Campus Living. Whilst working in the Florida real estate industry, he realised that for every person retiring in the state, a much larger proportion of the population did not move south because they wanted to stay close to their families. He decided, therefore, that an opportunity existed to open a retirement community further north. His first development was on the site of a former theological seminary in Charlestown, Maryland. This site gave him the idea that as colleges are designed to foster community amongst young people, why not seek to achieve the same concept for people wanting to retire? Hence in addition to the apartment blocks for the residents, the site offers six dining areas, an indoor pool, exercise rooms, billiard halls and the provision of a whole range of activities including bridge, macramé, stained glass painting and gardening.

EXISTING SMALL BUSINESSES

Many people have experienced, when visiting large hotels, hiring cars from firms such as Hertz or Avis, or when shopping in large retail stores, being asked to provide their views about the quality of the products or services which they have purchased. This type of questioning is a form of market research which large companies undertake because they often face difficulties differentiating their offering from the competition. These firms recognise that survival is often dependant upon offering a superior level of service quality. To ensure a quality of service strategy is being effectively executed, it is critical to regularly collect market data in order to determine whether customer satisfaction is being achieved.

It is a much rarer experience to encounter this type of market research activity when purchasing goods and services from small firms. Furthermore a research study survey of small businesses, especially amongst microfirms which have between one and nine employees, would reveal that only a very tiny proportion of owner/managers purchase market research reports on their sector of industry or use techniques such as focus groups or surveys to gain a detailed understanding of customer attitudes. Yet if one visits many of these firms and persuades the owner/manager to discuss his or her business, one will often be amazed by the depth of knowledge that many of these individuals have accumulated about their market, customer needs and the strengths and weaknesses of their competitors. The question that arises from this observation is: how are some firms, who apparently ignore all of the procedural conventions about market research, able to acquire such knowledge?

The answer to this question is that successful owner/managers are usually deeply committed to participation in what Carson *et al.* (1995) define as personal contact networks (PCNs). These networks evolve from the social behaviour of the owner/manager, building formal links (for example, being a member of a trade association) and informal ones (for example, drinking in the bar of a local hotel) with others within their business sector. Contacts within these PCNs will include similar businesses, suppliers, customers and members of the professions such as accountants and solicitors. These networks are not a tangible asset, but instead remain intrinsically linked with individual owner/managers. Knowledge acquisition via the network is largely unstructured, unplanned and highly informal. However, from this source the owner/manager is able to acquire the information necessary to sustain plans for the future survival and growth of their business operations.

EXAMPLE: EXPLOITING NETWORKS

The power of such networks to support information and knowledge acquisition among small firms has been demonstrated by a comparative study of the clothing industry in France and the UK (Fletcher and Hardhill 1995). This study demonstrated that small firms in the French clothing industry exhibit a pro-active orientation towards further developing their firms, investing heavily in staff training and exploiting new technologies as the basis for expanding both domestic and overseas sales. Their behaviour can be contrasted with similar firms based in the East Midlands who appeared to have adopted a reactive response to changing market conditions and consequently are performing poorly in comparison with their French counterparts. The study revealed that a key factor influencing the performance of French firms was their detailed under-standing of market trends and the benefits of continually seeking to further upgrade internal competencies. It was concluded that a critical reason for this attitude amongst the French firms is their strong commitment to the exploit-ation of social networks to access market information and identify ways of improving performance. This was not the case with the East Midland firms who appeared to be totally inactive in terms of seeking to participate in any form of sectoral networking.

Another key source of information exploited by the French firms is Minitel. This is an online data system which from the early 1990s has been sponsored and funded by the French Government as a mechanism for improving informa-tion interchange between firms. Through the system, which can be considered equivalent to an early version of the World Wide Web, French companies can access their banks, interrogate commercial databases, obtain guidance on legal issues and communicate with customers.

ACCOUNTING INFORMATION

Most management texts tend to present the marketing function in isolation, making little attempt to link this task role with other managerial processes associated with the operation of a business. Furthermore the usual message communicated by authors is the importance of satisfying customer need. Rarely is attention given to the commercial reality that delivering satisfaction only has a benefit if concurrently the firm's transactional activities generate an adequate level of profit. Similarly writings about market research, although mentioning the cost/benefit relationships of secondary data (existing informa-tion) versus primary data (new information generated by activities such as customer surveys), contain minimal reference to the fact that ultimately the purpose of collecting any data is to reach decisions most likely to optimise a firm's profitability.

In view of these observations, it is not really surprising to find that many small firms (a) are somewhat resistant to the claims made by marketing academics about the importance of their discipline and (b) perceive little benefit in expending time or resources seeking out data to assist their marketing management activities. Another unfortunate outcome is that many owner/managers are rarely made aware that their accounting system, even in the smallest of businesses, can provide an invaluable source of data for analysing markets.

The concept of exploiting accounting data can be illustrated by the example of a person who decides to make aromatherapy candles. These are candles to which a fragrance is added during manufacture. The reason for selecting the candles example is that the business, at a later stage in its trading history, forms the basis of the free e-business computer simulation which readers can obtain from the publisher of this book. At startup, the example business is run by a single person who sells the candles as a gift product to friends, relatives and local gift shops. The numbered elements which constitute the trading process are shown in Figure 2.1. What triggers the trading activity is the receipt of an order (1). The owner then starts making the candles, if necessary ordering more raw materials (3) should there be insufficient supplies on hand. Upon completion of the order, the owner delivers the product (2). Once the order has been shipped, the owner then does the bookkeeping. This involves recording any expenses which have been incurred (4, 5) and sending an invoice to the customer (6).

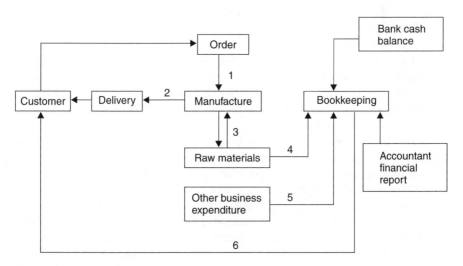

Figure 2.1 Business processes for the startup candle business

By reviewing the financial records of the transaction flows shown in Figure 2.1, the owner of the business would be able to extract data on issues such as:

- sales trends over time;
- the nature and location of customers;
- average purchase quantities by customer type;
- profitability of order by customer type;
- comparative profitability of items in the firm's product mix.

As well as low awareness about the value of accounting data as a source of knowledge about market performance in many small firm, another characteristic of many microbusinesses (those with less than ten employees), is the fact of the owner/manager rarely being enthusiastic about maintaining detailed financial records. Paperwork is held to a minimum and a large amount of the day-to-day information relating to trading activities tends to be stored in the owner/manager's head.

Two factors which clearly impact on the performance of a small business are cash flow and profitability. Many small businesses adopt the simple method of using their bank statement to provide them with information about the prevailing cash situation. If the bank statement indicates the cash balance is low or negative, then the owner/manager will take steps such as chasing outstanding invoices and/or postponing payment of outstanding bills from suppliers. The limited financial skills of many owner/managers mean that the task of analysing financial records and preparing the firm's accounts is often delegated to an accountant. To minimise professional fees, it is frequently the case that the accountant is only requested to prepare a profit and loss statement and balance sheet at year-end as part of the process of managing the owner/manager's income tax filing. The implication of this situation is that it is only once a year, after 12 months of trading, that the owner/manager is provided with detailed information about the firm's financial transactions (Turner 1997). Hence, even if one can persuade owner/managers of the benefits of using the accounting system to generate market data, in many cases the delegation of the task to their accountant means these individuals are rarely in position to be able to extract knowledge about their customers from this data source.

If a startup business is successful, business growth will ensue and the firm will possibly begin to hire more staff. These new staff will take on many of the day-to-day tasks that were previously fulfilled by the owner/manager. This latter individual will tend to retain total control over key marketing decisions such as pricing, negotiating with customers and promotion. In most cases the business structure will still remain relatively informal, with key information tending to be communicated verbally and the only formal business records being the financial information contained within the book-keeping system. The usual outcome is that as the firm continues to grow, marketing management problems will begin to emerge. These can include incorrect prices being quoted, deliveries being late and customers receiving the wrong products. The owner/manager will probably find that more and more of his or her time is spent fire fighting the latest business crisis (Gadenne 1998).

In those cases where the owner/manager recognises that effective management of growth requires a change in management style, the usual solution is to seek advice from the firm's accountants. Understandably the involvement of accountants will tend to result in a solution which is orientated towards placing greater emphasis on the use of financial information as the basis for guiding business operations in the future. This will typically be achieved by the accountant persuading the owner/manager to replace the simple book-keeping operation with an accounting system. In most cases the accountant will recommend that the new system should be computer-based, using a standard commercial package such as Sage or Pegasus. The resultant impact on information flows within the business is described in Figure 2.2.

Installation of the accounting system will only be of benefit if the owner/manager is prepared to utilise the data that can be generated to assist decision making within the firm. Unfortunately many owner/managers are extremely cost conscious and hence are most likely to purchase the cheapest version of an accounting software package. Unfortunately a major drawback of low cost, basic small business accounting software is that the generated reports contain information in a highly consolidated form. For example it is not

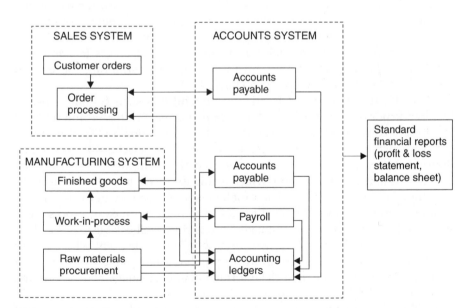

Figure 2.2 Evolution of a formalised accounting-based information system

feasible to use a standard profit and loss account statement to examine questions such as which are the company's most profitable customers or to analyse the mix of product sales to determine which order combinations are likely to generate the highest gross profit margin. It is not that the data are not available within the accounting system. The problem is finding a way of extracting the data in a format that can be used to assist the decision making process. Although in theory the sales staff could attempt to use the accounting system to extract data on the status of orders in process, they tend to find that it is still easier to rely on informal information exchange such as visiting the production department to ask about the expected shipment date for the latest order to a key customer.

MARKETING DECISION SYSTEMS

A frequently mentioned characteristic of small firms is their ability to rapidly reach decisions and have a level of flexibility which permits fast response to changing market conditions. Attributes which provide the basis of these characteristics are that there are few, if any, layers of management through which information must pass before a decision can be made, and the willingness of many owner/managers to base their decisions on an extremely limited amount of information. Under these circumstances, the right decision will be made if the owner/manager exhibits a high standard of intuitive reasoning. In many cases, however, the intuitive decision, although adequate, could often have been better if the owner/manager had been provided with a marketing decision support system capable of (a) offering rapid access to additional information presented in a relevant format and (b) permitting the user to pose 'what if' questions (Gupta and Harris 1989).

To be effective, Gupta and Harris recommend that such systems must be required to perform the three functions of (a) information storage and retrieval in a format convenient to the user, (b) data quantification and (c) permitting the construction of alternative scenarios that allow selection of an optimal decision. Many years ago, it was recognised that computerised accounting systems contained information which could be used to enhance decision making within organisations. The problem is finding a way of extracting the data in a format that can be used to assist the decision making process. The solution, known as database management, is now well established. Furthermore the costs of this technology have now fallen to the point where all but the very smallest of firms can afford to purchase more advanced computer packages able to translate financial information into a management accounting format (Hicks 1993).

As illustrated in Figure 2.3 a database management system is a set of programs that act as an interface between existing computer files and a set of

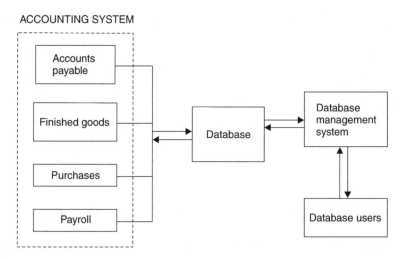

ACCOUNTING SYSTEM

Figure 2.3 A basic database system

integrated files known as a database. By assembling all available information into a single location, a database management system can be used to extract specific information which can be used to generate reports or support analysis of the implications of the decisions which are being made during the day-to-day running of the business. Should a small firm decide to acquire this level of analytical capability, this can be achieved either by adding database software to their existing accounting system or purchasing a more sophisticated accounting program with a database management system incorporated into the software package (Peel and Wilson 1996).

Although there are a number of analytical platforms available, the commonest type encountered in business is based around what are known as 'relationship' databases. The basic logic of this type of system is that information is stored in different tables. The problem is that each table only contains some of the information that is required to undertake an analysis. For example one may have a table which contains facts about suppliers (name, address, and so on) and another about the raw materials used in manufacturing. Thus if one wanted to develop an analysis of what and how many products are purchased by each customer, it is usually necessary to extract these data from two different sources. What is required in this situation is information (or a 'field') which is common to both tables. In this case one might use the ID number of the customer because each number is unique. Once this ID is also incorporated into finished goods files, one can then exploit the powerful capability of relationship databases; namely their ability to relate (or 'join') these two sources of data to generate an analysis showing which products have been purchased by which customers (Microsoft 1993).

Another important aspect of relationship databases is the simplicity of the programming language. If one was using a traditional file orientated system it would be necessary to write a complex program to execute the data manipulation process. Relationship databases use a language known as SQL for querying, updating and managing databases which is based around easily understandable commands such as 'select', 'from' and 'where'. Additionally many of the more popular software packages such as Microsoft Access have macros (automated sequences of commands) which automatically generate SQL statements as one is constructing the database management templates.

INFORMATION MANAGEMENT AND THE INTERNET

The advent of the Internet means that small firms have an opportunity to offer existing customers access to a 24 hour, 365 day a year purchasing facility and to attract new customers because the technology permits the firm to dramatically expand geographic market coverage. When considering a possible move into e-business, however, a small firm should recognise that establishing a totally automated, fully integrated transaction management website of the type operated by firms such as Amazon.com should be considered as a longer-term objective which may take some years to achieve. Most small firms would be advised to begin to acquire expertise by gradually progressing through the different phases of website development as shown in Figure 2.4.

Figure 2.4 proposes that the entry point to gaining operational website experience is often that of the firm establishing a static site providing generic information of interest to potential customers. Anybody seeking to purchase

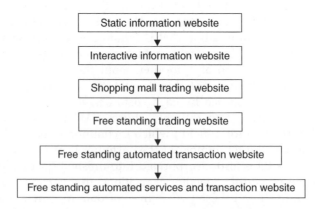

Figure 2.4 Possible progression phases in gaining website operational experience

32

product at this stage would have to follow the conventional process of contacting the firm via traditional means such as the telephone or being directed to their nearest local stockist. This first website will usually be static because at this stage the owner/manager will not have either the time or expertise to make very frequent changes to content. As a result, website repeat visitor levels are likely to be quite low.

At the time the small firm decides to start selling products online, it is often the case that instead of building their own transaction system the organisation rents space on a website that carries a number of other firms. Known as shopping malls, these sites have the advantage that they usually offer simple software that the firm can use to build the customer product ordering system. Typically these sites also offer an automated credit card transaction approval facility. Orders placed on the site are e-mailed back to the company which then manually executes the order fulfilment process.

Most small firms do not base their website at their own premises, but prefer instead to have the site hosted by a technologically more experienced third party. Organisations which host websites for firms are usually known as Internet Service Providers (ISPs). To the website visitor it appears that the online order placement service is available 24 hours a day, 365 days a year. Most small firms, however, do not have automated order acceptance and processing systems. What actually occurs is that the ISP e-mails the details of each order received to the company. During normal working hours, an employee then manually reviews the details in terms of correct price and order quantity. In the case of retail sites, most orders are purchased using a credit card and usually the ISP will already have checked the validity of the card with a third party card approval service. Once all the necessary manual checks have been made by the small firm, the order is processed using the same system as that for offline sales. The final action is that the customer is sent an e-mail confirming acceptance of their online order.

An example of this type of approach is provided by Yorkshire butcher Chris Battle (Anon. 1999). At the firm's family-owner shop, Chris and his wife developed a process for making traditional style bacon by smoking the product over oak shavings. In early 1997 the Battles joined the Classic England online shopping mall (www.classicengland.co.uk). The site cost less than £2000 to create and within a short period the Internet has generated significant revenue growth with the majority of sales coming from overseas customers.

For many small firms a back-office manual order confirmation and shipping system will be totally adequate for supporting their online transaction system. In the UK, for example, a number of small specialist retailers have established a website with a manual back-office order fulfilment system as the basis for expanding their customer base beyond that of customers who visit their retail outlet. Some are attracting customers from elsewhere in the UK and others have found the Internet is a platform through which to enter new overseas markets. As long as online customers are a small proportion of total business, manual back-office systems remain totally appropriate for managing online transactions. As the volume of online purchase traffic begins to grow, however, the small business may need to revisit its approach to managing the order fulfilment aspect of the customer satisfaction process. The reason for this situation is the nature of the purchasing behaviour exhibited by online customers. These can be characterised as expectations that a website has the capability to immediately provide:

- all the necessary information concerning product suitability;
- clarity over the pricing implications of alternative product options;
- the cost implications of alternative delivery options;
- automated confirmation of order acceptance and delivery date;
- response concerning subsequent customer enquiries about apparent failure to fulfil promised delivery dates.

An example of this trend is illustrated by the case of the London-based grocery home-shopping service, Food Ferry (Anon. 1999). In late 1988 the company faced online orders rising from 4% to 10% of the company's total turnover. What the firm soon found was that visitors to their site at www.foodferry.co.uk had much higher service expectations than their traditional offline customers. For example the online customers wanted more detailed factual information about ingredients, recipes and the nutritional value of products they wished to purchase. At the launch the firm decided against investing in an automated back-office. The outcome was that by early 1999, the demands of online customers began to damage other areas of the firm's operations because employees were spending more and more time downloading Internet orders and manually re-entering these into the firm's distribution management system.

For any small firm considering moving to an automated Internet back-office system, it is assumed that prior to this move action has already been taken to upgrade the organisation's marketing management software such that upon an employee keying in an order, the system automatically executes actions such as reviewing stock levels, approving customer credit rating, issuing an invoice and generating a delivery note. As illustrated in Figure 2.5, automation of the online order entry system merely requires the addition of a software tool to translate the data into a form which is understood by the firm's accounting system. The translator will usually execute the task of issuing an order confirmation e-mail to the customer. If the firm has contracted out the product delivery role to an organisation such as FedEx or UPS, the translator can also automatically inform the relevant shipping company that an order is ready for collection.

Having made the first move into website automation, the small firm is then in a position to begin to review what other aspects of the operation can be automated to achieve the aim of fulfilling customer service quality expectations.

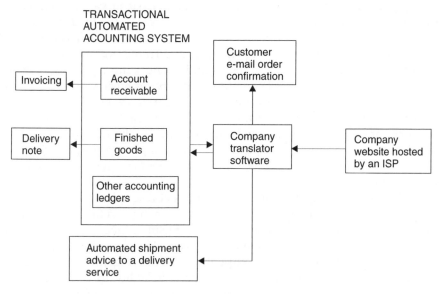

Figure 2.5   Online order entry automation

A very probable immediate opportunity will be in the area of stock control. If the firm has a computerised finished goods stock management system, then where on-hand finished goods are insufficient to meet a customer order the stock system can be interrogated to determine a likely product replenishment date. In many cases, a firm's on-hand stocks are critically dependent upon in-bound shipments from suppliers. Assuming that key suppliers operate a computer-based order acceptance system, then another area for Internet automation is to build into the firm's stock management system, automated order placement links with key suppliers. Contained within the firm's stock management system will be minimum acceptable on-hand stock levels for key supplies. Immediately any key supply falls to this minimum level, the system automatically generates a replenishment order and also monitors the response from the relevant supplier to determine whether the order will be fulfilled as specified.

MARKET RESEARCH

Market research is concerned with collecting data (the raw material of market research) which then needs to be transformed into meaningful information that can be used for making marketing decisions. Hence the process involves not only collection of the raw data from various sources, but also the application of specific techniques of data analysis of varying degrees of sophistication. The early use of market research was in the field of fast moving consumer goods (FMCG) marketing where it was identified as being vital to the measurement of marketing effectiveness. To this end it was employed in evaluating the impact of advertising and changes in price on sales. More recently market research has been utilised in services businesses to assess the impact of marketing activities on business performance and in particular to measure service quality. A distinction which must be drawn in market research, however, is the difference between the application in large versus small businesses. Although the same fundamental principles apply, there are likely to be limited resources in the smaller business which may constrain the options available.

Marketing information gathered using market research methods facilitates the process of achieving success by considering changes in the business environment. The environment within which a business operates is constantly changing. Such changes in circumstances can affect both the behaviour of customers and the nature of competition. Identifying these changes can enable more effective planning and reduced volatility in the demand for a business's products. Research can also assist in identifying particular strengths of the business and areas where improvements in specific areas of operation could be made. For example it may be possible to establish current levels of customer satisfaction and assess the effectiveness of marketing mix variables in contributing to satisfaction. Areas of weakness can also be identified which can then be resolved to permit attainment of improved marketing activities.

The range of products and markets to be served by a firm is a critical issue. Marketers usually adopt the process of market segmentation to subdivide the market and to classify different customer types. Segmentation involves selecting a particular part of the market upon which to focus on and to develop a specific market offer to meet the needs of customers in that segment. Market research is vital to successful segmentation and targeting of markets and in developing the right positioning to meet customer requirements. Once the business has been in existence for some time, it may also become necessary to evaluate the contribution of all of the items in the product range. Using research to do this, decisions can be made about whether or not to continue offering all of these products. At the same time decisions can be made about finding potential new markets for existing products and identifying potential new product opportunities.

For a small business the main benefits that can be expected from using information generated by market research are as follows:

- increased sales volume – selling more units;
- increased sales value – increasing the turnover in terms of monetary sales generated;

- increasing the perceived value that the customer receives from the market offer thus enabling higher prices to be charged;
- attracting more customers;
- keeping more customers;
- getting existing customers to spend more.

Further marketing benefits can come through the effective integration of a firm's marketing activities. In particular this may be achieved through:

- targeting promotional resources;
- estimating price sensitivity;
- reviewing existing products and improving new product development;
- assessing sales force and distributor value;
- evaluating customer service benefits.

It is important that market research is recognised as an investment rather than a cost with no return. Many small business owners perceive market research as an unnecessary expense. There are, however, substantial operational benefits to be gained from its use. If this fact is appreciated, it is also important to realise that research does not have to cost a large amount of money to achieve some useful insights into a business's markets and marketing activities. Data already available to a business may be of great value; but this information may require some basic collation and analysis. Simple analysis using calculators and spreadsheets is quite often sufficient to enable data to be converted into valuable information, and standard computer databases available to small businesses can be used to make access and management easier. In many instances the owner/manager can undertake the research and analysis themselves. On occasion, however, it may be necessary to buy the expertise of a market research professional.

The framework for the implementation of marketing research in small businesses is that of *information auditing*. This simple process focuses attention on information needs and how these can be satisfied using appropriate research methods. Whatever the stage of the business's life, information auditing can be used to trigger a review of marketing within the firm. Thus an information audit is advised not just at startup but throughout the entire life of the business.

The information audit process has four distinct phases which can be asked as a series of questions:

1. What does the firm need to know?
2. What does the firm already really know?
3. What's missing?
4. How can identified information gaps be closed?

Table 2.1 Marketing information requirements checklist

Market/customers	Competitors	Intermediaries	Suppliers	Products/services	Marketing mix
Market definition	Who are they?	Who are they?	Product factors	What are they?	Tools employed
Market size	Market share	Where are they?	Prices	Sales	Product
Market trends	What do they provide?	Do they have access	Service factors	Profits	Price
Driving forces	Direct/indirect	to markets?	Reliability	Revenue	Distribution
Seasonality	Market power	Do they support	Relationship	Cost	Advertising
For market and your	Market positioning	merchandise?	Importance	Margin	Promotion
own customers:	Competitive stance	What margins?	Promotional support	Contribution to firm	Publicity
How many?	Marketing strategies	Agents, distributors or		Interdependence	Sales force
Who are they?	Marketing resources	retailers?		Stage of life cycle	Direct mail
What do they buy?	Key strengths	Expected service		Benefits offered	Service
How much do they buy?	Key weaknesses	support		Usage advantage	Staff
How often do they buy?		Buying terms		Degree of competition	Premises
Where are they?		Bargaining power		How many are there?	Operations
How do they buy?				Do we need them all?	Effectiveness of the mix
Segments: different				New product	Individual elements
types				opportunities	As a whole
How satisfied are they?					Positioning
How responsive are					
they to mix variables?					

Source: Megicks and Williams (2000).

As described more fully in Table 2.1, the information audit should cover the issues of:

- market/customers;
- competitors;
- suppliers;
- intermediaries;
- products/services.

TYPES OF RESEARCH

Secondary (desk) research involves searching out, collating and analysing information that already exists in internal and external sources. There are multitudes of external sources of desk research information. These days most people start by searching the Internet. The best websites to visit will often depend on the nature of your business. Useful sites for desk research can be classified into three types:

1. *Government websites* often provide a useful starting point. In the UK, the Department of Trade and Industry website (www.DTI.gov.uk) contains useful data on the size and structure of market sectors, as well as information on consumers, European markets and regulations. The British Trade International (also known as BritTrade) site at www.tradepartners.gov.uk provides country and sector information on export market prospects, and can define specific export opportunities and trade partners. BritTrade is an offshoot of collaboration between the DTI and the Foreign Office. All Government sites contain information on sources of Government support, including grants and information provision; they can also provide you with a list of other useful websites for your research.
2. *Company websites* of prospective customers and competitors also provide valuable insights and leads.
3. *Information supplier websites* give away some market information as a 'taster' but for in-depth information one is often asked to subscribe to their services. Most major metropolitan and university libraries subscribe to a number of the recognised syndicated report titles which the small firm can often access at zero or minimal cost. Examples of such publications in the UK are MINTEL, Retail Business, Keynote and EuroMonitor.

Including the cost of staff time, secondary research costs about one tenth as much as primary research. Primary research means going out into the marketplace and collecting new information direct from potential and existing customers, competitors, and other useful sources (such as financial

Table 2.2 A comparison of research types

Secondary research	Primary research
• Seeks existing (published) data	• Provides original data
• Uses Internet or libraries	• Uses 'live' interviews or discussions
• Often not exactly what is needed	• Can be tailored to your exact needs
• Sometimes incomplete or out of date	• Expensive to collect
• Cheap and relatively quick to collect	• Quite time-consuming to collect
• Best conducted internally	• Often best delegated to specialists

analysts, industry experts). This type of research may require specialist techniques, or large sample sizes, which means the process may have to be delegated to an outside, specialist market research company. A summary of the differences between secondary and primary research is provided in Table 2.2.

To collect exploratory data will probably require qualitative market research. This is usually conducted with small numbers of customers. It tends to focus on the 'softer', less tangible aspects of the market, and is designed to explore attitudes and the motives underlying behaviour – particularly buying behaviour – in some depth. It is often used to involve customers in the development of new products. Qualitative research is about gaining insights by probing beneath the surface of what goes on in the marketplace, rather than trying to describe the market as a whole. It is neither necessary nor practical to conduct qualitative research among large samples.

Conducting qualitative research involves developing a list of topics for investigation, and exploring those topics through observation of, or discussion with, customers. It has become popular in recent years for market researchers to observe consumers purchasing and consuming products over periods of days and sometimes weeks, in shops, offices, leisure outlets and even private homes. This 'anthropological' approach to market research has led to some interesting insights, particularly on how consumer products are actually used. It is probably the most accurate way of researching behaviour. However, observation alone tells you nothing about consumers' motives. One method researchers have used to try to understand the motives underlying consumer behaviour as it is occurring, involves providing respondents with diaries or video cameras, with instructions on how to use them. Unfortunately all these methods are time-consuming and expensive, and – to be really effective – need to be conducted by well-trained researchers.

The most common method of collecting qualitative field data is face-to-face discussions with small groups of consumers/tradespeople by the interviewer (or 'moderator') who encourages respondents to describe their experiences in their own words. Qualitative research questions need to generate individualistic responses, and encourage people to talk openly. Qualitative interviews can be conducted by telephone, and a great deal of activity is currently taking place conducting qualitative research using the Internet. However, it is generally considered that visual responses and direct interaction provide for greater accuracy. In addition, the researcher may wish to gauge respondents' reactions to real or prototype products, promotional concepts, or other forms of 'stimulus' material. There are two formats for these face-to-face discussions: depth interviews and focus groups. Depth interviews are often the only practical way of conducting qualitative research in business-to-business sectors. It is difficult to get business people in a group together, particularly when they live and work at a distance from one another. Even when this is possible, respondents may work for companies in competition with each other, and so be guarded and defensive in their responses. It is easier to develop a rapport with respondents, and gain an understanding of their behaviour, when they are interviewed inside their organisations. Focus groups are more popular ways of collecting qualitative information from consumer markets. Groups of between eight and twelve consumers (sometimes fewer) are recruited – usually by specialist market research interviewers – and invited to a discussion venue, where a moderator encourages them to interact and explore their attitudes to the products or services being investigated. A short recruitment questionnaire filters out inappropriate respondents (such as non-users of your product) and ensures that the group reflects the target market being investigated (in terms of age, social group and so on).

Although qualitative research is invaluable for gaining insights into the market, most small businesses feel more secure when trying to understand their market in more numerical terms. They may also be more confident about making decisions based on feedback from sample sizes large enough to be representative of their market as a whole. The collection of such data usually involves the use of quantitative market research, collected from relatively large numbers of individuals or companies, using structured questionnaires that can be analysed relatively easily. Quantitative research is conducted across a large sample, so questionnaires need to be easy to analyse. The available question structure options include:

- standard 'yes/no' responses (or other dichotomous questions) which are useful for separating the market into groups by 'filtering out' non-users of your product, for example;
- multiple choice questions which are useful to establish, for example, market size, and distinguish between frequent and occasional users. In most cases multiple choice questions are presented in the form of scales offering a range of potential responses (for example, a scale ranging from 'strongly disagree' through to 'strongly agree');
- open ended questions in which respondents are asked to provide a detailed personal view about an issue.

Quantitative data acquisition can be implemented in a variety of ways. The best option will vary from survey to survey, depending on what information

Table 2.3   A summary comparison of research techniques

Qualitative research	Quantitative research
Why respondents do x	How many respondents do x
Explaining and understanding	Describing and measuring
Interpretative/impressionistic	Precise/definitive/scientific
Taps consumer creativity, dynamic, flexible	Standardised, repeatable
Depth/richness of understanding	Subgroup sampling or comparisons
Intensive	Structured
Quota sampling of individuals/groups	Probabilistic sampling to represent a segment
covering a range of opinions	of the market
Topic guide, open ended questions	Pre-coded questions on structured questionnaire
Interpretation	Numerical analysis/statistics
Provides ideas, insights, hypotheses	Provides conclusions

is wanted from the study, and who is being sampled. Interviews can be conducted by telephone, or face-to-face, using business premises, homes, shopping centres or other 'central locations'. If the firm has a website then it may consider including a short 'exit' questionnaire, which visitors can choose whether or not to complete, just before leaving the site. One can also fax or email questionnaires, provided that reliance on these methods does not bias the sample. Table 2.3 gives a summary comparison of research techniques.

DISCUSSION QUESTIONS

1. Why is market research an invaluable tool in terms of assisting the planning and ongoing management of the marketing process?
2. How can accounting systems be utilised as a market research tool? Review how further information becomes available to the small firm which initiates web-based trading activities.
3. Compare and contrast the techniques associated with secondary versus primary data generation.

REFERENCES

Anon. (1999), 'E-commerce brings home the bacon', *The Sunday Times*, London, 24 January.

Carson, D.J., Cromie, S., Mcgowan, P. and Hill, J. (1995), *Marketing and Entrepreneurship in SMEs*, Prentice Hall, London.

Fletcher, D. and Hardhill, I. (1995), 'Value-adding competitive strategies: a comparison of the clothing SMEs case studies in France and Great Britain', *International Small Business Journal*, Vol. 14, No. 1–2, pp. 33–52.

Gadenne, D. (1998), 'Critical success factors for small business: an inter-industry comparison', *International Small Business Journal*, Vol. 17, No. 1, pp. 36–51.

Gupta, J.N.D. and Harris, T.M. (1989), 'Decision support systems for small business', *Journal of Systems Management*, Vol. 40, No. 2, pp. 37–42.

Hicks, J.O. (1993), *Management Information Systems: A User Perspective*, West Publishing Company, St Paul, Minnesota, 3rd edn, p. 130.

Kotler, P. (1994), *Marketing Management: Analysis, Planning, Implementation and Control* Prentice Hall, Upper Saddle River, New Jersey, 8th edn.

McClune, J.C. (1995), 'The entrepreneur express', *Management Review*, March, pp. 13–20.

Megicks, P. and Williams, J. (2000), *Marketing Research Handbook for Small Businesses*, Plymouth Business School, University of Plymouth, Plymouth.

Microsoft (1993), *User's Guide, Microsoft Access*, Microsoft, Seattle.

Peel, M.J. and Wilson, N. (1996), 'Working capital and financial management practices in the small firms sector', *International Small Business Journal*, Vol. 14, No. 2, pp. 52–69.

Turner, R. (1997), 'Management accounting and SMEs: a question of style', *Management Accounting*, July–August, Vol. 75, No. 7, pp. 24–6.

3

RISK ASSESSMENT

LEARNING OBJECTIVES

· ·

After studying this chapter you should be able to understand:

1. the vulnerability which small firms face in relation to the behaviour of larger firms;
2. how the Microsoft versus Netscape browser war illustrates market vulnerability;
3. the implications of e-commerce for the future performance of small firms;
4. how to define market threats by the application of the Porter contending forces model;
5. how to construct a market system map as another approach to the mapping of market risk;
6. the components which constitute the supply chain within a market;
7. how macroenvironmental variables can impact the ongoing performance of core market systems.

CHAPTER SUMMARY

· ·

Small firms face the ongoing threat that larger firms may decide to dominate a market sector. The outcome of such events is illustrated by the Microsoft versus Netscape battle for the web browser market in the 1990s. Another threat facing small firms that are suppliers to larger firms is that the latter may decide to revise their procurement policies and/or adopt new manufacturing strategies. More recently small firms are also finding that e-commerce represents another potential threat to their ongoing existence.

Michael Porter has presented his 'five forces' model to demonstrate the sources of threat facing firms. The *Good Book Guide* case is provided to illustrate the impact of contending forces on the operation of a small business. Another way of mapping threats is to build a market system model. This model is constituted of two elements. One element is the core market system which contains the components which comprise a market sector value chain. Surrounding the core market is the macroenvironment. Contained within the macroenvironment are variables such as economic conditions, legislation and technology which can influence the ongoing performance of the core system.

INTRODUCTION

Given the opportunity most large firms would like to enjoy being in a monopoly position in their respective market sectors. This is because as a monopolist, they would have significant control over the market and thereby, be relatively immune from any external threats. As, however, most Western governments abhor a monopoly, the realistic, critical objective for most large firms is to achieve a sufficiently dominant market position. In this way they can control their own destiny whilst concurrently avoiding becoming enmeshed in a row with governments claiming they are using their market position to stifle competition.

An illustration of the activities associated with seeking market dominance is provided in the case of the battle between Microsoft and Netscape in America. Microsoft is a firm which sought to achieve market dominance and in the process fell foul of a government. Even in the early years of its existence, the firm's President, Bill Gates, recognised the benefits of achieving market leadership in the computer software industry. As the firm's products became the industry's global standard, the company's revenue growth was guaranteed because the firm's product range would be specified by all the leading manufacturers of PCs.

The battle between Microsoft and Netscape provides an effective demonstration of the advantages of company size in terms of dictating market destiny. Netscape was initially a small firm which grew in size as the result of implementing the highly entrepreneurial strategy of giving away free copies of their easy-to-use web browser, Netscape Navigator. As a result, their software rapidly found a home on 45 million PCs around the world. A fundamental reason for Netscape's success was that the firm developed a browser which would run on any computer operating system.

This situation apparently disturbed Microsoft because they appeared to be worried that if software developers began to write applications which were compatible with Netscape Navigator, this would cause it to become a universal platform. The potential implication of this situation would be to render as irrelevant operating systems such as Windows (Eddy 1999).

To add further fuel to the fire, Microsoft was preparing to launch the latest version of its operating system, Windows 95. The scene was now set for a major battle between two organisations, each seeking to dominate a technology convention which underpins the IT industry. On 7 December 1995 Microsoft announced that it had developed its own browser, Internet Explorer, which would be given away to customers. Even though Explorer was available at no charge versus Netscape Navigator, then being sold for $39, most users appeared to perceive the latter software as significantly superior to the Microsoft offering. Additionally, at this time the majority of Internet service providers, through whom most users gain access to the World Wide Web, were using Netscape software. The exception was America Online (AOL) which had a proprietary product, but was seeking to purchase a better browser. While Netscape sought to sell its browser to AOL, Microsoft's counter-offer was to supply Explorer free. Furthermore in return for signing an exclusive deal, AOL would be given space on the Windows 95 product. It is alleged that Microsoft's next move was to approach other Internet service providers offering packages which went well beyond just offering a free browser.

Then in 1998, Microsoft announced its next move of integrating Explorer 4 into the Windows operating system in preparation for the launch of Windows 98. Furthermore Microsoft offered large discounts on licensing fees to computer manufacturers to encourage them to bundle together the two programmes. This appears to have been the last straw for Netscape. The company announced that from then on their browser, now known as Communicator, would be given away free while the firm would now focus on marketing other software products and services.

All of these events subsequently became items of evidence in the US Department of Justice's antitrust suit against Microsoft. The initial outcome of this law suit was the court's decision that Microsoft should be split into two separate trading entities, one marketing its operating systems and the other supplying application software. Following an appeal it seems likely that Microsoft will avoid being split into two companies. Nevertheless the firm can still expect to pay out massive damages to other companies which think that Microsoft damaged their commercial operations.

As demonstrated by the Microsoft versus Netscape battle, most small firms have to accept that life is extremely risky. This is due to the facts that (a) events outside the firm can determine success or failure and (b) most small to medium enterprises (SMEs) lacks sufficient power within the marketplace to have any real control over their own future destiny. The lack of control over destiny is specially the case in business-to-business markets, where it is often a change in behaviour among larger firms that is the commonest reason why owner/managers are forced to totally re-evaluate their future plans. Possibly the commonest influence of large firm behaviour on small firm performance is that the former decide to change their procurement practices. Thus, for example, small manufacturers may suddenly lose a major contract because their customers, large original equipment manufacturers (OEMs), decide to move their procurement operation offshore and in future source their products from developing nations. This is due to the fact that these overseas firms can deliver products at a much lower price than the suppliers that the OEM has relied upon in the past.

EXAMPLE: SUPPLIER SURVIVAL IN THE CAR INDUSTRY

This requirement that small firms must continually assess operating risks, by monitoring external market variables and implementing new strategies before an adverse trend impacts performance, is exemplified by the UK engineering firm Frederick Woolley Ltd (Renton 1999). Based in the Midlands, ten years ago the company was a thriving sub-assembler within the UK motor manufacturing and motor parts industry, producing products such as link leads for car headlights. One of the problems they faced was that both car manufacturers and parts-service groups such as Kwik-Fit were increasingly turning to Eastern Europe as a source of cheaper products. More recently there has also been the added uncertainty surrounding the future of the Rover Car Group and Nissan's UK operations.

To survive, the company realised it had to move away from high volume production of low value goods and seek to manufacture higher value products such as complete cable harnesses. The company has successfully moved into the cable harness business by beginning to supply the bus manufacturing industry. This experience will in the near future hopefully permit its entry into the car cable harness sector. As well as seeking new market opportunities, Frederick Woolley has also recognised the need to improve efficiency in serving traditional customers. This has been achieved by involvement in the Society of Motor Manufacturers & Traders' initiative to modernise the firm's engineering skills and to upgrade capability to link electronically with major customers. In fact the company has been so successful in adopting new manufacturing and data management skills that it has entered into a joint venture with a consulting company to open a learning centre offering training in best practice to other engineering companies.

For small firms wishing to assess the threats presented by changes in their external operating environment, it is important to recognise that although market structures may change, the underlying philosophy of the firm's business operations will usually not have to undergo any fundamental revision. This is because most small firms will continue to acquire inputs, add value during the transformation of these inputs into outputs, and generate profits by obtaining a price in excess of operating costs. Hence what the small firm should seek to achieve is to determine what changes in the external environment may occur and to evolve an appropriate response capable of sustaining current revenues in the face of such change.

In the case of e-commerce markets, the small firm has the additional need, when developing an appropriate response to changing market circumstances, to assess the potential threat posed by other firms exploiting electronic technology to implement market actions such as:

- reducing their promotional costs;
- more rapidly providing customers with information;
- being accessible to respond to customer on a 24 hour/365 day basis;
- providing much detailed information in response to customer enquiries;
- being able to deliver much more customised information.

A similar approach will be necessary when analysing the way competitors may exploit e-commerce to achieve the aims of:

- reducing prices and/or increasing the speed of product delivery;
- enhancing purchase convenience and/or the quality of service;
- expanding market coverage;
- offering greater product choice;
- setting new standards for convenience and service quality;
- expanding the range of products or services in the marketplace.

MAPPING COMPETITIVE THREATS

Possibly the most widely known conceptual model for mapping the threats posed by the changing behaviour of competitors is that evolved by Michael Porter (1980), the Harvard Business School professor, during his study of strategic change in turbulent markets. As summarised in Figure 3.1, Porter has proposed that competitive threats can be classified into five major types; namely:

1. other producer firms already operating within the market sector seeking to increase market share;
2. customers using their buying power downstream to dominate the terms and conditions of purchase;
3. a supplier moving upstream and using their control over critical resources to dominate terms and conditions offered to customers;
4. substitute goods entering the market;
5. a new entrant arriving in the market.

Kleindl (1999), for example, in his analysis of competitive dynamics in the virtual marketplace, has demonstrated how Porter's contending forces model can be utilised by small firms seeking to determine the potential source of e-business threats in existing markets. As posited in Figure 3.1, the small firm undertaking

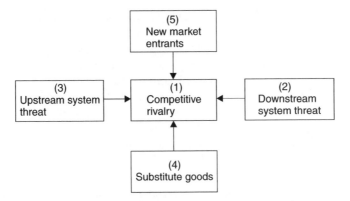

Figure 3.1 Contending competitive forces model

an e-business competitive threat assessment should review the potential impact of each of the following sources of future electronic competition:

1. *competitive rivalry*, which may result when a competitor is the first company to offer customers an online, automated product ordering facility;
2. *downstream system threats*, which can occur as the result of customers acquiring detailed information on prevailing prices being offered by different suppliers, not just in one country, but also from around the world. If price variations exist in a market sector and this fact becomes widely known to customers, then eventually the supplier can expect these customers to begin to exert pressure to force prices downwards;
3. *upstream system threats*, which can occur when larger firms, such as those in the airline industry, decide to by-pass traditional intermediaries and market their product direct to the final customer;
4. *substitute goods threats*, which may occur when small manufacturing companies in developed nation economies face competition from overseas producers who, by being based in a developing nation, can use the Internet to offer lower priced goods;
5. *new market entrant threats*, which may occur in situations where large firms use the Internet to gain a foothold in small niche markets which previously were not accessible because in the past the marketing costs associated with traditional techniques such as personal selling were much greater than the revenue generated.

EXAMPLE: LIVING WITH THE INTERNET

An illustration of the potential impact of e-business on future performance of a small firm is provided by the case of the UK direct marketing book firm Good

Book Guide (Smith 1999). The original business concept was the global marketing of the firm's *Good Book Guide*, mailed as a 36 page catalogue twelve times a year. Customers pay an annual subscription to receive the *Guide* and this operation generates a significant proportion of total income. Within the catalogue are impartial book reviews and recommendations. The firm's other major revenue stream is selling books, tapes and CD-ROMs. The customer profile is that 85 per cent of purchasers live outside the UK, 85 per cent have a degree and over 33 per cent have incomes in excess of £33,000. Applying the competitive threats model to the business, one can identify the following rapidly growing e-business threats:

1. *Competitive rivalry* from other direct marketing book firms creating an Internet presence and building market share by aggressive promotion of their online facility.
2. *Downstream system threat* as existing customers' use of the Internet causes them to see that major price variations exist in the book business. As this fact becomes widely known to customers, then eventually the Good Book Guide can expect these customers to begin to exert pressure to force prices downwards. Another downstream threat comes from traditional bricks and mortar book stores such as Barnes & Noble in the US and WH Smith in the UK establishing online operations.
3. *Upstream system threat* posed by the fact that many major publishers have already established informational sites and some can soon be expected to offer an online purchase facility.
4. *Substitute goods* entering the market. Already for example a number of consulting and computer software firms are offering free books written by their staff as a way of attracting site visitors who may then be in the market for fee generating services. Another substitute are the MP3 music sites where the visitor can mix and purchase their own customised CD-ROMs.
5. *New market entrants* gaining a foothold in markets previously not accessible to them. In the case of books, of course the classic new entrant is Amazon.com who were the first firm to recognise the potential of the Internet to establish an online direct marketing operation. They have subsequently been followed by other firms, many from the small firms sector who have established operations focusing on specialised niches such as art, nutrition and home decorating.

Although the Good Book Guide spotted these threats back in 1995, their initial reaction was that they could not see how one could generate any profits from e-business. Two years later the firm did establish a simple website offering an online purchasing facility to existing subscribers. Even then, however, the firm did not feel it could afford the huge investment required to match operations such as Amazon.com until it was more certain that the investment could be recovered from new sources of incremental revenue. The scale of impact of delaying this move was reflected in sales. These declined from £6.4 million in 1996 to £5.8 million in the following and subsequent years. Of even greater concern is that profits have been eroded and cash reserves have fallen by over £300,000.

MAPPING THE CORE MARKET

An inherent problem facing most small firms is that their scarcity of staff resources and minimal experience in market research often mean the business has insufficient capability to rapidly identify and then respond to external threats. In many cases it is only after sales or profits have begun to decline that the owner/manager allocates time to trying to understand the causes of poor performance.

What small firms must recognise is that in this day and age, changes external to the firm now occur much more rapidly than in the past. Furthermore the rapidity of change is even greater in e-commerce markets than in traditional, non-electronic, terrestrial markets. Hence survival necessitates that many owner/managers, if they wish their firm to remain in business well into the 21st century, must commit more time and resources to researching the sources of potential threats.

The increasing frequency with which small firms now face new market threats means that the owner/manager needs to acquire a very clear understanding of the factors which influence future performance. One way this can be achieved is to build a map of the market system and to identify the role of the firm within it. As shown in Figures 3.2 and 3.3, the role of a firm can be that of an end user, an intermediary, a supplier, or a producer. The first three of these are dealt with in the remaining subsections in this chapter; the fourth is dealth with in Chapter 4. Analysing the market system map permits identification of likely variables of key influence. During any efforts to evolve actions to improve future performance, it is these variables which will need to be managed in order to implement an effective response to the external threats which can be expected to confront the small firm.

As illustrated in Figures 3.2 and 3.3, a core market system is constituted of the organisations and customers who are participants in the market sector supply chain (Kotler 1997). Figure 3.2 provides a map of a typical consumer goods market system and Figure 3.3 a map of a typical business-to-business market scenario. As well as understanding the components that constitute the system, the small firm will also need to map information and transaction flows. The reason for this is that the evolution of an appropriate response to any threat will usually involve revising the nature of the firm's provision of customer information and/or the purchase transaction process.

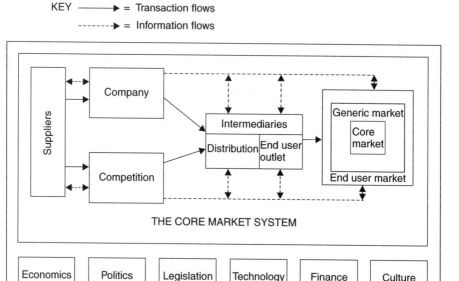

Figure 3.2 A map of a consumer goods market system

The end user market

The end user market is the point of ultimate consumption within the core market system. As shown in Figures 3.2 and 3.3, it contains two elements, the generic and the core market. Within the core market are those customers who are actively purchasing the product or service. Consequently the source of influence on customer behaviour is the product performance, price and promotional messages that are being presented by all of the firms operating in the market sector. Surrounding the core market is the generic market. This is constituted of the total population which is the source of both potential and actual users. Actual users are those individuals who have already migrated into the core market. The generic market is a critical influencer of product demand, because as this market grows or declines in size, this will impact the number of customers entering the core market. Thus, a small retailer specialising in the supply of children's shoes who is thinking of creating a website to increase sales revenue might define the size of the generic market in terms of the number of households within the shop's trading area which (a) contain children and (b) have access, via a PC or a digital television, to the Internet.

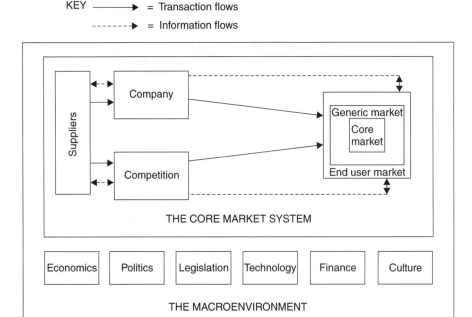

KEY ⟶ = Transaction flows

╌╌╌╌▶ = Information flows

Figure 3.3 A map of an industrial market system

Any change in this generic market (such as a decline in the number of children per household or an increase in the number of households acquiring digital TV) will eventually have a direct impact on the size of the retailer's core e-market.

The owner/manager should also recognise that customers rarely all exhibit exactly the same purchase behaviour. There are numerous ways of classifying customers. One common approach is known as market segmentation. This involves dividing the market into subgroups of customers exhibiting common, unique product needs. In the case of a small firm seeking to survive in a market sector being influenced by the advent of the Internet, one approach might be to segment the market on the basis of the degree to which customers seek information and/or use the Internet to make purchases. Thus it is proposed in Figure 3.4 that customers might be divided into the following four possible types:

1. *Low interest Internet user*: Members of this group have minimal interest in e-commerce and might just run a fast simple search about shoes on the Internet before going shopping. Their main way of acquiring information will be through the traditional media and the purchase will be made at a retail shop.

(2) High interest Internet information user	(4) High interest Internet information user/purchaser
(1) Low interest Internet user	(3) High interest Internet purchaser

Figure 3.4   An example of an e-commerce end user segmented core

2. *High interest Internet information user*: Members of this group will use the Internet as the primary source of product information but visit a retail outlet to make their purchase.
3. *High interest Internet purchaser*: Members of this group will use traditional information sources to acquire product information. This activity may even involve visiting retail shops in the product search process. Having selected their product they will then visit an Internet site, which they know offers the best possible value, and place an order.
4. *High interest Internet information user/purchaser*: Members of this group can be expected to implement all phases of the information search and purchase transaction process by using an e-commerce site.

Knowledge of variations in customer behaviour is critical to the successful development of a response to an emerging market threat. In the e-market scenario described above, if the small firm decides to attempt to influence customers from all four groups, this will require actions that (a) involve a promotional response covering both e-based and traditional media channels and (b) ensure products are distributed through both traditional and e-based, online outlets. The complexity of the actions to cope with managing both traditional and e-commerce market segments will vary depending upon the nature of customer behaviour and the firm's future sales targets.

Intermediaries

The primary role of intermediaries is to act as a link in the transaction chain between supplier and the end user. In business-to-business markets, where the value of the product is high, the number of customers relatively low and/ or product is customised to meet variations in product requirement (for example, a small engineering company supplying OEMs in the car industry), then usually the supplier deals directly with the customer. The outcome is that no intermediaries are required in the transaction process. This contrasts with most consumer markets where the intermediaries often play a critical role in the management of supply chains.

In many consumer goods markets, as illustrated in Figure 3.2, there are two roles specified for the intermediary: namely distribution and provision of end user outlets. In the case of some consumer goods markets, these responsibilities are fulfilled by different organisations (such as a cash and carry wholesaler who supplies independently owned, small corner shops). Over the last 20 years, however, the trend in many market sectors has been for the distribution and end user outlet role to become the responsibility of one organisation. For example, major supermarket chains which operate centralised buying and distribution systems are also owners of retail outlets. These organisations want suppliers who have the scale of resources to offer a broad range of products and the capability to deliver these across an entire country. Being unable to fulfil this requirement often means that most small firms are often squeezed out of any sector where a small number of inter-mediaries have managed to dominate a market. If a small firm wishes to survive in this type of market system situation then possible actions can include:

- developing a specialist product that can be sold through smaller specialist retailers (for example, upmarket craft goods sold through gift shops);
- identifying products with potential mass market appeal that cannot be supplied by their larger competitors (for example, farms and small proces-sors who have moved into supplying organic foods);
- by-passing the intermediaries and selling direct to customers. In the past this has usually been achieved by creating a direct marketing operation. More recently the same objective is now being achieved by the small firm establishing a website.

In determining future possible interactions with intermediaries, the small firm should always assess any decision in relation to the issue of what the customer wants in terms of information provision and purchase transaction fulfilment. Thus in upmarket sectors such as the consumer fashion goods industry, customers may still prefer to visit a retail outlet offering exclusive goods and having shop staff delivering a personalised service. Hence a small fashions goods manufacturer would probably be well advised to build a close working relationship with these small specialist retailers and not seek to gain distribution in mass market outlets. Concurrently, however, with the advent of e-commerce, this small manufacturer may need to examine whether there is an opportunity to establish a website to offer an online purchasing facility. The other alternative is to provides website visitors with detailed information and then direct them to their nearest specialist retail outlet to purchase products.

A major issue now facing the small firm owner/manager is whether there are benefits in reducing or ceasing to use intermediaries and to market goods and services direct to the end user using the Internet. Clearly this decision has major implications both for the firm and the intermediaries used to service the existing, conventional market system. For the small firm, a possible risk in offering goods online is that conventional intermediaries will react adversely and terminate their trading relationship with the supplier. Hence the firm will need to carefully determine whether conventional intermediaries have a role to play in the marketing process prior to establishing their own e-commerce operation. To reach a decision on this issue, the small firm will need to review the revenues that might flow from e-commerce versus the sales that might be lost as a result of alienating existing customers in traditional distribution channels. This evaluation has caused some small firms not to offer a transaction facility online, but instead, when people visits the company's website wishing to purchase goods, they are directed to a vendor further down the distribution channel (Kalin 1998). In relation to this issue, Gartner Group has estimated that more than 90 per cent of manufacturers do not sell their product online to end user markets. The main reason is their concern to avoid channel conflict with their existing terrestrial wholesalers and retailers (Weinberg 2000).

For many small firms, the future will probably be that of involvement in hybrid channel models where the customer utilises a combination of the best opportunities offered by online and offline transaction systems. Support for this perspective is supplied by the results of a research study undertaken by Ernst & Young (Hamel and Sampler 1998). This revealed that currently, 64 per cent of Internet users research products online and then buy them at stores or by telephone. Thus in the case of the clothing industry, the customer will probably visit a retail store when seeking out a new item. If, however, they want to replace a favourite pair of jeans, then very probably they will purchase the replacement product by contacting the manufacturer's website.

Over the next few years it can be expected that as more small firms come to understand the opportunities offered by e-commerce, this will lead to very significant changes in the role of the intermediary within virtually every market system around the world (Bloch *et al.* 1996). In some cases within the new systems, manufacturing firms will take over functions traditionally undertaken by intermediaries. The possibility of by-passing existing channel members with the resultant shortening of distribution channels is known as 'disintermediation' (Benjamin and Wigand 1995).

The problem facing many small retailers and industrial distributors is that many operate as intermediaries offering personalised services to customers in their trading area who need significant assistance to reach a purchase decision. Thus as their current suppliers, often large firms which are beginning to focus on using the Internet as a medium for selling their products or services directly to end users, these small firm intermediaries may face a very uncertain future.

In both North America and Europe, for example, one very large group of small firms are the independent travel agents who operate one or more retail outlets. For many years these small intermediaries were the usual place used by end users to purchase their air tickets and vacation packages. Even before the advent of e-commerce, the major airlines established telesales operations that permitted customers to make direct bookings. The advent of airline websites now means that many end users can make their booking from the comfort of their own home and thus save themselves a trip to their local travel agent's outlet. The reaction of some small travel agents has been to place greater emphasis on their capabilities to manage their customer's total travel needs, booking journeys and accommodation for business travellers and holiday packages in the consumer sector. Unfortunately the airlines have now moved to provide online facilities that can also offer a complete travel service. This has been achieved by creating websites that can be used both to search out and to book other elements of a travel package such as car rental and hotel reservations. Under these circumstances, it is probable that small independent travel agents may have an extremely tough time attempting to survive in a world where increasingly the Internet is permitting their traditional customers to deal direct with providers of travel services.

Bloch *et al.* concluded, however, that one alternative is for small entrepreneurial intermediaries to place much greater emphasis on positioning themselves as offering more effective buying services to the customer. These authors point out that when a customer contacts a single supplier, they only receive information specific to that supplier. Thus if the small intermediary is able to undertake a wider search of alternative offerings, the customer can then, by contacting this intermediary, rapidly evaluate which is the best purchase option relative to the various offerings being made by different suppliers. This is a skill which many small intermediaries have already acquired. What they need to do, however, is to also offer the same convenience of purchase that is currently being offered by suppliers who have sought to implement a disintermediation strategy by moving online. Thus to match the convenience of large suppliers but at the same time offer customers greater choice, the small intermediary will have to develop a sophisticated online system that permits visitors to undertake online searches for the most appealing travel package option. The cost of such systems is quite high. Hence one possible scenario is for a group of small firms to pool their financial resources and establish a collaborative hub Internet operation for use by their customers.

Suppliers

One aspect of the role of suppliers in any market is their ability to influence prices by the creation of raw material scarcities. OPEC's (The Organisation of Petroleum Exporting Countries) restriction of oil supplies, for example, and their concurrent demand for higher crude oil prices in the 1970s, triggered a global recession. This event caused many companies to carefully assess the impact of scarce resources on the future positioning of products in their respective markets. For example in the US, some small housebuilders found that one way to compete against their larger competitors was to build new houses which offered much higher standards of insulation. This made their houses very attractive to people seeking to avoid having to pay high energy bills.

More recently, however, small firms have begun to realise also that suppliers, as well as possibly being able to constrain input resources, can also be a major source of new opportunities. Most of the recent advances in the modern computer's data processing capability, for example, have not come from the laboratories of the computer manufacturers, but instead from the entrepreneurial behaviour of their suppliers. Hence over the last few years, large firms in business-to-business ('B2B') markets, who in the past tended to adopt an adversarial attitude to their small downstream distributors, have begun to recognise that the latter's knowledge of customer need means there are significant benefits in adopting a relationship orientated approach. In this way both parties openly exchange data that can be used to evolve more effective products and services with greater appeal to end user customers. This change in management practice is often described as 'building stronger supplier-customer chains'. It usually involves firms mutually determining how to optimise responsibilities for the various stages of the value-added processes associated with the production and delivery of goods to end user markets (Storey 1994).

The advent of the Internet has accelerated the trend for building stronger customer-supplier links. Virtually every large manufacturing and service organisation around the world is introducing an e-procurement strategy. Some are building their own systems. Others are linking into third-party procurement extranets. These are websites that are closed to the general public and can only be accessed via passwords and prior approval by the host. Unfortunately this trend can concurrently represent a new threat for the smaller firm because if the small firm does not develop the capability to electronically interface with its OEM customers in business-to-business markets, then in the near future it will have no customers.

MACROENVIRONMENTAL THREATS

The macroenvironment, an outer shell surrounding the core market system, contains the generic variables which can have massive impact on the future performance of the small firm. The problem facing any owner/manager seeking to understand these variables is that it is often difficult either to measure their actual current impact on the core market or to forecast how that impact may change over time.

The solution adopted by large firms is to employ teams of specialists who are assigned roles such as those of econometricians engaged in forecasting the impact of economic trends on future sales, or lawyers able to predict how the introduction of impending new employment legislation will influence future operating costs. In theory a small firm owner/manager can get similar guidance by hiring external advisers from the financial and legal communities. The majority of small firms, however, tend to feel they cannot afford to pay the fees charged by these professions. Fortunately many governments are now recognising the need for small firm support services to provide advice on macroenvironmental variables likely to impact business performance. This support is usually provided in the form of a free or subsidised service. Furthermore government agencies such as the Department of Trade & Industry in the UK and the Small Business Agency in the US are now moving to exploit the power of the Internet to ensure small firms can obtain low cost access to an ever expanding array of relevant data.

Thus the average owner/manager should develop an understanding of which macroenvironmental variables are most likely to impact performance. They can then determine how, by accessing relevant government agency databases, the firm can create some form of monitoring system to accumulate relevant knowledge about those variables which represent the greatest source of potential threat to future operations.

Another critical advantage which large firms have over small firms in terms of minimising the impact of macroenvironmental change is that where the former's operations represent a significant component of a country's economy, senior managers are often able to influence the behaviour of governments. Through mechanisms such as making political donations or employing lobbyists, these firms can often persuade governments of the apparent merits of actions such as implementing protectionist legislation, introducing import tariffs, offering export subsidies and making grants available to support new, sector specific capital expenditure on factories and machine tools.

Economics

In all market systems, prevailing economic conditions determine whether customer demand will grow, remains static or decline. A tragically repetitious example of the impact of this variable is provided by the building industry. Here the cyclical nature of the housing market in many parts of the world means that as an economy downturns, demand for new housing declines with the almost monotonous outcome that many small building firms are

forced into bankruptcy. A similar pattern can also be found in the leisure industry, where again any economic downturn is often accompanied by many
small hotels being forced to close their doors and cease trading.

The underlying explanation of this tragic scenario in both these sectors is
that few small firms have sufficient financial reserves to fund ongoing operations whilst they await the next economic upturn. Those small firms which
do survive such economic debacles typically exhibit two characteristics. First,
during periods of economic growth, their owner/managers avoid excessive
expenditure on items such as new assets, but instead strike a careful balance
between purchases and accumulating financial reserves. Second, these owner/
managers are usually more astute at reading the indicators of an economic
downturn. This causes them to move earlier than their counterparts in the
market sector to restructure their operations in readiness for a period of adverse
trading conditions.

Politics

The survival of small firms in most countries is heavily influenced by the policies
being implemented by their respective governments. In the UK, for example,
the previous Conservative Government, up to 1997, sought to place constraints
on the size of the welfare state, which in turn created problem for those small
firms supplying products and services to the public sector. This can be contrasted with the recent decision by the Labour Government to invest in programmes to modernise the National Health Service and increase the resources
allocated to education. These same small firms, who have faced difficult times in
the past, will clearly benefit from the UK Government's recent policy changes.

Predicting the future behaviour of governments is rarely easy because
politicians have a tendency to instantly revise their stance on issues if there is
a probability that their current opinions could result in losing the next elec-
tion. Thus, for example, some years ago the UK Labour Government was
elected on a platform which included seeking to closely align the country's
economic and social policies with those of other members of the European
Union (EU) such as France and Germany. The poor performance of the euro
since the new currency was launched, plus the Danish Government's failure
to gain approval in a referendum to replace the kroner with the euro, has
subsequently caused the UK Labour Government to adopt a somewhat more
conservative position on the issue of European integration.

Legislation

Legislation is the basis on which governments create statutes and guidelines
that provide a framework for regulating the behaviour of both consumers

and businesses. One problem confronting small firms is how they can stay up to date on changing legislation and thereby avoid being fined for non-compliance. For example, in the UK the whole area of employee legislation is already a minefield for the smaller firm in relation to such issues as unfair dismissal and the employment rights of part-time employees. Now, as of 2 October 2000, all firms have to cope with the implementation of the Human Rights Act which incorporates the European Convention on Human Rights into the domestic law of the UK. The problem is that although the Act was designed primarily to protect the rights of private citizens in their day-to-day lives, such as the freedom of speech and freedom of assembly, what may happen is that small firms will now have to expend funds on professional advisors in order to ensure that in their treatment of employees, the firm does not fall foul of the new Act. Their alternative is to remain blissfully unaware of the Act. Then at a later date they may face massive legal costs and possibly court-imposed fines because, for example, a disgruntled employee brings a legal suit claiming that their employer has infringed their human rights by refusing to give them time off to practice their religious beliefs.

The other problem about legislation is the costs which small firms face in fulfilling all the associated legal obligations. Most legislation will involve all firms in massive administrative costs. The fulfilment cost per employee for large companies is relatively small because these costs are spread across a large workforce. Small firm have to undertake the same tasks as their large firm counterparts but, because of the small size of their workforce, costs per employee can be huge. This situation can be illustrated by the costs facing UK employers who are responsible, under British tax law, for managing all aspects of the paperwork associated with calculating, collecting and remitting employee income tax, national insurance contribution, statutory sick pay and maternity leave. It is estimated that in most large firms managing these tasks costs somewhere in the region of £2–5 per employee per year. This can be contrasted with a firm employing between five and ten employees where the task costs are likely to be in the region of £250–300 per employee per year. Furthermore because many owner/managers do not feel they can afford to employ individuals to administer these statutory responsibilities, it is not unusual to find that owner/managers will spend over 60 per cent of their own time dealing with the burdens imposed on them by the state.

The area where small firms are most likely to face an exponential growth in new legislation is that of e-commerce. Governments are already frantically trying to find ways to tax those domestic operations who have moved their websites to an overseas location. Following the 1998 Ottawa ministerial conference, the Organisation for Economic Cooperation and Development (OECD) is examining many of these issues with the aim of recommending an international agreement in relation to how tax liabilities on payments of goods purchased via an e-commerce channel can be managed. Even if all the complexities of these issues can be resolved, however, there still remains the problem of whether the customer or the supplier will be responsible for remitting the collected taxes to the appropriate authorities.

In the US the consultants Ernst & Young estimate that in 1999, at individual state level, the tax exemptions associated with Internet trading caused the states across America to lose $170 million in tax revenue. Some states are lobbying Congress to take action over this issue. They are being supported by some 'bricks and mortar' retailers who feel it is unfair competition to permit their online rivals to escape payment of taxes. The magnitude of the problem is no smaller in Europe where value added tax (VAT) can account for up to 40 per cent of a country's tax revenues. This situation means that European politicians will probably be very supportive of the view that tax on Internet goods should be levied where the customer is based.

Recent court rulings in Europe have also not helped build the confidence of online traders (Anon. 2000) about their ability to avoid falling foul of legislation which was originally intended to protect business and consumer rights in terrestrial environments. E-commerce operations entering the German market are concerned by a recent Bavarian court ruling that hosts of commercial websites are liable to face fines if for example, racist material is placed on their site by a third party. Another example is that of a clothing firm which was found to be in breach of German consumer protection laws by not offering its normal 100 per cent replacement guarantee for clothing that wore out.

EXAMPLE: SURVIVING TECHNOLOGICAL CHANGE

Standard Photographic Ltd is a UK firm which specialises in the supply of photographic film (Smith 2000). The company, based in Leamington Spa, buys 40 million rolls of film per year from the major film producers and repackages these as 'own brand' film for retailers such as Boots, Dixons, Superdrug and Tesco. Standard also operates two other businesses. One is the conversion of photographic paper. It purchases master rolls of paper from Fuji which it then cuts into the sizes used by specialist mini-laboratories, publishing houses and hospital x-ray departments. The other operation is film processing in which the firm handles all of the mail order processing of Fuji photographic slides in the UK.

What is beginning to worry the firm is the growing threat of digital photography because over time, as more people move into this technology, the sale of film for traditional cameras can be expected to decline dramatically. The company's response, having recognised this technological threat, is to seek to diversify into new areas of business. Already the company has moved to acquire the technology that will permit it to provide the photo-developing service of printing photographs from digital files for online operations such as jungle.com. A review of existing competencies has also identified the fact that in acting as the supplier of 'own label' products for major retailers, Standard has acquired a superior competence in the area of Just In Time (JIT) logistics management. This skill will be in increasing demand as more and more firms begin to sell their goods via the Internet. Hence Standard's latest move is to establish a new distribution management operation, iNet Distribution.

Technology

All firms live in a world where new technologies are emerging that can have a significant impact on future operations. At the extreme, as illustrated above by the Standard case, are those technologies that can make obsolete a small firm's entire product range. The more usual impact of technology, however, is to offer a new way of implementing internal business operations that can have a significant impact on employee productivity (for example, the impact of robotics in manufacturing firms). Unfortunately technology's ability to reduce operating costs can represent a major threat to the average small firm. This is because it is often the case that the small firm does not have the financial resources to adopt the new technology. Consequently owner/managers are forced to sit helplessly by whilst a better funded competitor acquires the technology and subsequently moves to exploit achieved cost savings by reducing its market prices.

It can be the case that ongoing survival requires being a 'market follower' and purchasing the new technology. However, although acquisition of the new technology will reduce costs, the firm will receive no benefit from its investment because any cost savings are lost through the need to adjust market prices. This situation is already beginning to arise in e-commerce. Early small firm entrants into the field were able use online transactions as a way to service customer needs at a cost lower than that achievable using traditional business processes. However an annoying attribute of e-commerce is that customers can rapidly acquire market information on alternative price offerings. Through the willingness of customers to 'click around for the best deal' many small websites have already been forced to reduce online prices to retain their customer base. The outcome of this trend in many sectors is that small firms, having been forced to establish a website to counter the threat of the existing online activities of their competitors, now find that the intense price competition in many cyberspace markets means the firm is forced to reduce prices. Thus the situation now exists where small firms, having created an e-commerce operation capable of reducing transaction costs, find they are forced to pass on any savings to the customer in the form of major price cuts. The outcome is that increasingly, small firms are finding that e-commerce, instead of offering new opportunities, is in fact a new technology which offers only one outcome: a reduction in overall profitability.

Finance

Financial trends are possibly one of the most critical variables in terms of their potential impact on the day-to-day operations of the average small firm. This is because many small firms are excessively dependent upon overdraft and medium term loans from their banks to fund their operating and capital asset deficits. As a result many small firms are especially vulnerable to events such an upward move in interest rates. Additionally many bankers insist that their lending terms must include the demand for a personal guarantee linked to the owner/manager's domestic assets such as their house. This means that unlike their counterparts in large firms, who just have to worry about job security during periods of adverse trading, those in the small firm sector are faced with not just a loss of the business, but also their family's entire stock of personal possessions.

Another source of financial threat is fluctuating currency rates. Even for small firms which only operate in a domestic market, this can be a problem, if for example they are buying components from abroad and suddenly there is a fall in the value of their country's currency. The firm then faces higher raw material costs, and given that this is caused by a currency fluctuation, not a general rise in prevailing industrial sector operating costs, it is often difficult to pass on these rising costs to the customer in the form of higher prices. During 2000 this was the scenario facing many small European electronics companies who source their components in America and have to live with the rapidly rising value of the dollar in the world's financial markets.

For small firms which rely heavily on overseas markets as a major source of total revenues, the potential threat of fluctuating currency rates can often be even more devastating. Most small firms lack the financial sophistication of their large firm counterparts in areas such as using futures to smooth out currency variations. This means that many small firms quote their prices based upon the prevailing value of their own domestic currency. If this currency then begins to appreciate (for example, the £'s appreciation against the euro during 2000), firms suddenly find that their prices have become uncompetitive. The result is that existing contracts are cancelled and even the most loyal of overseas customers begin to look elsewhere for alternative sources of supply.

Culture

Since marketers first began to analyse market opportunity, it has always been apparent that different social groups within countries and between populations in different countries will exhibit variation in buying behaviour. One of the key variables contributing to this situation is the cultural background of individuals, because this will determine their wants, values, attitudes and beliefs. Hence the owner/manager must continually monitor how culture may be impacting customer behaviour. For example a small traditional retailer specialising in selling collectibles such as art or pottery may find younger customers are being lost because this age group has started to use the Internet. Similarly in business-to-business export marketing, some small firms can expect to find increasingly that key customers wish to shift to utilising online procurement systems, but the small firm only has the capability to offer the facilities of a sales force or a telesales operation to administer the customer order placement process.

DISCUSSION QUESTIONS

1. Why does e-commerce represent a potential threat to the future existence of many small firms?
2. Develop a core market system map for a small meat pie company which uses wholesalers to distribute products to small grocery stores and independent bakery goods outlets.
3. Describe the macroenvironmental variables which could impact the performance of a small engineering firm which produces the metal ducting used to create air conditioning systems in factories and office buildings.

REFERENCES

Anon. (2000), 'First America, then the world'. *Business Week*, 26 February, pp. 159–62.

Benjamin, R. and Wigand, R. (1995), 'Electronic markets and virtual value chains on the information superhighway', *Sloan Management Review*, Winter, pp. 62–72.

Bloch, M., Pigneur, Y. and Segev, A. (1996), 'On the road to electronic commerce – a business value, framework, gaining competitive advantage and some research issues', unpublished paper, Leonard N. Stern School of Business, New York University, New York.

Eddy, P. (1999), 'The selfish giants', *Sunday Times Magazine*, 14 March, pp. 43–8.

Hamel, G. and Sampler, J. (1998), 'The e-corporation', *Fortune*, 7 December, pp. 80–1.

Kalin, S. (1998), 'Conflict resolution', *CIO Web Business*, February, pp. 28–36.

Kleindl, B. (1999), 'Competitive dynamics and opportunities for SMEs in the virtual marketplace', *Proceedings of the AMA Entrepreneurship SIG*, University of Illinois at Chicago, Chicago, pp. 21–7.

Kotler, P. (1997), *Marketing Management: Analysis, Planning, Implementation and Control*, Prentice Hall, 9th edn, Upper Saddle River, New Jersey.

Porter, M.E. (1980), *Competitive Strategy: Techniques for Analysing Industries and Competition*, The Free Press, New York.

Renton, J. (1999), 'Surviving on industry's cutting edge', *The Sunday Times*, 7 November.

Smith, D.S. (1999), 'Web of competition traps bookseller', *The Sunday Times*, 25 July.

Smith, D.S. (2000), 'Photographic company aiming to develop with dotcom orders', *The Sunday Times*, 1 October.

Storey, J. (ed.), (1994), *New Wave Manufacturing Strategies: Organisational and Human Resource Management Dimensions*, Paul Chapman Publishing, London.

Weinberg, N. (2000), 'Not.coms', *Forbes*, 17 April, pp. 424–5.

4 SMALL FIRM INTERNAL COMPETENCIES

LEARNING OBJECTIVES

After studying this chapter you should be able to understand:

1. how small firms are influencing Western nation economies;
2. the common errors made by governments in the provision of support programmes for the small firms sector;
3. some research on factors influencing the performance of small firms;
4. a competency model for defining the internal variables impacting small firm performance;
5. the alternative orientations available for managing customer needs.

CHAPTER SUMMARY

Over the last 25 years, the small firms sector has become the dominant source of employment in most Western nation economies. This had led many governments to evolve support programmes to assist owner/managers. Many of these support programmes have made the mistake of assuming that management practices in both the large and small firms sectors are the same. In reality differences exist. Owner/managers are motivated differently than managers in large firms. Another error has been to assume that all small firms wish to operate as entrepreneurs.

The resource-based view of the firm contends that the internal competencies of a firm determine the nature of market performance. A review of four studies of factors impacting small firm market performance gives us materials which provide the basis for evolving a competency model of the small firm. Within the model important areas of competency include strategy, financial resources, innovation, human resources management (HRM) practices, quality, employee productivity and information systems. These competencies are of little benefit, however, unless the small firm also adopts an appropriate orientation for managing customer needs.

INTRODUCTION

In the period immediately following the Second World War, the Western world's economies were dominated by the large multinational corporations. Beginning in the early 1970s, however, these organisations, in the face of increasing Pacific Rim competition, began to implement strategic actions such as delayering to improve flexibility, downsizing to improve productivity, and relocating assembly operations offshore to lower labour cost areas of the world. The eventual outcome has been that the small firms sector has replaced that of large firms as the primary source of employment in most Western nation economies. Within the European Union, for example, over 60 per cent of the workforce is employed in the SME sector, with over 90 per cent of such jobs being in firms which employ less that ten persons.

As governments came to recognise the critical importance of the small firms sector within their respective national economies, they began to allocate a larger and larger proportion of their economic development budgets to funding a diverse range of SME research and support service initiatives. Unfortunately, even to this day, some agencies engaged in the provision of support to the SME sector tend to perceive that the only difference between large and small firms is the former having more '0s' in the numbers in their balance sheets. As a result, some of these agencies place too great an emphasis on development of new competencies within small firms which reflect the latest trend in large firm management thinking. Their reasoning is that such concepts will also be extremely valuable in assisting the performance of SME sector organisations.

In the UK, for example, in the 1980s, after large firms discovered the benefits of Total Quality Management (TQM), the Government was persuaded there was a need for small firms also to strongly embrace the concept of acquiring competency in the effective management of quality. The solution was to promote the merits to small firms of training staff in the processes required to become eligible for registration under some form of accreditation scheme such as BS 5750 or ISO 9000. The UK consultancy fraternity clearly made massive financial gains from being hired to deliver this initiative. Unfortunately subsequent research has demonstrated that for many small firms, management of quality through accreditation has had little or no impact on market performance. Furthermore in the most extreme situations, subsequent to receiving some form of accreditation, operating costs increased to the point where small firms were placed at a competitive disadvantage in relation to other businesses who had not sought to install a highly structured, formalised quality control system.

INTERNAL ORGANISATIONAL DIFFERENCES

In recent years, some governments have at last begun to listen to the wiser, more experienced small firm advisors and researchers when these individuals have communicated the message that small firms cannot be treated as down-scaled versions of multinational corporations. Thus in the UK, following years of effort by individuals such as Professors Curran, Gibb and Storey, the need to evolve management concepts that are directly relevant and applicable to the SME sector is finally being accepted by Government agencies developing new support schemes. Possibly four of the most important areas of internal organisational difference that need to be registered with support agencies and educationalists working in the SME sector are as follows.

First, although most large firms tend to have similar aims and objectives such as achieving market leadership and delivering an adequate return to their shareholders, the motivations which drive owner/managers are often very different. Some owner/managers, for example, have a lifestyle aim of wishing to create a business that leaves them free to play golf or go sailing at least two days a week. Others are concerned with enjoying a comfortable retirement and spend their time organising a directors' pension scheme based around the creation of tax efficient capital asset sale and leaseback schemes. Then there is another group of individuals who specialise in purchasing poorly run businesses at a knockdown price, upgrading the management team, installing effective control systems and once the business begins to recover, selling the enterprise for a significant profit.

Second, it is a common mistake to assume that the entire small firms sector can be considered as an homogeneous entity within which one can apply the same standard management paradigms to all situations. Even today, regrettably, this error is still to be found in some Government support initiatives (e.g. many new business startup schemes). In reality, however, there are huge variations in the nature of the management processes across the SME sector in relation both to the size of the small firms (thus a micro-enterprise consisting of three employees is clearly a very different proposition, even to a firm employing 15 individuals), and the sector of the economy in which the small firm operates (for example, a small hotel in the leisure industry versus a manufacturing firm producing high technology sub-components for the aerospace industry).

Third, it is not uncommon to hear the view articulated by both academics and support agency personnel that most small firms are orientated towards implementing a growth strategy which can lead to the creation of new job opportunities. This perspective probably explains why across Europe there is a plethora of government schemes making funds available to stimulate small firm expansion. However, if one talks to the average owner/manager, it soon becomes apparent that most are in fact 'growth adverse'. Their reasons for adopting this position are, however, very diverse. For example, some owner/ managers have achieved a satisfactory lifestyle and do not want the added responsibilities which would accompany any expansion of their business. Others recognise that they lack the skills to provide the quality of leadership necessary to effectively implement a growth strategy. In some other cases, the owner/manager accepts that their business has never really developed a genuine competitive advantage. Hence any further growth could probably only be achieved through the highly risky action of becoming more price competitive.

Fourth, another common misconception is that the majority of small firms are entrepreneurial. In fact, as demonstrated by (a) the highly conventional nature of most new business startups (for example, landscape gardening, industrial cleaning, house painting and so on) and (b) the strong appeal of entering the sector through the purchase of a conventional franchise (for example, the fast food industry, retailing, printing services), the vast majority of small firms seek to avoid the highly risky business of challenging prevailing market conventions.

THE RESOURCE BASED VIEW OF THE FIRM

A number of researchers examining the issue of what makes firms successful have concluded that a characteristic shared by growth firms is that of having an outstanding ability to manage internal organisational processes. Tom Peters (for example, 1992) has popularised this concept in his various writings where he presents examples of firms which have clearly discovered the importance of orchestrating internal activities to deliver superior customer satisfaction. Prahalad and Hamel (1990) have conceptualised the importance of managing internal processes better than competition. In their model they describe the internal influencers of success as firms having acquired superior core competencies. Goddard (1997) has subsequently proposed that in successful firms, core competencies are:

- imbued with experiential and tacit knowledge (that is, employees have an internalised understanding of how to effectively undertake their assigned organisational tasks) that competitors would find impossible to replicate;
- what the company does better than, or differently from, other companies;
- embedded in the organisation's *modus operandi*;
- limited to only two or three key activities within the value chain;
- the source of the company's ability to deliver unique value to customers;

- flexible enough to straddle a variety of business functions;
- the basis for defining market opportunities that the firm is uniquely equipped to exploit.

In the case of e-commerce, this new technology offers both a new promotional medium and an alternative channel through which to consummate the product purchase and delivery process. Consequently, applying the core competency concept implies that success in cyberspace markets will be influenced by the degree to which the small firm can develop unique capabilities by exploiting superior technical knowledge and internal organisational routines as the basis for supporting competitive advantage. This perspective leads to the conclusion that e-commerce provides an important example of how the 'resource based' view of the firm will provide the basis for determining whether a firm will achieve market success (Hitt and Ireland 1985; Mahoney and Pandian 1992).

Although e-commerce exhibits some unique technological features, the processes which it supports are not new to the world of marketing. A web page, for example, delivers promotional information using the same format as a magazine or a newspaper. The key differences are that the former has the facility to provide much more information and that the user, if they so desire, can undertake interactive searches for more data. Many websites go beyond communicating a promotional message by offering the additional feature of permitting the customer to place an order. Here again, processes associated with this activity of product identification, provision of delivery information and payment using a credit card are the same procedures that the customer will already have encountered when ordering goods through a direct marketing operation.

PERFORMANCE AND COMPETENCIES

There exists an extensive body of academic literature concerning the factors influencing the performance of small firms. Many of these factors can be classified under the three major headings of organisational development, functional management skills and sectoral economics.

A common element in the organisational development school of thought is to examine the relationship between the goals of the entrepreneur and the objectives of the organisation (Steinmetz 1969). In many instances, the discussion of relationships assumes the need for a move from an entrepreneurial to a 'professional' management style. However, given the debate on the need of larger organisations to move in the opposite direction and become more entrepreneurial (for example, Slevin and Covin 1990), some doubts must exist about whether this growth model philosophy should be offered as a normative theory through which to guide the activities of SME sector owner/managers.

The functional management school emphasises the need for the smaller firm to adopt a more formalised approach to activities such as strategic planning and the installation of effective control systems (Brock and Evans 1989). Although this rational decision making approach has received extensive coverage in the literature, there is still only limited evidence to support the view that clear links exist between the acquisition of these competencies and the subsequent growth rate of the firm (Carland *et al.* 1989).

Sectoral economic studies usually seek to identify factors of influence within an industrial system as the basis for predicting potential for growth. Researchers have often been able to demonstrate clear relationships between the perform-

Table 4.1 Summary of findings concerning characteristics exhibited by SME sector growth firms

---

Coopers & Lybrand (1994)
- perceive their markets as intensively competitive
- are flexible decision makers
- seek leadership through offering superior quality in a niche market
- deliver superior pre/post sales service
- use technology-driven solutions to achieve a superior position
- emphasise fast, frequent launch of new/improved products and draw upon external sources of knowledge to assist these activities
- emphasise application of technology and techniques such as cross functional teams, process re-engineering to optimise productivity
- recognise the need to invest in continual development of their employees
- rely mainly on internal profits to fund future investments

Cranfield study (Burns 1994)
- seek niches and exploit superior performance to differentiate themselves from competition
- operate in markets where there is only average to low intensity competition
- utilise clearly defined strategies and business plans to guide future activities
- rely mainly on internally generated funds to finance future investment

Comparative study of German and UK food processing firms (Brickau 1994)
- German firms emphasise acquisition of detailed knowledge of external factors capable of influencing performance
- they can clearly specify their competitive advantages
- they seek niches exploited through a superiority positioning
- they use strategies and plans to guide future performance
- they concurrently seek to improve products through innovation and enhance productivity through adoption of new process technologies
- they fund investment mainly from internal fund generation

Study of New Zealand exporting firms (Lindsay 1990)
- emphasise R&D to achieve continuous innovation and gain control of unique technologies
- orientate themselves towards achieving 'world class' superiority in specialist niches
- use structured plans based upon extensive information search to guide future performance
- exhibit a very entrepreneurial management style and encourage employee-based decision making
- strongly committed to using superior quality coupled with high productivity as a path to achieving competitive advantage

---

ance of original equipment manufacturers (OEMs) and growth rates of small business sub-contractors in sectors such as the car, computer and consumer electronics industries (for example, Storey *et al.* 1987). Overall, however, these studies do not appear to provide the basis for a generalised predictive model for the management of SME sector organisations (Doctor *et al.* 1989).

These three schools of thought have all made significant contributions to the evolution of theoretical paradigms for the understanding of management processes within smaller firms. Unfortunately they also appear to share the common weakness that it is difficult to apply these various concepts to evolve a predictive model for determining the competencies which support a successful growth strategy within the SME sector (Gibb and Davies 1990).

One possible alternative solution is to adopt the holistic view that common key characteristics exhibited by growth firms are a reflection of internal capabilities of the organisation (Chaston and Mangles 1997). A review of the literature, to identify internal capability factors which may influence the performance of small firms, revealed four studies in which the researchers used an extensive sample frame, their methodology was evolved through careful pilot testing, and the data were presented in a quantitative form which permitted some degree of statistical validation of the results. The findings from these projects, summarised in Table 4.1, have been used to evolve the visual descriptive model of small firm growth presented in Figure 4.1.

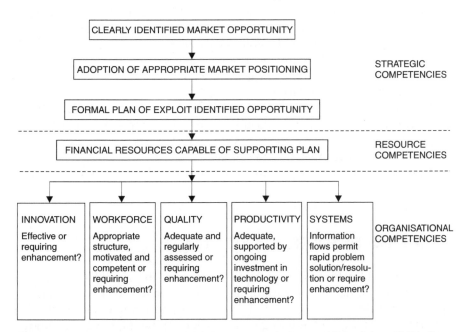

Figure 4.1 Qualitative model of characteristics exhibited by SME firms seeking to achieve market growth

STRATEGIC COMPETENCE

The long term survival of all organisations is critically dependent upon their ability both to identify new market trends and to determine how the internal capabilities of the organisation can be utilised to exploit emerging opportunities. This leads to the idea that the best entry point into the proposed model in Figure 4.1 is for the owner/manager to exhibit the strategic competence to identify a market niche which can be occupied by offering an appropriate product or service. During this analysis phase, in many cases the firm will be presented with a number of alternative options. In such cases what is required is to select that which the owner/manager believes offers the greatest source of long term opportunity.

This concept can be illustrated by examining the issue of evaluating strategic opportunity in the world of e-commerce. Ghosh (1998) has proposed that the following four distinct strategic marketing opportunities exist:

1. establishing a direct link with customers (or others with whom the firm has an important relationship) to complete transactions or exchange trade information more easily (for example, a small company distributing office supplies creating a website which permits the firm to sell supplies online to larger corporate customers);
2. utilising the technology to by-pass others within a value chain (for example, a small winery selling products direct to consumers via a website in place of marketing the product through retail outlets);
3. developing and delivering new products and services (for example, a golf course which offers online virtual reality golf games to people before they actually come to play the course for the first time);
4. becoming a dominant player in the electronic channel of a specific industry by creating and setting new business rules (for example, a supplier of specialist spare parts for rare sports cars who is first to create a website to market products to car enthusiasts and sources a much broader range of products by creating electronic links with other small suppliers across the world).

FINANCIAL RESOURCE COMPETENCE

The academic literature often contains reference to the view that small firms face immense difficulties in raising the finance needed to support ongoing operations. A closer investigation of these claims, however, often reveals that the firms which are encountering such problems either (a) have been under-capitalised from the outset or (b) the owner/manager lacks the necessary financial management skills required to ensure an appropriate balance between their ongoing trading activities and their working capital position (Peel and Wilson 1996; Kargar and Blumenthal 1994; Dodge *et al*. 1994). This observation is in contrast with the attribute exhibited by successful small firms. These latter organisations rely mainly upon internally generated profits, only occasionally need to turn to external sources to supplement internal financial reserves, and encounter few problems in raising more money when an injection of external funds is required.

The one area where small firm financing has faced a problem in the past, other than possibly within the USA, has been in the raising of small amounts of equity capital. This situation has been caused by the fact that institutional investors tend to be interested only in propositions requiring an equity injection of at least £500,000. Increasingly, smaller amounts of equity capital are now more readily available from the private investors. Additionally in both America and Europe this sector of the market has been expanded through the creation of lending networks known as the Business Angels scheme. Even by the late 1990s, however, some types of entrepreneurial propositions could still expect difficulties when seeking their first injection of equity capital. In the UK, for example, this situation currently confronts firms in the high technology sector or those owned by individuals belonging to ethnic minorities.

Another factor which can be an obstacle for small firms is that the owner/manager lacks the competence to develop a financial plan which is perceived as commercially viable by external lenders. Most recently this scenario has been illustrated by events in the small business e-commerce startup sector. For an e-commerce financial plan to be successful it is critical that the organisation has a complete understanding of the financial resources required to fund the level of investment which is needed to support an e-marketing strategy. For those owner/managers lacking Internet trading experience, initial examination would tend to indicate that creation of a website is an extremely low cost proposition. All that seems to be needed is to register a domain name and to then use off-the-shelf software from suppliers such as Microsoft to construct the organisation's web pages.

This observation is correct if the small firm merely wants to use the Internet to launch a static brochure into cyberspace. Unfortunately if the website is also required to attract visitors and generate sales, a much larger scale investment will be required. This investment will be used to (a) establish the hardware/software systems that can provide instant response to the diversity of demands which will be placed on the site by potential customers; (b) create the capability to update the site on almost a daily basis in order to sustain customer interest; and (c) ensure integration of the firm's internal information management systems such that customers receive a seamless service from the point of initial enquiry through to final delivery of purchased products (Seybold and Marshak 1998).

Even once the small firm has attracted the initial investment or bank loan to establish an effective Internet operation, there still remains the problem of sustaining visits to the site by both new and existing customers over the longer term. Merely being able to appear high on the list of sites identified by a customer using a search engine such as Yahoo or Alta Vista is not sufficient. For most online marketing propositions, the only way to generate a high level of site visitors is to continually invest in building customer awareness through expending funds on traditional promotional vehicles such as advertising, public relations and sales promotions (Chaston 1999b). This fact seems to have escaped the notice of many e-entrepreneurs, which is why the world is currently observing a spate of e-commerce closures (for example, the recent bankruptcy of the UK online sports goods operation www.boo.com) or of e-businesses being taken over by much larger firms.

INNOVATION COMPETENCE

To prosper and grow all organisations need to continually engage in finding new ways of improving their products and process technologies. Even once a firm has moved onto a growth track, complacency is not an option. This perspective is illustrated by one of Britain's most successful founders of a new business, Anita Roddick of Body Shop (South 2000). She spends at least four months every year sourcing new products from around the world. Currently she and her in-house team of innovators are focussing on natural skin products for women over 50 because they have realised that this sector represents a void in the firm's current portfolio.

Finding ways of improving internal operations should be given equal priority with new products in the battle to use innovation to stay ahead of competition. This philosophy is also illustrated by another example from Body Shop. In April 2000, the company launched a new operation designed to exploit the Internet and e-commerce to improve the company's ability to deliver retail services on a global basis. The first activity will centre on the US, followed in a few months' time by the opening of a UK website. To be effective, innovation should underpin and add support to a firm's existing mission and strategy. It is for this reason that the Body Shop electronic venture will focus on the dual objectives of retailing products and concurrently acting as a portal communicating the importance of operating socially and environmentally responsible businesses.

It should be recognised that exploiting innovation as a strategy for staying ahead of competition can be extremely expensive, especially for small firms involved in e-commerce. In this latter sector it is estimated that even firms which have already created successful, transaction-based websites are still having to spend 10–12 per cent of total revenue on R&D to stay ahead of competition (Anon. 1999a).

HUMAN RESOURCE MANAGEMENT COMPETENCE

It is often the case that whilst highly successful owner/managers are driven by the desire to achieve market recognition for their endeavours, they also have a tendency to ignore the need to concurrently establish an appropriate internal working environment capable of optimising both employee motivation and job satisfaction. As demonstrated by its success in intensely competitive markets such as Japan and the USA, New Zealand contains more highly entrepreneurial firms as a proportion of the total small firm population than possibly any other country in the world. It seems more than a coincidence, therefore, that within these firms, one frequently encounters owner/managers exhibiting a management style orientated towards fully involving the entire workforce in all key decisions. These owner/managers also place heavy emphasis on the continued development of all employees being a critical component in sustaining the ongoing success of their organisations.

In most market sectors, because the majority of firms understand the nature of customer need and use similar internal operations in the process of adding value whilst converting inputs to outputs, it is extremely difficult to achieve a long term sustainable advantage over competition. A key variable which can make a difference is the overall competence of a firm's workforce (Curran 1989), for example, the skills exhibited by employees in (a) the speed and accuracy with which products and services are delivered to customers and (b) obtaining the best possible performance from the machinery and equipment used in value-added processes.

It is critical that human resource management (HRM) practices within small firms are focussed on continually investing in upgrading of employee skills in order that all staff are capable of fulfilling their job roles to a standard that exceeds that achieved by competition. By achieving this goal, specific benefits can accrue to the small firm (Kerr and McDougall 1999). These include increased flexibility within the workforce (which permits people to be interchangeable, undertaking a number of core roles within the operation); an enhanced level of job satisfaction (which in turn promotes more effective working practices); and improved managerial skills at all levels within the firm.

Furthermore emphasis on good HRM policies permits the owner/manager to acquire greater understanding of what causes certain employees to consistently achieve high performance standards within the organisation. This knowledge can then be applied to ensure that all employees have the competencies necessary to make an effective contribution in sustaining the firm's market lead over competition.

An important issue is for owner/managers to recognise that the specific nature of HRM problems requiring resolution will vary both between firms in the same sector of industry and between different sectors of industry. For example at the moment, the greatest HRM problems facing firms in the e-commerce industry are the recruitment, retention and ongoing skills development of the technical staff responsible for the development and operation of e-commerce systems. For as recently reported (Anon. 1999b), even in Silicon Valley, California, the greatest constraint facing small firms wishing to gain competitive advantage in their Internet operations is the availability of computer staff with knowledge of the latest advances in network systems operations, telecommunications and programming. To promote an orientation towards ongoing learning by employees and to maximise staff retention levels in the sector firms are finding it critically important to create a work environment appropriate for the knowledge workers responsible for the development and operation of electronic technologies.

'Techies' are well known for their love of informality, freedom to work strange hours and immediate access to pizza and Coca Cola. Hence even the most conservative of e-commerce owner/managers are being forced to recognise the requirement of creating a work environment that promotes satisfaction across their workforce. Thus when one visits a small e-commerce firm one should not be surprised to find employees bringing their dogs to work, programmers being worked on by masseuses, a well stocked kitchen or canteen offering 24 hour access to food, huge refrigerators filled with an exotic range of alternative drinks and facilities for playing billiards (Anon. 1999a).

QUALITY COMPETENCE

Correction-based quality management, which essentially is the practice of waiting until something goes wrong and then initiating remedial actions to correct the fault, is founded on what is now considered to be an outmoded concept. It has been replaced by moving to prevention quality, whereby the organisation develops processes to minimise the occurrence of the mistakes that have been causing product defects to occur (Schonberger 1990).

The leaders in evolving prevention quality approaches have been the Japanese. The performance standards which they have set in world markets have meant over the last ten years, large Western nations have been forced to focus upon improving quality in order to survive. For example, Rover Group Cars seeking to respond to quality standards set by Honda and Toyota; and British Airways fighting to win back business customers lost to competitors such as Singapore Airlines.

In both consumer and 'B2B' markets, customers have experienced the reality that most large firms have improved their quality standards over recent years. This has caused the majority of customers to develop even higher expectations of the quality of services which they require from their suppliers, whether these be a big multinational or a member of the SME sector. Thus the ability of small firms to sustain customer loyalty is critically dependent upon their internal competencies in relation to all aspects of quality management.

Parasuraman *et al.* (1988) have determined that the critical variables influencing whether customers perceive that their expectations are being met include reliability, tangibles, responsiveness, assurance and empathy. In seeking to manage these variables it is important for small firms to recognise that most customers have an expectation that they will receive a greater level of personalised service than that which might be available when purchasing equivalent items from a large firm supplier. Hence small firms must have systems in place that ensure employees avoid making errors at the client interface whilst undertaking activities such as responding to an initial enquiry, order fulfilment, responding to customer questions, ensuring on-time delivery, handling product returns and meeting after sales service commitments.

In the case of small firms involved in e-commerce it is increasingly apparent that the requirement to fulfil quality expectations is even higher than in an equivalent terrestrial trading environment. This is due to the fact that if a website fails to fulfil expectations of quality, then at the click of a button the potential customer can instantaneously travel to a new location offering a higher level of service quality (Shapiro and Varian 1999). An additional problem facing the e-commerce firm is that the inexperience of many online customers means they are likely to make more mistakes and therefore need even more help resolving problems which their errors originally caused (Bartholomew 2000). For example, Ernst & Young estimate that about two thirds of people abandon their online shopping carts because they become confused or concerned about their purchase decisions. The other cause of service problems is that some small firms fail to make the investment required to ensure that they effectively link their website to their back office operation. The outcome in this situation is that errors or delays occur during the delivery cycle and this experience causes customers to seek out an alternative, more efficient online supplier.

PRODUCTIVITY COMPETENCE

Productivity is usually measured in terms of level of value-added activities per employee. By increasing productivity, the firm can expect to enjoy an increase in profitability (Hornell 1992). Given the major influence of productivity on organisational financial performance, it is clear that this is an area of internal competence that will have significant influence on market performance.

In relation to the management of the marketing process, possibly the two most important elements of the productivity equation are customer interface productivity and logistics productivity. In the case of customer interface productivity, the trend is towards using technology to ensure the small firm can rapidly and effectively respond to meeting all aspects of customer need from product enquiry through to ordering. Where the interface requires a high level of employee involvement it is critical that these individuals have been trained in their task role. There is a growing trend to assist these staff by providing them with computer-based tools such as access to online databases whilst talking to the customer.

Achieving customer satisfaction also demands that once an order is placed, employee productivity of back office staff involved in order processing, order assembly and product delivery is of the highest level. Again this can be achieved both by investing in staff training and by utilising technology such as computer-based, automated invoicing and shipping systems to support the task role.

In reviewing how to achieve productivity standards that are higher than those of competition, T.J. Rodgers, the founder and President of Cypress Semiconductor Corporation of San José, California, proposed in a *Harvard Business Review* article (1990) that there is a need to:

- hire outstanding people and hold on to them;
- encourage everybody in the organisation to set themselves challenging goals and to meet them;
- allocate key resources such as people and money to those areas most likely to provide the greatest opportunity for further productivity gains;
- reward people to encourage superior performance, rather than using more conventional reward systems such as pay rises based upon years of service to the firm or promotions based upon seniority. This is because these latter types of policy have the tendency to demotivate superior performers.

Rogers recommended that as well as ensuring that these operating philosophies are effective, there is a critical need to track performance of the organisation. Furthermore performance measurements must not be executed in isolation because such data are of little practical benefit unless they can be compared to information on performance achievements of other firms in the same industrial sector. This usually means that performance tracking within a firm should be based upon calculating ratios such as revenue per employee, revenue per unit of fixed asset, profit per employee and return on investment. This approach, because one can obtain published accounts of any limited company, permits the owner/manager also to undertake comparative productivity assessments of competitors.

An interesting perspective presented by Rogers is that as organisations grow in terms of hiring more people or acquiring additional equipment, the time will come when further expansion may begin to be accompanied by a decline in productivity. In his opinion, this occurs because the firm becomes too large to manage effectively. In the semiconductor industry, Rogers feels the break point is in the region of an annual revenue of $100 million. Thus as his company has grown, he has evolved the business into separate autonomous trading entities, on the grounds this is the only way to retain an achieved level of productivity per employee which is significantly higher than any other firm in the semiconductor business.

EXAMPLE: BEING DIFFERENT

Many small manufacturing firms are founded by engineers who often gain their greatest satisfaction from continually modifying and revising their firm's production processes. Although driven more by a fascination with how unconventional production techniques can improve on long standing sectoral conventions than by any real desire to significantly influence production costs, the outcome is that this group of owner/managers frequently introduces new operating procedures that can dramatically increase employee productivity. An example of this scenario is provided by a UK firm, Rigibore Ltd, which produces the drill bits for machine tools used in high precision engineering companies. The conventional way of designing a new drill bit, which can take several weeks, is to take the customer's drilling specification, make lengthy calculations, manually generate the design drawings, and finally have a specialist machine setter calibrate the machine for manufacturing the new design. Under the leadership of the firm's managing director, Rigibore has developed a proprietary CADCAM system which permits total automation of the process from design through to manufacture. The firm can now produce a new drill bit in hours, which provides an amazing employee productivity advantage over their more conventional competitors who will take several weeks to complete the same task.

INFORMATION SYSTEM COMPETENCE

A characteristic of the small firms sector is that insufficient managerial attention is given to establishing formalised information management systems. To a large degree this can probably be attributed to an apparent aversion that many owner/managers feel to spending time recording and documenting the day-to-day details of the various activities which constitute their business operations.

Possibly one of the most dangerous areas of poor information management relates to the firm's financial activities. Because many small firms lack any form of formalised accounting system, other than the annual financial reports produced by the firm's accountants, this failing is the reason why so many small firms get into financial difficulties. Without any internal systems, the owner/manager may be unable to undertake even the most basic types of financial assessment, such as reviewing debtor levels or identifying adverse trends in the average age of outstanding debts.

The availability of extremely low cost PCs and accounting/project management packages is beginning to have some impact on improving the quality of small firms' information systems. Nevertheless at the current time it is still quite unusual to find examples of small firms which have adopted the philosophy of using information systems as a route through which to achieve competitive advantage.

Participation in e-commerce provides an important catalyst for increasing the adoption rate of information systems within the SME sector. This is because for those firms which decide the Internet can provide the primary channel through which to attract new customers and retain the loyalty of existing customers, poorly integrated information systems are not an acceptable option. Success can only occur if all data flows are integrated. Continuous investment is demanded to achieve the goal of further upgrading and enhancing the company information systems. Without such investment it is extremely unlikely that the firm will be able to implement a strategy for beating the competition (Young *et al.* 1997).

EXAMPLE: THE BENEFITS OF BEING CONNECTED

The dramatic decline in the cost of the hardware and software for creating networks for linking together PCs means that smaller, more forward thinking firms are exploiting this aspect of IT as the basis for improving organisational performance (Hurst and Hayward 2000). One example is the architectural practice Marks Barfield which uses networks to link together its project teams and contractors around the world. To assist communication the firm has installed an ISDN connection to the Internet. This system permits instant delivery of working plans and diagrams. To handle e-mails the practice uses an Intel router which sends and receives mail, sorts mail and redistributes the message to the appropriate recipient.

Wise Buddah is a small firm employing 34 people which claims to be the biggest independent producer of music programming in the UK. The company produces over 1200 hours of programmes for radio stations such as those of the BBC. Five all-digital audio production studios are based in two buildings in London. To link together all the operations in these two buildings, the firm has created a private digital network. This system is complemented by staff using wireless telephones to make and receive voice and text messages. Each employee also has a single mail box on their PC to receive fax-mail, e-mail and voice-mail.

Richardsons is an accounting practice based in Oxfordshire. The practice has found that as clients have moved from communicating via snail mail to fax or e-mail, their expectation is for the practice to turn work around much more rapidly. In an attempt to move nearer to achieving this aim, Richardsons have installed a Microsoft Small Business Server 4.5 which links together the firm's 35

PCs. A central intranet permits file sharing and also has stabilised the increasing costs associated with employing support staff. A central digital library provides access to reference materials such as tax legislation updates, client case histories, tax returns and scanned-in correspondence. These pooled resources mean that client files can be shared and audit teams are able to work more effectively.

COMPETENCE TO FULFIL CUSTOMER NEEDS

In considering customer needs, over recent years a number of researchers have come to question classicist strategic marketing theory on the grounds that it places undue emphasis on the management of single transactions. Studies of the marketing process in service sectors such as finance and retailing have revealed situations where customers do not exhibit strong transactional orientated buying behaviour. This situation has thereby permitted small supplier firms to exploit opportunities for building long term relationships based on working in close partnership with purchasers.

During the 1980s, in considering both industrial and service markets, theorists began to focus on the idea that firms who were placing emphasis on single transactions should in fact be attempting to build long term relationships with customers. A strong impetus to this alternative philosophy was provided by Reichfeld and Sasser (1990). They demonstrated that a transaction orientation could result in focusing excessive resources on attracting new customers when in fact the real benefits of marketing come from programmes directed at retaining existing customers (or in their terminology ensuring achievement of 'zero defections').

As a result of studies of the marketing processes employed by both industrial and service firms, a new school of thought has emerged which examines how the firm can orchestrate internal resources and processes to create and sustain customer loyalty. Collectively this new orientation, which has both American (Berry 1983) and Nordic (Gummesson 1987) roots, is known as relationship marketing. Supporters of this new form of marketing argue that in order to survive in markets which have become more competitive and more turbulent, organisations must move away from managing transactions and instead focus on building long lasting customer relationships (Webster 1992).

Some disciples of the 'new marketing' have suggested that traditional concepts based around the approach of focusing resources on the '4 Ps', which may have been appropriate for North American consumer branded goods markets of the 1950s and 60s, are no longer relevant in today's world. Gronroos (1994), for example, proposes that 'The usefulness of the 4 Ps as a general theory for practical purposes is, to say the least, highly questionable.' A somewhat less extreme position, however, has been proposed by Nevin (1994) who feels firms should adopt a segmentation philosophy, ranging from building strong relationships with key customers through to continuing to utilise the traditional '4 Ps' approach for those customers seeking a standardised, generic product proposition.

Jackson (1985) has presented a similar view about the need to recognise that only certain market scenarios will permit application of a relationship marketing orientation. For her, transactional marketing is probably more appropriate in those cases where the customer has a short time horizon and switching suppliers is a low cost activity. In contrast, where the customer has a long time horizon and the costs of switching are high, then the purchase decision will involve a careful search for a supplier who is prepared to invest time and money to build a strong, lasting relationship with the customer. If one accepts Jackson's perspective, then the debate between transactional versus relationship marketing is one of choice. Thus in virtually every industrial and/or service sector situation there are price oriented customers who respond well to a transactional marketing philosophy, whereas there are other purchasers with whom a strong long term relationship can be created. The objective for the small firm under these circumstances is to select the marketing philosophy that is most suited to existing internal competencies or the nature of the product proposition to be offered to the market.

The same proposal on internal capability and nature of product offering can be made in the context of an entrepreneurial versus a non-entrepreneurial marketing orientation. Some small firms are best suited to manufacturing standardised goods at a competitive price. Other firms are extremely competent at managing 'leading edge' technology and clearly this skill can be best exploited by adopting an entrepreneurial orientation of regularly launching new, innovative products.

By drawing on Chaston's (1999) theory of alternative customer needs, it is possible to evolve a matrix of the type described in Figure 4.2. This conceptual model suggests that the following customer needs orientations exist in small business markets:

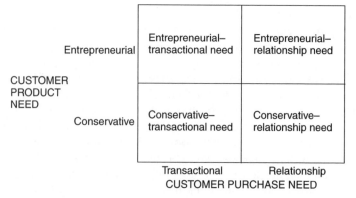

Figure 4.2 A customer need matrix

1. *Conservative-transactional orientated customer needs*
   - Price/quality/value product combination superior to that of competition
   - Standardised products
   - Low prices
2. *Conservative-relationship orientated customer needs*
   - Product/service combinations which deliver complete, customer specific solutions
   - Product solutions based on standard specification for industrial sector
   - Being offered even more effective solutions to solve customer problems
3. *Entrepreneurial-transactional orientated customer needs*
   - Products offering outstanding superior performance versus competition
   - Products offering better performance than existing products
4. *Entrepreneurial-relationship orientated customer needs*
   - Product contributes to ensuring customer output delivers superior performance relative to competition
   - Assistance to customers to achieve even more innovation that can extend the performance boundaries of their existing products

Achieving high standards of competence across all areas of activity is the desirable goal for every excellent small business. It is, however, extremely unlikely that any small firm has either the time or resources to achieve this aim. Under these circumstances, the owner/manager will need to carefully assess the needs of key customers and then decide which competencies should receive priority for further enhancement in terms of supporting the organisation's marketing strategies. Thus the conservative-transactional orientated small firm producing standard products and seeking to deliver a strategy of offering the best possible price/quality combination would probably be well advised to give priority to the organisation's information management systems and to optimising internal productivity. These competencies will also be of importance to conservative-relationship orientated firms, but additionally attention to service quality competence will be needed in order to deliver a strategy based around working in close partnership with the customer (Chaston 1999).

Entrepreneurial-transactional orientated small firms should probably give the highest competence priority to that of managing innovation in order to fulfil the strategy of always offering superior products. Given that customers in this sector of the market are more concerned with product performance than low price, then this type of firm need probably not be as concerned about concurrently achieving high ratings for employee productivity. Similarly entrepreneurial-relationship firms will also need to pay attention to innovation competence. In this latter case, however, the philosophy of working in close partnership with customers will also demand high levels of competence in the area of service quality (Chaston 2000).

Further empirical support for the concept that the importance of competencies will vary by market circumstance is provided by Borch *et al.* (1999)

in their study of the competitive strategies of Australian small firms. These researchers concluded that the influence on business performance of certain competencies was common to all firms across all sectors. These included an ability to ensure capitalisation is adequate, the requirement of managerial competence to ensure profit levels are appropriate to the degree of risk facing the firm, and an ability to make decisions about selecting the optimal source of external funds. In the case of small manufacturing firms, sector specific competencies included (a) the ability to acquire knowledge about competitors' activities and (b) having the process technologies to support being able to price products at a competitive level. This can be contrasted with small service sector firms, where the role of employees interfacing with customers is of critical importance. Successful service firms are those which have evolved an effective HRM operation that (a) ensures employees are involved in decision-making, (b) permits accurate appraisal of employee performance and job satisfaction and (c) creates effective systems for the delivery of appropriate ongoing employee skills development.

DISCUSSION QUESTIONS

1. Review the various errors which have been made by governments seeking to provide support services to assist the small firm sector.
2. Discuss the internal competencies known to influence the market performance of small firms.
3. Describe the different types of customer need which may be encountered. How might the competencies of small firms have to differ in order to service these variations in customer need?

REFERENCES

Anon. (1999a), 'Inside IBM: internet business machines', *Business Week*, 13 December, pp. 20–4.

Anon. (1999b), 'Barriers in e-commerce', *Today* (newspaper), New York, 6 August, pp. 8–9.

Bartholomew, D. (2000), 'Service to order', *Industry Week*, 3 April, pp. 19–20.

Berry, L.L. (1982), 'Relationship marketing', in Berry, L.L., Shostack, G.L. and Upah, G.D. (eds), *Emerging Perspectives on Service Marketing*, American Marketing Association, Chicago, pp. 25–8.

Borch, O.J., Huse, M. and Senneseth, K. (1999), 'Resource configuration, competitive strategies and corporate entrepreneurship: An empirical examination of small firms', *Entrepreneurship Theory and Practice*, Vol. 24, No. 1, pp. 29–62.

Brickau, R. (1994), *Responding to the Single Market: a Comparative Study of UK and German Food Firms*, Unpublished Ph.D. dissertation, University of Plymouth, Plymouth.

Brock, W.A. and Evans, D.A. (1989), 'Small business economics', *Small Business Economics*, Vol. 1, No. 1, pp. 7–21.

Burns, P. (1994), 'Keynote address', *Proceedings 17th ISBA Sheffield Conference*, ISBA, Leeds.

Carland, J.W., Carland, J.C. and Abbey, C. (1989), 'An assessment of the psychological determinants of planning in small business', *International Small Business Journal*, Vol. 7, No. 4, pp. 23–33.

Chaston, I. (1999), *New Marketing Strategies*, Sage, London.

Chaston, I. (2000), *Entrepreneurial Marketing*, Macmillan Business, London.

Chaston, I. and Mangles, T. (1997), 'Core capabilities as predictors of growth potential in small manufacturing firms', *Journal of Small Business Management*, Vol. 35, No. 1, pp. 47–57.

Coopers & Lybrand (1994), *Made in the UK: The Middle Market Survey*, Coopers & Lybrand, London.

Curran, J. (1989), 'Employment and employment relations in the small firm', Kingston Business Research Unit, Paper No. 6.

Doctor, J., Van der Haorst, R. and Stokman, C. (1989), 'Innovation processes in small and medium-sized companies', *Entrepreneurship and Regional Development*, Vol. 1, No. 1, pp. 35–53.

Dodge, H., Fullerton, S. and Robins, J. (1994), 'Stage of the organisational life cycle and competition as mediators of problems', *Strategic Management Journal*, Vol. 15, pp. 121–134.

Ghosh, S. (1998), 'Making sense of the Internet', *Harvard Business Review*, March–April, pp. 127–135.

Gibb, A.A. and Davies, L. (1990), 'In pursuit of a framework for the development of growth models of the small business', *International Small Business Journal*, Vol. 9, No. 1, pp. 15–31.

Goddard, J. (1997), 'The architecture of core competence', *Business Strategy Review*, Vol. 8, No. 1, pp. 43–53.

Gronroos, C. (1994), 'From marketing mix to relationship marketing', *Journal of Academic Marketing Science*, Vol. 23, No. 4, pp. 252–4.

Gummesson, E. (1987), 'The new marketing – developing long-term interactive relationships', *Long Range Planning*, Vol. 20, No. 4, pp. 10–20.

Hitt, M.A. and Ireland, R.D. (1985), 'Corporate distinctive competence, strategy, industry and performance', *Strategic Management Journal*, Vol. 6, pp. 273–93.

Hornell, E. (1992), *Improving Productivity for Competitive Advantage: Lessons from the Best in the World*, Pitman, London.

Hurst, R. and Hayward, E. (2000), 'Get connected', *Real Business*, September, pp. 57–64.

Jackson, B.B. (1985), *Winning and Keeping Industrial Customers: The Dynamics of Customer Relationships*, D.C. Heath, Lexington, MA.

Kargar, J. and Blumenthal, R.A. (1994), 'Leverage impact of working capital in small businesses', *TMA Journal*, Vol. 14, No. 6, pp. 46–53.

Kerr, A. and McDougall, M. (1999), 'The small business of developing people', *International Small Business Journal*, Vol. 17, No. 12, pp. 10–22.

Lindsay, V., (1990), *Export Manufacturing – Framework For Success*, New Zealand Trade Development Board, Wellington.

Mahoney, J.T. and Pandian, J.R. (1992), 'The resource-based view within the conversation of strategic management', *Strategic Management Journal*, Vol. 13, pp. 363–80.

Nevin, J.R. (1994), 'Relationship marketing and distribution channels: exploring fundamental issues', *Journal of Academic Marketing Science*, Vol. 23, No. 4, pp. 334–7.

Parasuraman, A., Zeithmal, V.A. and Berry, L.L. (1988), 'A conceptual model of service quality and its implications for future research', *Journal of Marketing*, Vol. 49, Fall, pp. 34–45.

Peel, M.J. and Wilson, N. (1996), 'Working capital and financial management in the small firm sector', *International Small Business Journal*, Vol. 14, No. 2, pp. 52–68.

Peters, T. (1992), *Liberation Management*, A.F. Knopf, New York.

Prahalad, C.K. and Hamel, G. (1990), 'The core competence of the corporation', *Harvard Business Review*, May–June, pp. 79–91.

Reichfeld, S.S. and Sasser, W. (1990), 'Zero defections: quality comes to services', *Harvard Business Review*, September–October, pp. 301–7.

Rogers, T.J. (1990), 'No excuses management', *Harvard Business Review*, July–August, pp. 12–26.

Schonberger, R.J. (1990), *Building a Chain of Customers: Linking Business Functions to Create the World Class Company*, Hutchinson, London.

Seybold, P.B. and Marshak, R.T. (1998), *Customer.com: How to Create a Profitable Business Strategy for the Internet and Beyond*, Random House, New York.

Shapiro, C. and Varian, H.R. (1999), *Information Rules*, Harvard Business School Press, Harvard, Mass.

Slevin, D.P. and Covin, J.G. (1990), 'Juggling entrepreneurial style and organisational structure – how to get your act together', *Sloan Management Review*, Winter, pp. 43–53.

Steinmetz, L. (1969), 'Critical stages of small business growth', *Business Horizons*, February, pp. 12–19.

Storey, D.J., Keasey, K., Watson, R. and Wynarczyk, P. (1987), *The Performance of Small Firms*, Croom Helm, London.

South, G. (2000), 'What on earth is Anita Roddick up to now?' *Real Business*, September, pp. 14–16.

Webster, F.E. (1992), 'The changing role of marketing in the corporation', *Journal of Marketing*, Vol. 56, October, pp. 1–17.

Young, K.M., El Sauvy, O.A., Malhotra, A. and Gosain, S. (1997), 'The relentless pursuit of "Free Perfect Now": IT enabled value innovation at Marshall Industries', 1997 SIM International Papers Award Competition, http://www.simnet.ord/public/programs/capital/97papers/paper1.html.

5 MARKET POSITIONING AND COMPETITIVE ADVANTAGE

LEARNING OBJECTIVES

After studying this chapter you should be able to understand:

1. the alternative positioning available in relation to the variables of mass marketing, niche marketing, cost leadership and differentiation;
2. why differentiation represents a higher scale advantage than a cost leadership positioning;
3. the advantages enjoyed by mass market brands and how these are rarely available to small firms;
4. the claims of how the Internet might represent a source of advantage for small versus large firms;
5. the attributes of a niche marketing strategy;
6. how larger firms are acquiring the ability to customise their products and thereby are now also able to service the needs of niche market customers.

CHAPTER SUMMARY

The alternatives of mass versus niche marketing and of cost leadership versus differentation mean that firms are presented with four possible options when considering the selection of a market positioning. Cost leadership is a low order advantage because sustaining this advantage is difficult. Long term positioning security is more likely to accrue to firms opting to offer superior performance to customers. Mass market brands enjoy economies of scale, large promotional resources and an ability to control market environments. These options are rarely available to small firms. Initially it was thought that the Internet could resolve this competitive imbalance between small and large firms. Evidence is now emerging, however, that large firms are learning how to also dominate cyberspace trading channels.

Small firms have traditionally avoided confrontation with large firms by being able to occupy specialist market niches. By exploiting the benefits of TQM, JIT and lean manufacturing, large firms are now more able to produce a more diverse range of customised products. An example of this achievement is provided by Dell being able to offer an online facility that permits customers to purchase 'one off' PC designs. This ability within the large firm sector means that small firms can no longer feel safe by occupying a market niche. To survive they need to place greater emphasis on using their knowledge of markets to add value to their product offerings and on sustaining delivery of superior service quality.

INTRODUCTION

Marketers have long accepted that success demands identification of some form of competitive advantage capable of distinguishing the organisation from other firms operating in the same market sector. In seeking to evolve a model for describing alternative strategies for achieving advantage, Michael Porter (1985) combined two marketing concepts. The first was the perspective that small firms tend to specialise in serving only parts of a market (that is, niche marketing), whereas large firms usually seek to maximise the number of customers served (that is, mass marketing). The second concept involves the operational characteristics of the firm, in terms of generating sales by exploiting lower operating costs to market low price goods, versus offering a superior product, thereby commanding a higher price in a market.

By merging the concepts of mass versus focus (niche) marketing and superior performance versus cost leadership, Porter evolved a competitive advantage matrix of the type shown in Figure 5.1. This matrix is a visual representation of four possible generic competitive advantage options available to organisations: *cost leadership, differentiation, focussed cost leadership* and *focussed differentiation*.

Delivering low price by being a cost leader is based upon exploiting some aspect of internal organisational process that can be executed at a cost significantly lower than competition. There are various sources of this cost advantage. These include lower input costs (for example, the low labour costs associated with coal mining in Eastern Europe); and lower in-plant production costs or delivery costs reduced by the near proximity of key markets (for example, the practice of some major beer producers who locate micro-breweries in, or near to, major metropolitan areas). In the case of focussed cost leadership the company decides to occupy (a) specific niche(s) servicing only part of the total market (for example, a horticulture enterprise which operates an on-site farm shop offering low priced, fresh vegetables to the inhabitants of towns within the immediate area).

BASIS OF PRODUCT PERFORMANCE PROPOSITION

	Cost	Superior performance
Mass market	Cost leadership	Differentiation
Niche market	Focussed cost leadership	Focussed differentiation

MARKET COVERAGE

Figure 5.1   A competitive advantage alternative positioning matrix

Porter has proposed that focussed and overall market cost leadership represent a 'low scale advantage' because it is often the case that eventually a company's advantage is eroded by rising costs. For example, as an economy moves from developing to developed nation status, unions are able to persuade employers to pay higher wages or to improve terms and conditions of employment. Alternatively a company's market position is usurped by an even lower cost source of goods (for example, the Korean manufacturers in the 1980s being able to usurp Japan's position as a low cost car producing nation).

The generic alternative of offering superior products is usually known as differentiation. Porter argues that this is a 'higher scale advantage' because (a) the producer can usually command a premium price for output and (b) competitors are less of a threat, for to be successful they must be able to offer an even higher performance specification product. Focussed differentiation, which is typically the preserve of smaller, more specialist firms, is also based on a platform of superior performance. The only difference is that the firm specialises in serving the needs of a specific market sector.

The other attraction of differentiation is that there are a multitude of dimensions which can be exploited in seeking to establish a product or service which is superior to competitor offerings. Garvin (1987), for example, has proposed that in relation to superior quality there are eight different dimensions which might be considered: performance, features, reliability, conformance to quality expectations specified by customers, durability, serviceability, aesthetics and perceived quality. In addition to dimensions associated with the physical product, organisations can also exploit other aspects of the purchase and product utilisation process by offering outstanding service across the areas of ease of ordering, delivery, installation, customer training, maintenance, repair and post-purchase product upgrades.

MASS MARKETING

Drawing upon concepts pioneered by individuals such as Henry Ford in America, the marketing philosophy of many large firms is to dominate markets by manufacturing large volumes of standard goods that can be made available at prices affordable by the majority of a population. Richard Tedlow (1990), a business historian at Harvard Business School, has identified generic guidelines for the strategies appropriate for establishing successful mass market brands. By reviewing these guidelines one can determine why the average small firm should rarely expect to take business away from large firms. Tedlow's mass marketing guideline 1 proposes that large firm marketers will exploit the economies of scale associated with mass production to sell huge volumes of low margin goods which generate a high level of absolute profits. The lack of economies of scale within SME sector firms means that an equivalent profit opportunity is rarely available to a small firm. Guideline 2 proposes that the mass marketer can afford to expend funds supporting a high level of promotional activity as a mechanism through which to shape market demand. Here again the small firm rarely enjoys anywhere near the same level of absolute profits and is thus unable to fund promotional activity which can match the spending level of major brands.

Guideline 3 proposes that large firms, in seeking to create a high level of stability in the external operating environment, will often move to create a vertical system through which raw materials are sourced, production operations are managed and products delivered to the final consumer (for example, Coca Cola's operation, which involves supplying concentrate syrups to bottling companies around the world, who then manage both production and distribution of the product to end user outlets). Few small firms have either the resources or negotiating power to create equivalent vertical networks and this means they are more affected by fluctuations in market environments than their large firm counterparts. Guideline 4 proposes that, once an enterprise has achieved mass market dominance through being the first mover in a major market sector, this is followed by the creation of economies of scale barriers to ward off attacks from competition. In contrast small firms are rarely able to establish such barriers, and if a larger firm is interested in their market, it is usually impossible to counter their actions to steal market share from the smaller firm.

An example of this latter scenario is provided by Freddie Laker, a UK entrepreneur who was the first to recognise the opportunities of offering cut-price seats on international flights between Europe and the USA. Once Laker Airlines demonstrated the huge market appeal for the proposition, the established airlines such as British Airways responded with some aggressive, in some cases possibly illegal, strategies which eventually forced the smaller airline into bankruptcy.

THE FALSE GOLD OF THE INTERNET?

In the early years of the Internet, some of the first entrants into cybermarkets were small firms offering specialist goods and services. This trend caused some industry observers to predict that the low cost of entry into the world of cyberspace trading at last permitted small firms to compete on a level playing field with mass market brands. Over the last few years, however, it has become apparent that many major brands are now often more successful than small firms in exploiting the Internet.

Analysing this situation reveals that e-commerce is a purchase channel that tends to favour the brand leaders in many market sectors. A prime reason for this situation is that when customers start to use the Internet they are often very concerned about the potential risks associated with this new way of executing the purchase transaction. To reduce this risk, customers will usually select the company or brand name with which they have greatest familiarity. Additionally the major brands also have the promotional resources that permit the use of traditional channels such as television advertising to build awareness of their website address and of the nature of their online offering.

This trend in the online battles between small and large firms is demonstrated by events in the world of grocery shopping. In the USA, one of the first firms to offer online grocery shopping was the new small business entrant, www.peapod.com. They succeeded because none of the major supermarket chains was then considering offering an online transaction and home delivery service. This contrasts with the situation in the UK a few years later, when the early entrants into e-commerce were the national supermarket chains such as Tesco and Sainsbury's. Their online presence, linked to well established brand identities and heavy promotional spending, has meant that no small firm has been able to replicate Peapod's success in the UK.

A possible exception to the usual outcome in small versus large company online warfare can be found in relation to the smaller, specialist firm competing against the manufacturers of major fast moving consumer goods (FMCG) brands such as Lever and Procter & Gamble. These latter companies have extensive experience in developing and executing marketing strategies designed to ensure they can sustain the long term performance of their branded goods operations (Marsh 1999). It seems surprising, therefore, to find that apparently they have been somewhat slow in seeking to establish a significant presence on the Internet. Smaller firms in the same product categories, however, who have already moved onto the Internet should be very wary of what will happen over the next few years. These owner/managers need to realise that FMCG companies rarely attempt to lead their customers into making significant changes in purchase behaviour. Instead their more likely tendency is to monitor emerging market trends and then make a move only when they believe the time is right. Thus as the Internet gains in popularity with the major brands' target customers, FMCG firms can be expected not only to enter the world of online trading, but to accompany this move with a scale of promotional expenditure capable of totally burying many smaller firms.

Some small e-commerce firms have realised that that there is unlimited shelf space available through operating a single distribution point to service all online customer needs. This means the only constraint on the range of products that can be offered on a small firm website is sufficient working capital to fund the expenditure on inventories (Noto 2000). This situation permits even the smallest of firms to offer the customer a genuine 'one stop shop' purchasing experience. The Internet also has the capability to make vast quantities of information available to online visitors. Given that small firms often have specialist, in-depth knowledge of their market sector, there may be potential for them to defeat large brands by offering customers a broad range of products, all supported by a higher level of information than just product usage knowledge.

This view is supported by Christensen and Tedlow (2000). These authors feel it is probable that over time, national retailers who move online will force many existing smaller electronic outlets to migrate upmarket. In their view the most viable long term strategy for the smaller e-commerce retailer is to use their expertise to offer additional knowledge based, value added services. This then allows them to counter threats from larger firms who tend to compete using an aggressive price discounting strategy and only offering a limited level of online support to their customers.

THE NEW THREAT

For many years small firms have survived by identifying sectors of the market where customers are seeking specialist goods or services. In the past, the size of these specialist sectors has been such that large national or multinational firms had neither the interest nor the manufacturing flexibility to profitably service these types of market opportunity. Tedlow (1990), however, has shown that many leading mass market companies have moved from a profit-through-volume strategy approach towards a new operating philosophy based around segmenting the market and offering a variety of goods to the now more sophisticated and experienced customer. The first moves in this direction occurred in the 1960s when large multinationals perceived the bene-fit of adopting a market segmentation approach of using a broader product range to serve the varying needs of specific groups of customers instead of merely offering a single, standardised product to all customers. Initially large firms tended to use very simple taxonomies for segmenting markets, such as customer location or sociodemographics (Bonoma and Shapiro 1983). These early, somewhat crude approaches have now been replaced by techniques such as dividing customers into groups on the basis of their knowledge, benefits sought, attitudes or product usage rates.

In the early days of market segmentation, small firms faced few threats from large firms because of the latter's inability to manufacture products capable of adequately meeting highly varied, specialist customer needs. This was due to inflexible manufacturing philosophies making it prohibitively expensive to schedule production runs of numerous, different specification products. By the mid 1980s, in large part due to pioneering efforts by Japanese firms in the area of lean manufacturing, many large companies have acquired the ability to control the costs associated with frequent changes in the variety of products being produced. As this new approach to manufacturing management has been adopted around the world, large firms have started to entertain the idea of serving smaller and smaller customer segments.

The ultimate possibility offered by lean manufacturing is that in some market sectors, companies can consider the idea of one-to-one marketing. As large firms have begun to implement this new philosophy, small firms in sectors as diverse as health and beauty, sports cars, food products, computers, computer software and industrial chemicals are having to learn how to survive in a world where the new competitive threat is that of large multinationals.

In the past, a major advantage enjoyed by small firms has been that being close to their customers meant they were able to acquire an in-depth knowledge of individual customer needs. Traditional market research techniques have prevented large firms from acquiring a similar depth of knowledge about their customers. However, advances in technology have removed this obstacle because multinationals are now using electronic data collection to acquire data on purchases by individual customers. One catalyst in this area was the advent of electronic shop tills that permit the monitoring of purchase patterns of individual consumers using Universal Product Codes (bar codes). This has been followed by large firms using data generated from consumers using credit cards to make purchases and more recently, exploiting the information that becomes available from persuading customers to join loyalty schemes which employ smart cards to record individual in-store purchase behaviour.

By exploiting the rapidly declining costs for computer hardware and software tools, large firms are now able to rapidly analyse data collected electronically. This new trend is known as data warehousing or data mining. Baker and Baker (1998) have proposed that this new approach permits large firms to acquire a knowledge of individual customers equal to that previously only available to small firms, because data mining permits large firms to classify:

- customers into distinct groups based upon their purchase behaviour, and to model relationships between possible variables such as age, income and location to determine which of these influence individual purchase decisions;

- data into infinitely small clusters that define specific customer types, and use this knowledge to tailor the marketing mix meet the specific needs of individual customers.

The pace at which large firms are moving into one-to-one marketing has been further accelerated by the advent of e-commerce. Customers visiting websites are usually required to provide detailed information as part of the order placement process. This has greatly added to the ability of large firms to use data warehousing to gain in-depth insights into the behaviour of their customers. In commenting on this new world, Jeffrey Bezos, the founder of Amazon.com, the world's leading mass marketing bookshop, has used the analogy that the e-commerce retailer can behave like the small-town shop-keeper of yesteryear. This is because large firms can now develop a deep understanding of everybody who comes into the online store. Armed with such knowledge, like the shopkeeper in a village store, the large retailer can personalise service to suit the specific needs of every individual customer across a widely dispersed geographic domain.

In his analysis of the strategic implications associated with operating in the information rich world of e-commerce, Glazer (1999) has proposed that the winners will be the 'smart companies'. He defines these as organisations which have realised the power of IT to totally transform business practices within their market sector. They are the 'first movers' who exploit every advance in computer and telecommunications technology ahead of their 'dumber' competitors. In reality the ability to be a first mover is just as available to small firms as it is to their large firm counterparts. Furthermore given that small firms usually have the organisational flexibility to rapidly exploit newly emerging opportunities, then the small, smart firm should review the opportunities available from being first to offer their customers the benefits of:

1. one stop shopping, such that customer needs can be satisfied by a single supplier, thereby saving the customer time in searching out a range of goods from multiple sources. In many cases for the small firm to achieve this goal there will be a need to form a collaborative relationship with other businesses (for example, a group of small hotels creating a regional website for tourist visitors);
2. providing the customer with a menu of choices concerning modes of product form and different delivery options (for example, a smoked salmon producer diversifying into a whole range of smoked fish and meat products and via a website offering express or standard time delivery options);
3. proactively anticipating the changing market needs and developing even more effective information systems for more rapidly and more efficiently satisfying the customer (for example, a small yacht company, specialising in alternative materials such as carbon fibre and advanced plastics in the construction of hulls, offering a website on which visitors can examine

(a) product specifications for alternative utilisation of yachts from cruising through to racing and (b) the cost implications of different hull designs.

NICHE MARKETING

A niche market is a narrowly defined market containing a group of customers with highly specialist needs. When compared with market segments, niches tend to be smaller and consequently the limited scale of market opportunity means that only a small number of firms will seek to offer the distinct product benefits that are sought by potential customers. The traditional theory presented in most marketing texts is that the limited scale of revenue offered by many market niches is such that this type of opportunity is of little interest to larger firms. As discussed earlier, however, the advent of large firms being able to exploit advances in process technology to move into one-to-one marketing means that small firms need to be aware that national or multinational operations may seek to move into the more attractive niches which exist in some markets.

Fortunately a critical variable in the execution of a mass customisation strategy is an ability to produce the customised products required by the purchasers (Anon. 2000). To date only a small number of national or multinational organisations have acquired this capability. However if small firms want to see the implications of how this will increasingly occur in the future, then there is possibly no better example than that of Dell Computers. This company permits customers to design an individualised computer online. The online product order data are used to automatically schedule production, contact suppliers where components are not on hand and alert the logistics group to schedule the shipment of the finished product on a specific date.

EXAMPLE: UNDERSTANDING OPPORTUNITY

Identification and exploitation of new market niches is a skill that is rarely encountered in large firms. In most cases this activity is the preserve of the small firm entrepreneur, who often stumbles upon unfulfilled customer satisfaction and recognises that this can provide the basis for a new business.

Stephen Gordon graduated from college in 1978 and having quit his job as a psychologist started to renovate a six bedroom Victorian mansion in Eureka, Northern California (Marsh 1998). Whilst locating materials and furnishings for his project he soon realised that other people renovating homes in Eureka were frequently approaching him for advice and assistance. Thus in 1980 he opened a store called Restoration Hardware which stocked hard-to-find materials for house renovators. By the early 1990s the company had five stores in California.

By the mid 1990s Restoration Hardware had evolved into a chain of 41 furnishing stores operating across 18 American states.

Another example of an opportunistic niche is provided by French farmer Serge Griotto who discovered a freak of nature: a solitary red rice plant with mature grains the colour of garnet growing on his rice farm in the Camargue (Hardcastle and McLoughlin 1997). This plant was a naturally occurring mutation caused by a cross between a white rice plant and the Camargue's indigenous, inedible, wild red grass. Griotto exploited his find by creating a new product known as Camargue Red Rice which offers an unusual alternative to white rice because his product exhibits the unique properties of a nutty flavour, soft texture and the ability to retain the red colour when cooked. By the late 1990s the product had become established as a specialist rice especially suitable for use in salads and is now sold by most major supermarket chains within the European Union.

It is somewhat rare that an owner/manger encounters a niche which offers the scale of opportunity exemplified by Restoration Hardware and Camargue Red Rice. A more usual outcome is that the limited scale of market opportunity will mean the small business will never grow beyond a certain size. This latter scenario is demonstrated by Wolfe Video, a Californian distributor of R-rated gay and lesbian movies (La France 1999). Founded by Katherine Wolfe, the company distributes videos to speciality shops, major retail video stores and via a direct marketing operation. What the founder has realised, however, is that the identified niche is an extremely finite market opportunity which means that after 14 years of very hard work building a customer base, annual sales of $1.6 million only generate $100,000 in pre-tax profits.

EXAMPLE: THE IMPLODING NICHE

Highly experience owner/managers are always very sceptical of market niche opportunities that appear to offer the chance to generate extremely high levels of profit. Over the years, they have come to understand that the usual outcome for high profit niches is that strong market demand will either prove to be (a) a temporary phenomenon or (b) a long term opportunity, which means large firms will eventually seek to acquire ownership of the market sector.

A recent example of an imploding niche is provided by the e-commerce consultancy business in the USA (Koudsi 2000). Founded by individuals who previously worked for large firms, these new enterprises exploited the mushrooming demand by firms desperate for assistance in developing an Internet business strategy and to launch their first website. Having delivered these services during the late 1990s, by 2000 many e-commerce consultancies found that the demand for web design and development had been replaced by clients seeking to create integrated e-commerce systems which are merged into the firm's terrestrial operations. This latter type of market requirement requires a diversity of expertise that is usually only available in large consultancy businesses such as Price Waterhouse Coopers and Arthur Anderson Consulting.

One firm squeezed out by the implosion of the US e-commerce niche is iXL, based in Atlanta, Georgia. In September 2000, the company announced it would miss the next quarter's financial targets and planned to lay off 12% of the workforce. Two weeks later shareholders filed a class action suit claiming they had received false and misleading information from the company. Company shares then plunged in value by 38% to hit an all-time low of $5.

Although small firms have a reputation for being flexible thinkers able to proactively react to changing market conditions, even in these types of organisation, employees can sometimes be a major obstacle in the way of change. This is illustrated by events at Luminate, a US business software company (Daniels 2000). The company was founded in 1995 to exploit the demand for installing specialist software capable of monitoring performance of a sophisticated Enterprise Resource Planning (ERP) system produced by SAP of Germany. ERP is a technology that allows big firms to automate and integrate organisational processes.

By 1999, it became apparent that the market demand for SAP was on the decline which in turn would mean an eventual implosion of Luminate's market niche. The company's founder, Bruce Fram, realised that survival required Luminate ro move from installing software on the client's computer system and instead become an Application Service Provider (ASP) offering software to the market via an Internet site.

Fram's problems in implementing the fundamental change in strategy included amongst other things a categorical refusal by the firm's product development team to believe a move to web-based product delivery was necessary. As a result it took three months to persuade them to agree to write the new software. In hindsight, Fram admits he made a fundamental error is attempting to keep the employees from knowing that a major change in business direction was necessary whilst he worked with senior executives in the planning of the firm's proposed market repositioning. As a result employees could only guess that something was going on and this caused them to become concerned about the future security of their jobs. Finally having overcome internal employee resistance to change, Luminate launched the new web-based operation in March 2000. In the first two months of trading their first online product, Mamba, achieved a 25 per cent market share.

A distinct contrast to Luminate is Mercury Interactive, a firm that seems to revel in re-inventing itself on a regular basis. In the early 1990s the company's core business was testing Unix and Windows software. Then it moved to exploit opportunities in the Y2K (year 2000) market. Now the firm has moved on again. The current core business is enhancing the performance of websites by monitoring performance and identifying 'fixes' that can speed up online data interchange. Numbered among the company's client list are companies such as Cisco, Wal-Mart, Amazon and America Online (Rynecki 2000).

Most small firms operate as batch producers which means they often still retain a superiority in being able to more flexibly and rapidly respond to customers seeking an unusual product or service. Thus a small 'metal basher' in the metal ducting industry is still likely to be the preferred supply source by a construction company seeking a one-off ducting system for a project concerned with updating and renovating an old factory building. Similarly owners of rare, unusual classic cars are likely to get better insurance coverage by using a small independent broker than by seeking cover from a large multinational insurance firm.

Some small firms, having been successful in one market niche, then assume that they have sufficient expertise to expand into other market sectors. Regrettably what often happens in this scenario is that the firm lacks the ability to effectively manage a growth or diversification strategy and failure subsequently ensues. A recent example of this outcome is provided by the UK firm, Laura Ashley. The firm started life as a specialist producer of upmarket fabrics and furnishings. Having successfully established itself in this market niche, in the 1980s the firm embarked on a massive expansion, broadening its product range and concurrently seeking to expand market coverage into numerous countries around the world. Sadly the firm soon encountered severe trading difficulties, went through the process of hiring and firing chief executives and by the late 1990s became a shadow of its former self.

A common constraint facing niche players wishing to implement a growth strategy is an inability to cover the massive expenditure on promotion and channel expansion that is required to attract a sufficiently large number of new customers. The advent of e-commerce has, however, in some cases changed this situation. This is because by establishing a web presence, niche firms can now offer their products or services across the entire globe. One of the reasons why the approach can be successful is that in many cases, it is not necessary to spend heavily on traditional promotional campaigns to build awareness of the firm's web address. The ability to avoid promotional expenditure occurs because customers seeking very specialist needs are often prepared to spend hours using Internet search engines to find new sources of supply.

EXAMPLE: B2B NICHE OPPORTUNITIES

Most people tend to imagine the achievement of growth objectives in the computing and telecommunications industry is the preserve of multinationals such as IBM, Microsoft, Nokia, and AT&T. Nevertheless these sectors have also provided a rich spawning ground for small firms able to exploit a specialist technological capability as the basis for building a highly successful B2B small business (Daniels 2000). Furthermore in many cases, the customers of these specialist producers are often a sector's largest original equipment manufacturers (OEMs).

RF Micro Devices, based in Greensboro, North Carolina has developed a range of data transmitting semiconductors which are used in mobile telephones and wireless security systems. Cree Corporation in Durham, North Carolina holds 71 patents on blue light emitting diodes or LEDS. These are the components that provide backlighting in products as diverse as car dashboards and cell phone displays.

In the case of stories about successful small Internet businesses, the tendency of the popular media is to feature firms operating in consumer goods markets. In reality, however, the opportunity for e-commerce niche marketing is significantly higher in business-to-business markets (Stackpole 1999). One reason for this situation is that many business to business (B2B) markets contain highly fragmented groups of buyers and sellers, many of whom encounter problems finding each other because of time and/or geographic constraints.

An example of this type of market scenario is provided by the construction industry. At the end of a major contract, construction companies are often left with capital equipment. The probability of timing a sales call to coincide with the point in time when another company has just decided they need a used bulldozer is very low. The solution which has emerged in this industry sector is that construction firms can now use an 'Industry to Industry' website to dispose of the surplus equipment by featuring the items in an online global auction. A similar concept has emerged in the shoe industry, where manufacturers and retail footwear chains face major problems getting rid of excess stocks. The solution, which has been developed by iWork Networks Inc of New York, has been to establish an online auction system where buyers and sellers can rapidly reach agreement on the sale of shoes which are surplus to requirements.

Another reason for small firm success in B2B e-commerce markets is that of being the owners of technological expertise which is in demand among large OEMs (Patsuris 2000). For example, in the market sector of integrated online procurement systems, the two dominant players are Ariba and Commerce One. Also operating in this sector is a small company, www.IProcure.com, which specialises in the procurement of parts and services needed in the maintenance and repair of production equipment used in manufacturing plants. Unlike the large online procurement operators who offer the benefit of making savings in purchase of supplies, iProcure's unique proposition is an ability to electronically track and schedule maintenance procedures. This service can prevent the occurrence of expensive breakdowns and avoid key equipment being non-operative due to the non-availability of a critical spare part. The market appeal of iProcure has been validated by being selected as the supplier by the major diversified US multinational conglomerate ConAgra. They have hired the small firm because it is one of the few online procurement firms which has the necessary expertise to manage the complexities of ConAgra's machine parts and maintenance services.

COMPETITIVE ADVANTAGE REVISITED

Although a very useful conceptual tool, a very major risk associated with Porter's competitive advantage option model, as described in Figure 5.1, is that managers in mass markets and owner/managers in focussed markets may exhibit a blind allegiance to theory. Should this occur they may incorrectly decide that the alternative strategies of cost leadership and differentiation are mutually exclusive. Available case materials would suggest that in the past, many Western nation managers assumed that one should strive to be either a low cost leader or a producer of superior, differentiated goods. This situation can be contrasted with Pacific Rim firms whose Confucian approach to decision making appears to frequently result in the generation of superior, holistic solutions. In the case of competitive advantage, the advent of advances in flexible manufacturing permitted Pacific Rim firms to develop products which concurrently offer high standards of performance and low prices. Their ability to establish a dual benefit market positioning in areas such as video cameras, cars and televisions was a key factor in contributing to the achievement of their major global market share gains during the 1980s.

Fortunately, as if often the case in the SME sector, owner/managers have a tendency to act intuitively which means avoiding acceptance of inappropriate guidance from management gurus. Thus many small service sectors firms such as decorators and specialist retailers have always based their philosophy of operations on the promise of offering their customers both value for money and superior service quality.

Thus it would seem that both large and small firm marketers can significantly increase the number of competitive advantage options available to their companies by considering the opportunities offered by the dual options of (i) combining cost leadership with differentiation and (ii) product customisation. As shown by Figure 5.2, this action increases the number of competitive advantage options from four to nine.

Another potential drawback with the Porterian approach to defining competitive advantage is the risk that it may result in placing excessive emphasis on internal organisational competence. It may possibly, therefore, be argued that a superior approach would be to base consideration of competitive advantage options on a decision model that is orientated towards fulfilling customer needs (Chaston 1999).

Some academics have argued, especially in relation to the management of small firms, that organisations should only opt for meeting the needs of entrepreneurial customers. As with the debate over relationship versus transactional marketing, owner/managers can choose the nature of the product offering to be made in relation to whether they are seeking to meet the needs of entrepreneurial or non-entrepreneurial customers. This choice is necessary because some small firms are best suited to manufacturing standardised goods at a competitive price. Other small firms are extremely competent

PRODUCT BENEFIT

	SINGLE COMPETITIVE ADVANTAGE		COMBINED COMPETITIVE ADVANTAGE	M A R K E T
Mass market	Cost leadership*	Differentiation*	Value and superior performance	
One to one marketing = Customisation	Customised cost leadership	Customised differentiation	Customised value and differentiation	C O V E R A G E
Niche market	Focussed cost leadership*	Focussed differentiation*	Focussed value and focussed differentiation	

(*The original four Porterian options)

Figure 5.2 An expanded competitive advantage options matrix

at managing leading edge technology and clearly this skill can be best exploited by adopting an entrepreneurial orientation of regularly launching new, innovative products.

If one accepts the perspective that both transactional versus relationship and entrepreneurial versus conservative marketing are not mutually exclusive concepts, then this permits consideration of a hybrid model of how different forms of customer need can provide the basis for defining alternative competitive advantage options. Such an approach seems eminently more likely to benefit the evolution of new theories of marketing than the trait of exhibiting an unchanging allegiance to a single, purist philosophy. Acceptance of alternative views of the world then permits the suggestion that all of the following types of customer orientation may exist within a market:

1. *conservative-transactional* style customers who are seeking standard specification goods or services at a competitive price;
2. *conservative-relationship* style customers who, although seeking standard specification goods or services, wish to work closely with suppliers to possibly customise some aspect of the product or the purchase and delivery system;
3. *entrepreneurial-transactional* style customers who are seeking innovative products or services which can be procured without forming a close relationship with suppliers;
4. *entrepreneurial-relationship* style customers who wish to work in partnership with suppliers to develop innovative new products or services.

One way of presenting these alternative market positions is to assume there are two behaviour dimensions: the degree of closeness to supplier desired by the customer and the level of product innovation being sought by the customer. By using these two dimensions, it is possible to create a matrix of the type shown in Figure 5.3 to visualise the four alternative customer purchase styles.

The very different nature of the alternative customer orientations described in Figure 5.3 suggests that the following routes to competitive advantage may be available to firms in a market:

1. *conservative-transactional* competitive advantage achieved through offering a price/quality/value standard product combination superior to that of competition and/or superior service through excellence in production and distribution logistics. For example, a small replacement window company which specialises in installing extremely low price products and which exploits this expertise when bidding on public sector property refurbishment contracts.
2. *conservative-relationship* competitive advantage achieved through offering a product/service combination which delivers a superior, customer specific solution. For example, a small sports car manufacturer who rebuilds and thereby customises popular mass market sports cars for people who want to use their vehicles both on the road and also race them at amateur sports car meetings.
3. *entrepreneurial-transactional* competitive advantage achieved through offering a new product which delivers features and performance not available from standard goods producers. For example a small mail order publishing company which specialises in producing self learning texts on new ways to enhance the power and capability of standard software tools such as Word and Excel.

DESIRE OF CUSTOMER FOR A CLOSE RELATIONSHIP WITH SUPPLIERS

TYPE OF PRODUCT SOUGHT	Low	High
Innovative product	(3) Entrepreneurial-transactional customers	(4) Entrepreneurial-relationship customers
Standard product	(1) Conservative-transactional customers	(2) Conservative-relationship customers

Figure 5.3 An alternative customer need matrix

4. *entrepreneurial-relationship* competitive advantage achieved through offering a new product developed in partnership with the customer and contributing to the company also being able to launch new, innovative products or services. For example, a small software firm which works with its customers in the healthcare industry to develop uniquely specified hardware and software solutions that form the basis for creating integrated office management systems for doctors' surgeries.

RESEARCHING NICHE THEORY

Although there exists a multitude of firms occupying market niches, this fact cannot be accepted as absolute proof of the claimed advantages that exist for small firms seeking to avoid competition from other large and small organisations. Within the academic literature there has been only been a limited number of empirical research articles about validating theories concerning the selection of optimal strategies for supporting a niche position.

One strong promoter of the niche marketing concept is Bruce Henderson of the Boston Consulting Group. He is a firm believer in the view that niche management theory can be evolved by drawing upon biological theories concerning the survival of species. He has proposed that in any market, Gaus's Competitive Exclusion Principle applies and that only one firm which has a unique advantage can survive in any market niche. Unfortunately real world business examples such as the apparent existence of numerous firms all succeeding in the same market sector would seem to raise some doubts about the validity of Mr Henderson's perspectives.

There are in fact a number of reasons for this situation. Firstly, in applying biological paradigms to business situations it is necessary to recognise that in the animal kingdom it usually takes somewhere in the region of several hundred to several thousand years for a species to achieve a niche dominant position. As many business niches only last for somewhere between ten and fifty years, it is doubtful whether the rule of survival of the fittest has sufficient time to determine the destiny of firms. Secondly, as any field ecologist can explain by pointing to the observable niche overlaps in bird species in any back garden, Gausian theory only seems to works perfectly in laboratory experiments on the fruit fly *Drosophila*. In contrast it is very difficult to totally validate the exclusion theory in real world biological habitats where a number of species apparently happily survive side-by-side exploiting the same resources available within an ecosystem.

One of the problems in undertaking research on firms in market niches is that this requires longitudinal research over a number of years. Furthermore, unless firms are facing rapidly changing market circumstances, it is extremely difficult to identify how marketing strategies are being evolved to suit prevailing conditions. In an attempt to overcome these methodological problems, Mosakowski (1993) used published data from Initial Public Offerings (IPOs) and annual shareholder reports issued by small computer software firms. Her focus was upon determining which types of differentiation strategy are most likely to contribute to the survival and growth of niche players. By constructing a regression model, this researcher was able to statistically test a number of hypotheses.

The study concluded that in the computer software industry, there are four possible dimensions that can provide the basis for niche differentiation strategies which permit firms to outperform competition. One is to adopt a vertical market focus and concentrate on supplying companies downstream in a specific market sector such as the healthcare or aerospace industries. A second strategy is to adopt a customer needs orientation and seek to provide highly specialised product applications such as customised data management or computer imaging software. A third possibility is to specialise in the provision of superior service response models such that customers can be offered a more rapid resolution of their problems than if they contact any other software supplier. The fourth option is to develop the capability of staff to be effective managers of complex R&D projects that will be of appeal to customers for whom access to sources of rapid problem resolution is of critical importance.

An even larger scale longitudinal study of niche behaviour in the computing industry was undertaken by Lawless and Anderson (1996). These researchers focussed on small manufacturers in the PC industry to determine how the introduction of next generation technologies can impact market performance. Data for the study were taken from a commercial, industry tracking operation that publishes information on the industry, individual firms, specific models of computers and the incorporation of specific types of microprocessor. This data set was used as the basis for a cluster analysis to define the nature of specific niches that exist in the US PC market.

By the application of least-square regression, the researchers were able to test a variety of niche management hypotheses. They concluded that early adopters of a new technology will usually outperform those competitors who are late adopters. The willingness to be more innovative is usually rewarded in the form of higher sales and profits. The study also showed that in the PC industry, competition is more likely to come from other firms within the same market niche and not from new firms seeking to enter the niche. The associated implication of this finding is that firms which remain within a market niche can usually expect to outperform organisations which switch between niches in the search for new opportunities. Linked to this conclusion is the interesting fact that a firm which has operated for a significant length of time within the same market niche may find that this behaviour causes an erosion in market performance. The apparent explanation for this finding is that in niches facing rapid changes in technology, some of the oldest firms become somewhat slower than their younger, more nimble footed competitors in moving to update their technologies and product designs.

The researchers also sought to determine whether some of the biological theories about the influence of competitor densities within a niche can both influence business survival rates and the intensity of competition. Drawing upon the ecological theory which suggests species in densely populated niches will need to expend significant energies in acquiring sufficient food resources to survive, they hypothesised that the greater the population density of firms in a market niche, the weaker will be the performance of individual firms. They also developed the hypothesis that if a niche contains the same firms over an extended period, firms become familiar with each other's behaviour patterns and are able to co-exist by avoiding actions that might signal a desire for a head-to-head confrontation. Although these hypotheses seem both reasonable and logical, neither were found to show statistically significant results when entered into the linear regression research model.

DISCUSSION QUESTIONS

1. Describe the positioning alternatives that are available to firms. Which of these options is most likely to be of appeal to smaller firms?
2. Discuss why the Internet was originally perceived as levelling the playing field for the smaller firm. What evidence is now emerging to suggest this perception may prove to be incorrect?
3. Review why the different nature of the alternative customer orientations can provide the basis for differing routes through which to achieve competitive advantage. What attributes are required of firms seeking to deliver each of the described types of competitive advantage?

REFERENCES

Anon. (2000), 'All yours', *The Economist*, 1 April, pp. 57–61.

Baker, S. and Baker, K. (1998), 'Mine over matter', *Journal of Business Strategy*, Vol. 19, No. 4, pp. 22–7.

Bonoma, T.V. and Shapiro, B.P. (1983), *Segmenting the Industrial Market*, Lexington Books, Lexington, Mass.

Chaston, I. (1999), *New Marketing Strategies*, Sage, London.

Christensen, C.M. and Tedlow, R.S. (2000), 'Patterns of disruption in retailing', *Harvard Business Review*, January–February, pp. 42–6.

Daniels, C. (2000), 'The trauma of rebirth', *Fortune*, 4 September, pp. 367–9.

Garvin, D.A. (1987), 'Competing on the eight dimensions of quality', *Harvard Business Review*, Nov.–Dec., pp. 101–9.

Glazer, R. (1999), 'Winning in smart markets', *Sloan Management Review*, Vol. 40, No. 4, pp. 59–73.

Hardcastle, S. and McLoughlin, L. (1997), 'Variety act', *The Grocer*, 13 December, pp. 33–6.

Koudsi, S. (2000), 'Down and out', *Fortune*, 2 October, pp. 42–3.

La France, R. (1999), 'Can you be too focused?' *Forbes Magazine*, 31 May, pp. 53–4.

Lawless, M.W. and Anderson, P.C. (1996), 'Generational technological change: effects of innovation and local rivalry on performance', *Academy of Management Journal*, Vol. 39, No. 5, pp. 1185–1218.

Marsh, A. (1998), 'Not your dad's hardware store', *Forbes Magazine*, 26 January, pp. 26–7.

Marsh, H. (1999), 'Children's choice', *Marketing*, 15 July, pp. 27–9.

Mosakowski, E. (1993), 'A resource-based perspective of the dynamic strategy-performance relationship', *Journal of Management*, Vol. 19, No. 4, pp. 819–40.

Noto, A. (2000), 'Vertical vs. broadline e-retailers: which will survive?' Cnetnews.com, 2 March.

Patsuris, P. (2000), 'ConAgra picks Iprocure.com', *Forbes*, 7 March, pp. 7–8.

Porter, M. (1985), *Competitive Advantage: Creating and Sustaining Superior Performance*, The Free Press, San Francisco.

Robertson, T.S. and Barich, H. (1992), 'A successful approach to segmenting industrial markets', *Journal of Marketing*, December, pp. 5–11.

Rynecki, D. (2000), 'Yen stocks: the best of the bunch', *Fortune*, 4 September, pp. 120–3.

Stackpole, B. (1999), 'A foothold on the Web: Industry-specific Net markets', *PC Week*, 10 May, pp. 78–80.

Tedlow, R.S. (1990), *New and Improved: The Story of Mass Marketing in America*, Heinemann, Oxford.

6

MARKETING PLEARNING

LEARNING OBJECTIVES
....

After studying this chapter you should be able to understand:

1. the issue of whether formal structured planning is of benefit to small firms;
2. the learning benefits associated with participation in planning activities;
3. the three phases of process associated with the development of a plan;
4. the utilisation of the resource advantage planning matrix to determine competence-driven strategies;
5. how to use case materials to illustrate the process of marketing plearning.

CHAPTER SUMMARY
....

Conventional wisdom proposes that small firms can benefit from developing a detailed, classicist-type marketing plan. The research evidence to support this view is, however, somewhat less than conclusive. Possibly the real benefits of planning are not the outcome but the process itself whereby the small firm, through learning, gains a fuller understanding of current and future operations. It is proposed that this process might be called 'plearning'. It involves the three phases of learning: where the firm is now, where the firm should go, and how to achieve specified performance objectives.

The focus of planning should probably be that of determining which internal competencies provide the basis for achieving competitive advantage. One way of undertaking this type of analysis is to construct a resource advantage matrix. It may also prove useful to analyse the firm's value chain to identify sources of added advantage. A case study of a furniture business, Cummings Ltd, is provided as a detailed illustration of how to implement the marketing plearning process.

INTRODUCTION

Possibly the issue which has received greatest attention in the small firms literature is whether it is mandatory that small firms should develop a formal marketing plan to manage future business performance. The conventional wisdom is that a positive link exists between the existence of a plan and business performance (for example, Robinson 1979; Schwenk and Shrader 1993). This is also the view shared by small business support agencies, virtually all of which insist that the start point in any relationship with small firms seeking advice or training is that the client must produce a marketing plan.

A 1990s example of a small firms programme which placed emphasis on planning was the UK Department of Trade & Industry's Enterprise Initiative. This scheme provided 50% of the funds for small firms to hire the services of a consultant. A significant number of these consultants were assigned the task of creating a marketing plan. In many cases the outcome was similar to that encountered by one of the present authors when discussing the benefits of the programme with an owner/manager in South West England. This individual pointed to a large report which he was using as a door stop. When asked about the contents of the submission his response was, 'They took my ideas, added long words which I did not understand, which presumably were designed to impress the reader, and then had the nerve to submit a ridiculously inflated invoice.'

In contrast to the accepted wisdom that plans assist performance, some researchers have been unable to demonstrate the existence of any empirical relationship (for example, Fulmar and Rue 1974; Shrader *et al.* 1989). To account for this situation, some writers have concluded that variations between studies may reflect problems in research methodology (for example, Wood and LaForge 1979). Whichever view is the correct conclusion, what few small business researchers appear to accept is the opinion expressed by Mintzberg (1979). He concluded that a highly structured, formalised approach to planning is not a mandatory requirement for every organisation. Instead he suggests that the need to a adopt a specific approach to the planning process will vary dramatically across different organisational forms.

Organisational learning is an emergent discipline which focusses on the concept that firms can enhance performance by combining new knowledge with existing experience as the basis for evolving new solutions to encountered business problems (Chaston 2000). Learning as a role in the planning process within the SME sector is noted by Castrogiovanni (1996). He feels that the most important goal in the marketing planning process is not the generation of a formal document. Instead owner/managers should perceive planning as an opportunity to use organisational learning as the basis for reviewing recent events and determining a future direction for their organisations. To underline this conceptual approach, he suggested that perhaps the term 'marketing planning' should be abolished and replaced with the new phrase, 'marketing plearning'.

A PLEARNING MODEL

Learning should be perceived as a continuum. At one extreme the individual only considers prior experience when approaching a problem. This is known as a single-loop learning style. The other extreme is where the individual proactively seeks new sources of knowledge as the basis for bringing new insights to the problem under consideration. This latter style is usually known as a double-loop learning style.

In terms of which is the most appropriate style, this will depend upon circumstance. In some cases single-loop learning may be completely appropriate. This is often the case in the resolution of everyday standard operational problems. There are other situations, such as reviewing a possible future strategy for the firm, where a more effective philosophy might be to apply double-loop learning to ensure that new knowledge is being considered when reviewing various alternative marketing management scenarios.

A possible approach to evolving a marketing plearning model is to continue to utilise a modified version of the classic three phase marketing planning process. This would cause the small firms to seek to (i) learn more about where the firm is now; (ii) learn more about where the firm wishes to go; and (iii) learn more about possible actions to achieve specified future performance goals. A version of this simple plearning process is shown in Figure 6.1.

The core of the model assumes that there are three groups involved in the learning process. These are the firm's stakeholders (for example, suppliers, the financial community); the owner/manager; and the employees. The most productive form of learning is where there is interaction between all three groups, as this maximises exposure to sources of new knowledge.

In relation to learning about where the firm is now, two areas of information will need to be reviewed: identified signals of potential change in the market environment, and the recent performance history of the company. This latter area should encompass an examination of both external and internal organisational activities.

It is understandable that the activities surrounding determination of future aims will tend to be dominated by the values and attitudes of the owner/manager. This individual can, however, acquire a much broader perspective on the future by drawing upon the opinions of stakeholders: for example, the accountants' comments on how best to undertake any borrowing that may be required to fund future operations, and the employees' perceptions of what actions may be necessary in relation to upgrading their competencies to utilise changing technologies in execution of assigned tasks.

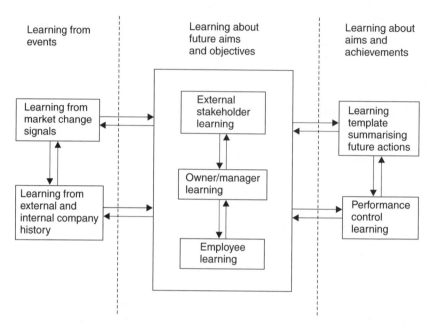

Figure 6.1 A marketing plearning model

All three sources of opinion should also be involved in the plearning processes associated with determining what actions will be required to deliver the future performance aims agreed for the firm. It may be useful to generate a template to summarise agreed actions. This template should not be in the form of the huge documents so beloved by management consultants and the boards of large firms. The recommended preference is for a very simple record of proposed actions which is probably not more than a few pages in length. The critical issue about this template is that all employees are made aware of its content. They can use this information to guide them in the fulfilment of their job roles. The other benefit of the template is that it provides a simple control system which permits rapid evaluation of actual events against specified aims when the new market plearn is being implemented.

RESOURCE BASED PLEARNING

Hamel and Prahalad (1994) have suggested that, 'Competition for the future is competition to create and dominate emerging opportunities... to stake out new competitive space.' They further recommend that, 'A firm must unlearn much about its past... recognise that it is not enough to optimally position a company within existing markets... develop foresight into the whereabouts of tomorrow's markets.' In offering guidance on how to achieve this aim, Hamel and Prahalad rely very heavily on the concept of understanding the probable nature of future market conditions and ensuring the organisation has acquired competencies appropriate for achieving ongoing success. Their definition of a successful firm is one which is able to accurately envisage the future, and acquire core competencies ahead of competition, thereby becoming the dominant player within an industrial sector. Clearly this is a conceptual philosophy which in practical terms only a minority of firms can ever aspire to achieve. Nevertheless the logic of the process of exploiting the capabilities of the firm as the basis for beginning to define a potential source of competitive advantage can be an extremely appropriate start point in the formulation of a marketing 'plearn'.

Day (1994) has developed an eloquent argument for proposing that a capability-based approach to planning is more likely to be a more productive source for determining competitive advantage than the competitive forces model tabled by Michael Porter. In defining capabilities, Day suggests that capabilities are complex bundles of skills and accumulated knowledge which, when integrated with the firm's organisational processes, permit the optimal utilisation of assets. He illustrates this perspective by pointing to Marriott Hotels which consistently achieve high ratings for their capability to deliver a level of service quality which sets them apart from their competitors such as Hyatt and Hilton. Day describes this superior service as the 'distinctive capability' that permits Marriott to out-compete other firms operating in the same market sector.

A similar perspective on the utilisation of distinctive capability to provide the basis from which to evolve a marketing plan has been presented by Hunt and Morgan (1995, 1996) in their resource based theory of competition. As illustrated in Figure 6.2, the internal resources of the firm determine market position and this in turn will influence financial performance.

In tabling their model, Hunt and Morgan have specified some observable variables which they feel overcome many of the problems associated with applying neoclassical economic theory to explaining the management of the marketing process. Firstly, they suggest that customer preferences are rarely homogeneous because customers usually exhibit variation in their choice of product features. Secondly, as most customers have imperfect information, this will lead to variances in buyer behaviour. Thirdly, firms, in seeking to achieve superior financial performance, should not act to maximise profit but instead use the benchmark of other firms in the same market sector to determine the exact definition of financial performance superiority. Fourthly, firms have a multiplicity of competencies and resources, which fact results in organisations adopting very different approaches to achieving alternative routes to competitive advantage in the same market sector. Fifthly, it is usually the distinctiveness with which firms utilise their resources and competencies that results in firms being able to occupy different market positions.

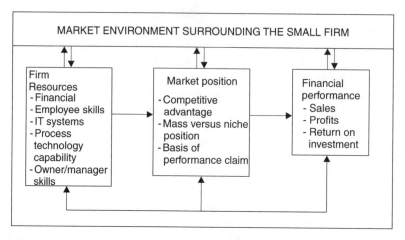

Figure 6.2   A resource based approach to small business planning

Hunt and Morgan have proposed that their model can be used to define alternative competitive positions by using the dimensions of (i) 'relative resource costs' (the degree to which a firm's operating costs are higher or lower than competition); (ii) 'relative resource produced value' (the degree to which the firm's financial performance is better or worse than competition). Although this is a very effective model, one potential risk is that the small firm marketer using the concept as a decision model might be directed towards placing too great an emphasis on financial performance. In view of the fact that the primary objective of the marketing process is to deliver products or services which are perceived to offer the highest possible value to the customer, it seems reasonable to propose that 'perceived value to customer' is preferable in a planning model than the concept of 'relative resource produced value'.

The start point in building a resource advantage planning matrix is to first determine which factors influence the degree to which (a) a product or service is perceived as offering value to the customer and (b) current operating costs differ from those of competition. Factors influencing relative perceived customer value will vary by both industrial sector and nature of marketing style being utilised by the organisation. Examples of reasonably standard factors which might be considered in virtually any situation include:

- level of actual performance the product or service delivers to the customer;
- range of benefits offered by the product or service;
- level of service quality being delivered;
- price;
- effectiveness with which information is made available to the customer.

In the same way as perceived value, factors influencing operating costs relative to competition will also vary by industrial sector and the marketing style orientation of the organisation. Examples of standard factors applicable in virtually any situation include:

- cost of producing a unit of product or service;
- raw material costs;
- employee productivity;
- distribution and logistics costs;
- cost of fixed assets per unit of output.

Having defined key factors, the next stage in the process is to rate these factors on some form of scale. Possibly the simplest approach is a scoring system ranging from a low of 1 through to a high of 10. Where a score approaches 10 for each dimension this indicates (a) much higher perceived customer value than competition and (b) much lower operating costs. Having executed the scoring, the average total score is found by dividing summated total scores by the number of factors used in the analysis. This generates an overall score for perceived customer value and relative operating costs. Data can then be interpreted by entering scores on a resource advantage planning matrix of the type shown in Figure 6.3. As can be seen, resultant positions in the matrix guide the organisation towards the possible adoption of the following nine generic strategies:

| | | Perceived value to customer | | |
		Low	Average	High
	High	(1) Immediately withdraw from market	(2) Phased withdrawal from market over time	(3) If feasible invest in major cost reduction project
Relative operating costs	**Average**	(4) Phased withdrawal from market over time	(5) Sustain market position	(6) Invest in cost reduction programme
	Low	(7) Examine how efficiency can be used to increase value	(8) Invest in market diversification	(9) Invest in retaining value and cost leadership position

Figure 6.3 A resource advantage planning matrix

1. *Cell 1* where the low perceived customer value and high operating costs suggest the firm has minimal opportunity for success. Hence the company (assuming it also has operations in other, more successful, sectors) should withdraw from this market sector immediately.

2. *Cell 2* where average perceived customer value and high operating costs imply poor future prospects, but where withdrawal should be a phased process because this will permit avoidance of major financial write-downs for redundant capital assets.

3. *Cell 3* where the high customer value that a company delivers is an opportunity that must be exploited. Hence the strategy is to initiate a major internal process revision project that can lead to a significant reduction in its high operating costs. If, however, this project does not deliver the required cost reduction, then a market sector departure strategy would be the next action.

4. *Cell 4* where, similar to cell 2, low customer value and only average operating costs imply poor future market prospects. Again market withdrawal should be a phased process because this will permit avoidance of major financial write-downs for redundant capital assets.

5. *Cell 5* where perceived customer value and operating costs are both at parity with other firms in the market place. For many organisations this type of classification applies to a core business area generating a major proportion of total revenues. Hence the existing operation should be managed to sustain current market performance (for example, if the competitors begin to offer perceived higher value, actions should be taken to match these increments). Similarly if competitors appear to be making efficiency gains, action should be taken to ensure parity of operating costs is sustained.

6. *Cell 6* where operating costs are only average but value to customer is perceived to be high. The organisation should initiate a cost reduction programme with the eventual aim of achieving much greater internal operating efficiencies than competition.

7. *Cell 7* where operating costs are low, but perceived value is below average. The firm's advantage in the area of internal operating efficiencies should be examined to determine whether this situation can provide the basis through which to offer additional customer value (for example, reduce prices, add additional services).

8. *Cell 8* where the firm can exploit lower than average operating costs as the basis for moving into new market sectors where achievement of offering higher than average perceived customer value is a viable option.

9. *Cell 9* is a highly attractive position for the organisation because high perceived customer value and low operating costs have both been attained. This will probably mean that the company has already achieved a market leadership position and therefore this mandates ongoing investment in order to protect the operation from any new competitive threats.

EXAMPLE: APPLYING THE RESOURCE ADVANTAGE MATRIX AT BRYMOR SYSTEMS (CHASTON 2000)

The UK replacement window industry is made up of a few national players such as Everest, and a large number of SME sector businesses. Brymor Systems Ltd is a small company which manufactures the component materials used by other small UK companies which fabricate and install new and replacement windows. The industry originally used aluminium as the standard material for window frames. The first significant technological advance was the introduction of double glazed frames, containing two pieces of glass which, by creating a thermal barrier, offer superior heat conservation properties. Approximately 50% of industry unit volume comes from sales in the domestic housing market, with the balance of sales split between industrial products (windows, shop fronts, office buildings, and so on) and the public sector (for example, local government and housing association dwellings).

Important trends in the domestic market were the introduction of low cost plastic (or PVC) frames, and for performance orientated end users, the introduction of composite frames made by coating aluminium with polyvinyl compounds. The industrial market mainly still considers that aluminium is the best material for meeting their specification for durability and variability of shape.

Brymor supplies (i) bar lengths of all four product types (aluminium, thermal break aluminium, PVC and composites) to customers who wish to fabricate windows, and (ii) window frame kits to customers who wish to install frames without any involvement in fabrication. From the first day of the company being created, the founders recognised that because Brymor was too small to capture the economies of scale available to its larger, national competitors, the firm would be unable to compete on the basis of low price. Thus they consistently operated on a market positioning of offering (a) high quality products; (b) exceptional customer service; (c) a free technical advisory service for customers confronted with a difficult or unusual window replacement contract. This strategic orientation has resulted in the firm developing strong downstream relationships with window fabricators and installers who make their purchase decision on the basis of factors such as product quality, just-in-time deliveries and provision of technical support to assist the resolution of any very significant technical problems which may be encountered during either the pre- or post-purchase phase. Although limited industry data prevent an accurate assessment of market share, Brymor is believed to be a market leader in the supply of premium quality, advanced design, bar lengths and kit form products.

Over the years, the company has invested in new technologies to sustain quality and further enhance its speed of response in order fulfilment. It was one of the first replacement window firms in the UK to invest in a computer aided design/computer integrated manufacturing system (CAD/CAM). Although the intended use for this system was to optimise the organisation's manufacturing productivity, it soon found that the system was useful when negotiating an order with customers needing one off designs to overcome complex installation problems.

Three years ago, the firm's problem solving reputation led them to be approached by architects and larger building firms involved in complex renovation contracts such as the refurbishment of older hotels and office buildings. Brymor had for some years been producing a range of conservatories for domestic homes. When an architect who was working on the renovation of a 150 year old hotel became aware of Brymor's involvement in this product area, he asked if it would be possible for them to develop a massive, customised conservatory reminiscent of the orangeries which had been popular in the Victorian era. By using its CAD/CAM system Brymor was able to develop, manufacture and deliver the components for the conservatory in eight weeks.

Currently the firm uses a sales force to call on major customers. These meetings are strategic in nature, focussing upon customers' future needs and how Brymor can assist in the resolution of complex problems. Customers are supplied with a detailed catalogue listing Brymor's product lines. Price lists which accompany this catalogue are updated on an 'as needed' basis. If a customer has a specific design need or installation problem, they contact Brymor's technical department by mail, telephone or fax. Orders are placed with the sales-service department, again using mail, telephone or fax. This department also acts as a contact point, advising customers on the status of product shipments and delivery dates. Over the last three years the firm has been investing time and resources in seeking to ensure that various computer systems used within the firm (for example, the accounting system, the sales management order entry system, the computer based manufacturing scheduling system and the CAD/CAM system) have been integrated in a way which permits automated information interchange between all company databases.

During this period of investment in building a more effective management information system, the increasingly competitive nature of the replacement industry has been putting pressure on Brymor's net profits. Hence the firm has decided to examine how involvement in e-commerce might generate additional sources of competitive advantage. To achieve this goal the directors implemented a strategic marketing planning exercise in which factors such as benefits offered to customers, quality of service, manufacturing costs and distribution efficiency were used to construct a RAM matrix. As can be seen from Figure 6.4, the firm has some products which fall in the phased withdrawal/resource withdrawal categories, a core thermal break business, an area for cost reduction, an enhanced value opportunity, a market expansion opportunity, and the need to retain leadership.

The directors recognise that there are few opportunities for introducing new products into the industry, or cost reduction benefits to be gained from purchasing new production equipment or developing new process technologies. Their decision, therefore, is to build upon their newly integrated information

Perceived customer value

		Low	Average	High
Relative operating costs	High	Immediate withdrawal - No product	Phased withdrawal - No product	Invest in major cost reduction - No product
	Average	Phased withdrawal - Aluminium products sold to price sensitive customers in industrial markets	Sustain position - Thermal break windows in both industrial and consumer markets	Cost reduction programme - uPVC products in both industrial and consumer markets
	Low	Value through efficiency - Aluminium products supplied to small fabricators / installers in domestic markets	Diversification - Large customised conservatories in industrial market	Leadership retention - Composite products

Figure 6.4   The Brymor resource advantage matrix

management system as the basis for examining how moves into e-commerce might permit enhancing perceived value by upgrading customer services and reducing operating costs. The focus of their planning is to undertake a cost/benefit analysis of the following areas:

1. establishing an online pricing and ordering system which would be of major benefit in decreasing operating costs across all market sectors. This system is perceived as having critical impact in being able to pass cost savings on to customers in (a) the aluminium product range sold to small fabricators/installers in the domestic market and (b) the uPVC market;
2. linking their logistics system with a national distribution company to both decrease time between order completion and delivery, and offer customers an online enquiry system for tracking goods in transit;
3. permitting major uPVC customers to interface with the production scheduling system to ensure large orders receive scheduling priority, thereby reducing the response time between order placement and shipment;
4. providing architects and building contractors with online access to the company's CAD/CAM conservatory design and manufacturing software;
5. offering an interactive online design and technology applications website service to assist customers for composite products to (a) more effectively

exploit the structural benefits offered by this material and (b) configure product designs and purchase orders to optimise quoted prices.

SELECTING CORE COMPETENCIES

Having matched markets to capability using an analysis tool such as the resource advantage matrix, the next issue confronting a firm is to undertake a plearning activity concerning which core competencies will be the driving force upon which to build future market success. A useful plearning tool for assisting the selection of core competency is Porter's (1985) value chain concept. This model, as shown in Figure 6.5, proposes that opportunity for adding value comes from (a) the five core competencies of inbound logistics, process operations, outbound logistics, marketing, and customer service and (b) the four support competencies of management capability, human resource management practices, exploitation of technology, and procurement.

Jarillo (1993) has posited that analysis of the precise value chain role an organisation will undertake within a market system is a crucial step in the determination of future strategy. A fundamental objective in this process is to ensure that the organisation is able to maximise its contribution to value added activities within the system. He further points out that the exact nature of opportunity may change over time. An example he uses to illustrate this point is the computer industry, where in the past the producers of hardware were able to enjoy a major proportion of the profits generated by value added activities. More recently, however, as knowledge of the technology associated

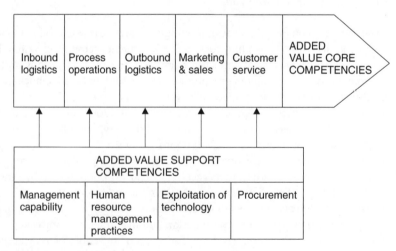

Figure 6.5 A value chain model for analysing competencies

with the assembly of 'boxes' has become more widely available, then greater profits have begun to accrue to those who have retained a 'lock on key technologies' (for example, Intel in the manufacture of microchips, Microsoft in the area of operating systems and software applications).

Jarillo also proposes that when and if the promised advances in information technology permit firms to rapidly and efficiently exchange information, then many firms should examine how their more peripheral activities might be sourced from other organisations with higher levels of competency. Thus firms operating in transactional markets might assess their value chain to determine if any activity such as sourcing raw materials might be assigned to an outside supplier. In relationship orientated markets, firms might examine how horizontal partnerships with other firms at the same level in the market system, and vertical partnerships with suppliers, can be utilised to identify how their specific value added activities, when linked with those of others, can optimise the determination of competitive advantage.

EXAMPLE: E-COMMERCE IN THE PRINTING INDUSTRY

The arrival of e-commerce has created a framework through which small firms can evaluate how information technology can be used to effectively manage the outsourcing of certain aspects of their value chain to lower operating costs. Alternatively, IT systems can be exploited to permit delivery of increased perceived customer value. Whichever route is taken, this action can release the managerial resources of the small firm to concentrate even more attention on optimising those core competencies associated with maximising the added value of activities retained within the organisation.

One example of exploiting e-commerce technologies is Reedform Ltd, a long established UK business print management company (ISI 1999a). In recent years the firm has seen a diminishing demand for traditional products such as business forms as customers move to computerise their administrative operations. Business print customers are time sensitive. Customers suddenly realise their stocks are getting low, or re-ordering delays occur because communications go missing. Reedform's solution was to evolve a system to assist customers become more involved in the self-management of their printing needs. The company designed a complete print management system which links Reedform's website directly with customers' PCs. Customers can place orders, make enquiries about stocks on hand and track the progress of their orders.

Card Corporation is based in Leeds, providing short run printing services such as business cards and stationery (ISI 1999b). Low volume print runs can be expensive because of the paperwork, proofing and time involved in managing the job from design through to production. Card's solution was to develop a fully interactive website for printing stationery and business cards. The front end of the website enables individuals and companies to design and order business cards and sta-tionery online. Customers control everything from typeface to background colour to print layout. Designs are pre-specified on the website, but customers seeking variations can contact Card Corporation by telephone to discuss alternative approaches. Behind the website, Card Corporation either prints product orders or transfers them to associates abroad for local printing and delivery. Despatch of finished goods is by post or courier. Regular customers can make payments on account and the website provides information on outstanding invoices. Infrequent or single purchase customers pay by credit card or a secure bank bureau service.

EXAMPLE: MARKETING PLEARNING AT CUMMINGS

Cummings Ltd is a small, upmarket furniture and soft furnishings retailer which owns outlets located in two market towns in Devon. Stephen Cummings took over as managing director when his father Frank, the founder, decided it was time for him to retire. Having held the leadership position for a year, Stephen decided it was time for a reconsideration of the company's future. To initiate this process he developed the following brief summary of the firm's trading history: 'My father, Frank Cummings opened the first store in 1957. To avoid competing with large national furniture chains Cummings has always specialised in offering a range of upmarket furniture and soft furnishings. A second store was opened in 1978. In both cases the company purchased the building in which the retail operations are based. The success of the two outlets led to the decision in 1992 that the company might have the capability to succeed in a large metropolitan area and a third store was opened in Bristol. In this latter case, high property prices prevented the purchase of a building. Instead the company signed a 25 year lease with a development company. Despite significant investment and a willingness to underwrite trading losses for some years, the move to Bristol proved disastrous and in 1998 the outlet was closed. Premature termination of the lease resulted in a significant financial penalty which was charged against the firm's retained profit reserves.'

'Although the two remaining outlets are trading profitably, there are two con-cerns which need to be addressed. Firstly, since 1988 year-on-year annual sales have remained virtually unchanged. Secondly, in both market towns, planning consents have been given for construction of two out-of-town shopping areas, and on both sites national furniture chains have established large furniture superstores. To date these stores do not appear to have had an appreciable effect on Cummings. Nevertheless there are no grounds to assume that sales might not be impacted in the future, if for no other reason than that shopper traffic has fallen in both town centres because the general public find parking is much easier at these out-of-town sites.'

Stephen mailed this brief summary of company history to all employees, the firm's accountant, bank manager and the managing directors of three of Cummings' key suppliers. In an accompanying letter he explained that he was hoping everybody would be willing to share their views on possible future opportunities for the company. To initiate these discussions he invited everybody to a late afternoon/early evening meeting to be held at a local hotel.

On the day of the meeting, Stephen opened the event by presenting a plearning model of the type shown in Figure 6.1 and asked participants to decide which of the following groups they would like to join:

- financial operations (facilitator the finance director);
- store operations (facilitator the merchandising director);
- furniture and furnishings procurement (facilitator the senior buyer);
- opportunities for new and improved products and services (facilitator Stephen Cummings).

He stressed that all groups should determine their own boundaries and not be concerned if they appeared to be covering issues that might also be of interest to other groups. Following a question and answer session, the groups were formed and spent the rest of the event planning their approach to the task of reviewing recent company history and possible new market trends in relation to their assigned areas of plearning. The agreed action was that the groups would each submit a short written summary of their findings and that these would then be jointly reviewed by the four facilitators. Some of the information contained in the subsequently produced reviews was as follows:

Financial operations

Current financial trading performance has remained unchanged for some three years. Annual sales are £2.3 million, cost of goods £1.5 million, gross profit £0.8 million (gross margin 35 per cent of sales), selling, general and administrative expenses £0.5 million, yielding a net profit, before tax, of £0.3 million (net profit 13 per cent of sales). These trading results compare poorly with most national furniture chains, which in recent years have been achieving sales growth in the region of five to ten per cent per year (although such growth does seem to come from the opening of new outlets around the country). However Cummings performs much better in terms of net profit at 13 per cent of sales because the average for the industry is in the region of six to seven per cent. Asset and liability balances are well managed and offer few opportunities for changes that could improve future return on investment. Nevertheless on the basis of current trading results it will take at least another three years before the retained profit reserves will return to the level enjoyed prior to the write-down of losses incurred in the closure of the Bristol operation. Hence, assuming the firm would not consider looking for an injection of capital by seeking out new investors, it is not felt that Cummings is at a position where the firm should consider any significant new capital investments in the next few years.

Store operations

Nationally consumer expenditure on furniture is not growing to any significant degree, as demonstrated by the following data (source: Mintel 1999):

	Total furniture	Living/dining	Kitchen	Bedroom
Sales £000	5817	2209	331	752

A similar trend is apparent in the case of the soft furnishings market:

	Wallcoverings	Fabrics	Carpets/floorcoverings
Sales £000	460	979	1572

Both stores are generating similar sales and profits. The mix between furniture and furnishings of 68/32 is very similar to the national market situation. Nationally younger couples and families probably represent a significant proportion of the customer base for multi-outlet retailers. Cummings is somewhat different in that its typical customers are older persons in the age group 45–60 and drawn primarily from the A and B social groups. These customers can be divided into three main groups: (a) professional couples and early retirees moving into the South West from elsewhere in the UK; (b) couples who have lived in the region for some years who are purchasing a more expensive house; (c) couples who are refurbishing their existing houses as their children begin to leave home.

On the basis of observations and comments by customers, the prime benefits of shopping at Cummings are a range of unusual products different to those stocked by most shops (especially the national chains), a willingness of staff to spend time helping select items, and the store's free decorating and furnishing advisory service. Over the last two years interest in unusual products is reflected by sales growth for imported goods (example sources: Italy, France, Sweden and the USA) and furniture and fabrics manufactured by smaller UK firms based in the South West.

Furnishing and furnishings procurement

Over recent years it has become apparent that customers are looking for greater variety in an attempt to furnish their houses in a way that makes them different from those of their friends and neighbours. In an attempt to meet these demands, purchases from national manufacturers have been de-emphasised and attempts made to build new links with two product sources. One source is overseas manufacturers who have been selected on the basis of their committment to regularly update their designs and an ability to ensure promised delivery dates are met. Most of these suppliers tend to produce furniture or furnishings which are very modern in their design. The other source is high quality traditional furniture and furnishings. Cummings customers living in older properties and those owning converted barns or cottages are usually interested in more traditional furniture and furnishings which reflect both unusual design and high quality craftsmanship. Fortunately, over the last ten years the South West has shown a major increase in small furniture and furnishing manufacturers capable of meeting this requirement.

New opportunities

The furniture and furnishings business is still a somewhat fragmented sector of UK retailing, with specialist independent stores still capturing some 15–20 per cent of total sales. There is, however, no room for complacency because the Swedish store group IKEA has shown that national chains can capture a significant share of the market if they give attention to improving the quality and design of products stocked whilst concurrently placing emphasis on delivering a high quality of customer service. Quite clearly the dominant UK player, MFI, is not a threat because this company is overtly positioned at the bottom end of the market. This, however, is in contrast with middle and upmarket department stores which in the past have been somewhat passive players in the retail market. These outlets are now recognising that both higher store traffic and higher revenues can be generated by offering a greater variety of higher quality products. Their activities, especially if these stores begin to bring to the provinces some of the products marketed through their London stores, could become a potential new threat to Cummings.

In terms of other market trends, there are two which might benefit from further investigation. The first is the growing success of mail order firms which also have a retail operation. The second, and potentially of even greater interest, is the Internet. In the USA firms such as www.furniture.com and www.garden.com have shown that people are very willing to use websites to purchase high price items. Furthermore, although Internet shopping for non-grocery products has only achieved a limited level of market penetration in the UK, this situation is likely to change dramatically over the next few years. A major catalyst will be that of more and more consumers gaining access to the Internet via new technologies such as interactive digital television.

Stephen Cummings undertook the responsibility of collating the feedback from the four groups and having completed this task, circulated materials to all individuals involved in the plearning process. Each group was asked to comment on (a) what annual sales objective Cummings should seek to achieve and (b) where they felt there might be potential for revenue growth. The consensus from this phase of plearning was that people felt Cummings should seek to return to a growth phase. Virtually everybody, however, felt that in the face of increasing competition from out-of-town national superstores and the possibility of more aggressive marketing by department stores, Cummings should not expect much, if any, growth from the current retail operation. Neither the board of Cummings nor stakeholders from the financial community felt it wise to consider opening a new store. Hence Stephen Cummings' proposal was that over the next three years the aim of the business should be to generate an annual revenue growth rate in the region of ten per cent per annum whilst concurrently seeking to ensure store sales remained at current levels. The implication of this suggestion was that all future growth would come from new activities such as mail order or online retailing.

Another short meeting was held with all participants at which it was agreed that the next phase of developing action plearning templates should be undertaken by a smaller team. It was agreed to form two teams, one for store operations and the other for new developments. The store team comprised a selection of representatives from the previously constituted finance, store operations and procurement groups. Everybody was adamant that Stephen should facilitate the new developments project and to assist him he recruited individuals from the finance, procurement and new opportunities groups.

These two new groups were given six weeks in which to develop action templates for their assigned areas of responsibility. In order to ensure that everybody had the chance to contribute and comment on the evolution of the action templates, it was agreed that the firm's IT manager would create an Intranet site which people could access both to monitor progress and contribute their perspectives. The following provides a summary of the content of the two action templates which were produced:

Store operations

Aims: To sustain current sales and profitability.

Positioning: To focus on a positioning of offering premium quality, unique, different and unusual products to upmarket customers seeking either imported, modern designs or traditional, craftsmanship quality goods manufactured by small UK manufacturers.

Stocking policy: To reduce to a minimum shop floor space for national brand products, keeping only those for which strong demand exists, in order to create more merchandising space for imported and traditional design items.

Operations: Opportunity exists to improve cash flow, reduce order placement/delivery cycles and enhance customer service by creating a fully integrated computer-based sales, product specification catalogue, accounting, stock management and procurement system. Although the core system will be a standard commercially available retail management package, over time modifications will be made to tailor the system to suit the specific needs of the Cummings operation. To achieve this goal an investment will be made in hiring a full-time software developer and in the provision of IT training for all staff at every level within the organisation. The estimated cost of these actions is a front end expenditure of £20 000 for hardware and software and additional salary costs of £30 000 per annum. Training provision is expected to cost £10 000 per year over a three year period. Preliminary estimates suggest that these actions will lead to a ten per cent savings in sales, general and administrative expenses. Hence the total costs of this project should be recovered over three to four years from the improvement in profits that the efficiency gains are expected to generate.

New developments

Aims: Through an investment in new developments, to generate incremental revenue that can support the overall goal of increasing sales by ten per cent per annum.

Positioning: To expand the Cummings retail catchment area outside of Devon through the use of new marketing techniques to communicate to a wider audience the stores' capability of offering premium quality, unique, different and unusual internationally sourced, modern designs or traditional, craftsmanship quality goods manufactured by small UK manufacturers.

Actions: Although mail order is a well established component of the UK furniture and furnishings market, an effective entry into this type of marketing operation requires significant expenditure on a catalogue, a direct marketing promotional campaign to attract customers and an online telesales centre to manage customer order placement. The scale of the investment versus the potential revenue in the early years of trading suggests this is not a concept which should be progressed. It should be noted, however, that many US websites have found that having created a loyal online customer base, a significant volume of additional revenue can be generated by mailing out a direct mail catalogue two or three times a year.

In contrast to mail order marketing, initial entry into the world of online retailing is made attractive by the fact that the major expenditure in hardware/software and a programmer is already covered by the proposed actions to update the store operations computer system. The operation can be located on an existing Internet service provider (ISP) site. The candidate ISP is very experienced in electronic retailing, which means it can in assist in the creation of a website offering product information plus online ordering facilities, the selection of an appropriate back office system, and training of Cummings' staff in ongoing website updating and maintenance activities. For customers seeking additional help this ISP can also provide access to a telesales operation. Year 1 costs for a full online support service from the ISP are £10 000 which will then decline to £2500 for subsequent years. Order fulfilment will

Table 6.1 Trading forecast for the proposed Cummings online operation

	£		
	Year 1	*Year 2*	*Year 3*
Sales	115 000	230 000	300 000
Cost of goods	74 750	149 500	195 000
Gross profit	40 250	80 500	105 000
Advertising/PR	50 000	50 000	50 000
Web operations	10 000	2500	2500
Distribution	5750	11 500	15 000
General expenses	65 750	53 560	67 500
Net profit	9000	26 850	37 500
Profit as per cent sales	7.8	11.6	12.5

be from both the Cummings stock and where feasible our suppliers' warehouses. Distribution will be outsourced to an experienced e-commerce logistics operation.

It is assumed that the average value of an online customer order will be one third of that placed by our terrestrial customers. This latter value of purchase is £500 per customer. Given that the online operation is required to generate £250 000 in annual sales (the ten per cent incremental annual growth target for Cummings), this means that the site would need to attract approximately 1700 visitors who place an order. Assuming a five per cent conversion from visitor to online buyer, there is a need to attract 34 000 visitors per annum. Although this target represents only 0.6 per cent of the total current UK universe of online women shoppers, it is recognised that with only a limited promotional budget generating this level of site visitors will probably take at least 24 months to achieve. Applying these assumptions, as shown by the following trading performance forecasts, over the first three years the site will yield an annual profit of £9000, £26 850 and £37 500 respectively, as shown in Table 6.1.

DISCUSSION QUESTIONS

1. How can learning within the firm be of assistance in terms of improving the future market performance of a small firm?
2. Describe the construction and application of the resource advantage planning matrix technique.
3. Review the components associated with the execution of the marketing plearning process.

REFERENCES

Castrogiovanni, G.J. (1996), 'Pre-startup planning and the survival of new small business', *Journal of Management*, Vol. 22, No. 6, pp. 801–23.

Chaston, I. (2000), *Entrepreneurial Marketing*, Macmillan, London.

Day, G.S. (1994), 'The capabilities of market-driven organisations', *Journal of Marketing*, Vol. 58, No. 4, pp. 37–53.

Fulmar, R. and Rue, L. (1974), 'The practice and profitability of long range planning', *Managerial Planning*, May–June, pp. 1–7.

Hamel, G. and Prahalad, C.K. (1994), *Competing for the Future: Breakthrough Strategies for Seizing Control of Your Industry and Creating the Markets of Tomorrow*, Harvard Business School Press, Boston, Mass.

Hunt, S.D. and Morgan, R.M. (1995), 'The comparative advantage theory of competition', *Journal of Marketing*, Vol. 59, No. 2, pp. 1–15.

Hunt, S.D. and Morgan, R.M. (1996), 'The resource-advantage theory of competition: dynamics, path dependencies and evolutionary dimensions', *Journal of Marketing*, Vol. 60, No. 4, pp. 107–15.

ISI (1999a), Reedform, DTI, London.

ISI (1999b), Card Corporation, DTI, London.

Jarillo, J.C. (1993), *Strategic Networks: Creating the Borderless Organization*, Butterworth-Heinemann, Oxford.

Mintel (1999), *Furniture Retailing*, Mintel Retail Intelligence, London.

Mintzberg, H. (1979), *The Stucturing of Organisations*, Prentice-Hall, New York.

Porter, M. (1985), *Competitive Advantage: Creating and Sustaining Superior Performance*, The Free Press, San Francisco.

Robinson, R. (1979), 'Forecasting and small business', *Journal of Small Business Management*, Vol. 17, No. 3, pp. 19–27.

Shrader, C.B., Mulford, C. and Blackburn, V. (1989), 'Strategic and operational planning and performance in small firms', *Journal of Small Business Management*, Vol. 27, pp. 45–60.

Schwenk, C. and Shrader, C.B. (1993), 'Effects of formal strategic planning on performance of small firms', *Entrepreneurship Theory and Practice*, Vol. 17, No. 3, pp. 63–4.

Wood, P. and LaForge, R. (1979), 'The impact of comprehensive planning on financial performance', *Academy of Management Journal*, Vol. 72, pp. 516–26.

7

PRODUCT MANAGEMENT AND INNOVATION

LEARNING OBJECTIVES

After studying this chapter you should be able to understand:

1. the relationship between innovation and acceptance of risk;
2. the issue of whether innovation will be conventional or entrepreneurial;
3. how to use an analysis tool for determining the degree to which both product functionality and product form may be modified by innovation;
4. the process of product portfolio management;
5. the factors influencing new product success;
6. the linear, sequential new product management model;
7. how time to market may be reduced;
8. the influence of marketing style on the probable type of innovation in which a firm may become involved.

CHAPTER SUMMARY

Innovation is critical to business survival. The owner/manager will need to balance the degree of innovation to be considered against a willingness to take risks. It is also necessary to decide whether innovation will be conventional or entrepreneurial. The nature of innovation will also require consideration of the degree to which both product functionality and product form will be modified.

Most firms have more than one product and hence there is a need to consider how best to manage these product portfolios. A modified version of the Boston Consulting Group matrix is presented to guide this process. Specific guidelines are known to obtain which influence the probability that innovation will succeed. Many firms utilise a linear, sequential planning system to manage new product development projects. This system can cause delays, and techniques are emerging to reduce 'time to market'. In applying these techniques the firm will need to recognise that marketing style will influence the probable nature of the innovations in which the firm should be involved.

INTRODUCTION

Innovation, whether directed towards the development of new products or the ongoing improvement of existing products, is possibly the most important aspect of the product management responsibility in any small firm. In a world where other firms, both large and small, are seeking to expand their share of the market, successful small firms often can only stay ahead of competition by offering products or services which deliver new forms of added value to their customers.

In formulating an appropriate product management strategy, the owner/manager will need to determine the scale of innovation which will implemented by the firm. Reaching a decision on the scale of innovation involves selecting an appropriate stance toward innovation at a point somewhere along a continuum. At one extreme is the decision to progress innovation based purely upon minor extensions to the current product portfolio. The other extreme on the continuum involves the firm in adopting the aim of wishing to make available to the market a completely new product or service.

Another necessary decision is whether the owner/manager wishes to adopt a conventional market management approach or to opt for an entrepreneurial orientation. This matter also involves the selection of a point somewhere along a continuum. At one extreme is the decision to progress development based purely upon conventional thinking. The other extreme on the continuum involves the organisation adopting a totally entrepreneurial approach, to create an unconventional product or service.

Combining the dimensions of (a) source of sales growth and (b) organisational behaviour generates an alternative medium term product management option matrix of the type illustrated in Figure 7.1. Cell 1 is associated with concentrating on exploiting currently conventional products. Product improvement activity will have minimal impact on the organisation's future performance. This path is probably the most frequently utilised of all of the options proposed in Figure 7.1.

Cell 2 proposes the option of emphasising the importance of new products, but retaining a conventional orientation to innovative activities. Small firms which adopt the Cell 2 position typically assume that as their new products gain market share, they will be able to move back nearer to a Cell 1 situation with new products reverting to being a significantly less important source of revenue growth.

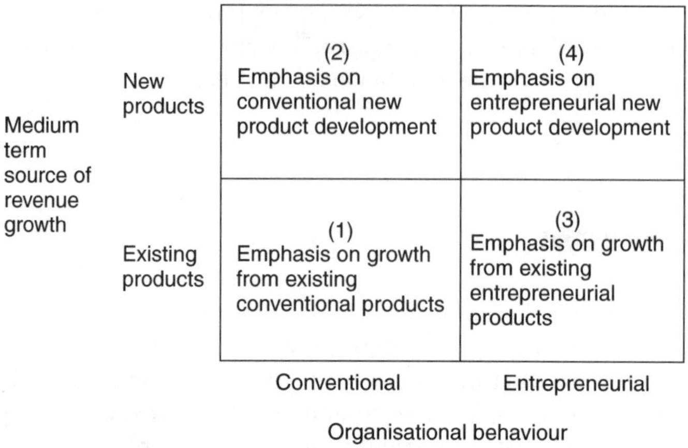

		Conventional	Entrepreneurial
Medium term source of revenue growth	New products	(2) Emphasis on conventional new product development	(4) Emphasis on entrepreneurial new product development
	Existing products	(1) Emphasis on growth from existing conventional products	(3) Emphasis on growth from existing entrepreneurial products

Conventional   Entrepreneurial

Organisational behaviour

Figure 7.1   Medium term new product option path matrix

Cell 3 suggests that an entrepreneurial small firm which has previously developed a range of unconventional products will, at least for the foreseeable future, concentrate on generating revenue growth without committing additional resources to the development of a completely new product concept. Cell 4 positions the small firm as concentrating the majority of its resources upon entrepreneurial new product development. It is possibly the riskiest of all of the options available within the matrix. Accordingly, most small firms will only adopt this position for a defined period of time in the hope that once the new products are launched, it can gradually move towards a Cell 3 situation where this latest generation of products will come to represent a long term source of revenue growth. A possible exception to this scenario, however, is the small firm run by an intuitive entrepreneur, who only achieves real personal satisfaction from trading activities which continually involve developing and launching radically new products.

The proposed model in Figure 7.1 is posited as a dynamic process, changing over time depending upon the circumstances confronting the small firm. What is possibly a very rare direction within the dynamic model, probably because it requires a fundamental shift in organisational culture, is for a small firm to shift product management style. Nevertheless one circumstance where this is likely to occur is when an entrepreneurial firm is so successful that its product strategy becomes the new convention within an industrial sector. One could argue, for example, that this is exactly the scenario which faces Microsoft. Having as a small firm established its suite of Windows-based programmes (Word, Excel, Access, Powerpoint, and so on) as the global standard in the world of computing, it now spends a significant proportion of its time exploiting these products and, on a regular basis, acting in a very conventional way by issuing updated, more powerful versions.

EXAMPLE: E-COMMERCE PRODUCT INNOVATION DECISIONS
....

An example of innovation as a natural extension of an existing product management strategy is provided by Axle Publishing Ltd (Innovation Awards 1999). This UK firm had already launched a successful magazine, *Property Broker*, for people in London wanting to buy and sell property without the involvement of estate agents. The promised benefit was that because homeowners could sell their property for the cost of an advertisement in the magazine, this provided a significant saving versus paying commission to an estate agent. Operating costs were kept to a minimum by using digital photography and advanced printing technologies.

The potential problems facing the firm were (a) the need to more rapidly bring together buyers and sellers and (b) the fact that some publications would not carry advertising for *Property Broker* because it conflicted with the interests of their other major advertisers, namely estate agents. The solution adopted by the firm has been to establish an Internet-based product which provides an electronic companion to the existing terrestrial market product.

Another example of extending an existing product proposition is provided by Cave Wood, a UK company involved in the international transportation business (Innovation Awards 1999). Their aim was to improve the efficiency and accuracy of information about consignments passing through their transit warehouse. The solution was a combination of electronic data interchange (EDI) and bar coding to communicate with their other partners in their pan-European distribution operation. Cave Wood automated their data management system, and this now means that customers are offered a new electronic product which permits them to access Cave Wood's information system to obtain real time updates on delivery times and the delivery status of shipments.

Information technology can also be used to create a new product form that can further expand a firm's level of market opportunity. An example of this scenario is provided by City Index, a leading City of London sports and financial bookmaker (Innovation Awards 1999). The company was originally established as a bookmaker with whom clients communicated by telephone. Observing the potential for using e-commerce to enhance customer communication and market coverage, the company established a new interactive online gambling website www.bluesquare.com Cyberspace gamblers are offered over a thousand different betting opportunities with selections drawn from traditional sports markets, political events and even possible future story lines in popular television soaps such as Eastenders. The website marketing objective is to use e-commerce to educate people towards understanding that betting is as much about entertainment as about gambling.

In the UK haulage industry a major headache is managing the paperwork associated with the servicing and repair of lorry fleets when vehicles hit problems away from their company depot. This problem exists because drivers use a diverse range of garage services at various locations across the country whilst making deliveries. It is estimated that invoicing errors are costing the UK haulage industry some £150 million per annum. Additionally some 20–30 per cent of all invoices submitted by garage and repair service operators contain errors, which means them having to be returned to the supplier for correction. The solution developed by a UK firm, OASIS, was to create a system using EDI, smart cards and code translation software to link together providers of garage services and their haulage industry customers (Innovation Awards 1999). Each driver carries a smart card carrying all the information required by a service or repair centre, including the haulier's maintenance authorisation limit. Upon completion of the work on a vehicle, the lorry fleet operator is sent an electronic invoice which is automatically downloaded into their accounting system for processing.

CONFIRMING STRATEGIC FOCUS

It was proposed earlier in this text that most small firms will opt to select one of four areas of possible strategic focus: product performance excellence, price performance excellence, transactional excellence and relationship excellence. Given the high risks associated with virtually any form of significant product or service innovation, it is probably much safer for a small firm to retain its existing strategic focus than to use new product development as an opportunity to totally reposition the organisation at the same time. Clearly, however, prior to finalising the project specification for any significant product innovation, the owner/manager should revisit this issue of current organisational positioning. This action is to ensure that an appropriate decision has been made concerning the strategic pathway along which to travel while seeking to identify an idea capable of supporting their small firm's future financial performance goals.

The owner/manager has to determine the degree to which market conventions are to be challenged. In reviewing this issue, the individual has two product dimensions to consider: the functionality of the product (the benefit offered to customers) and the form of the product (its physical nature). As shown in Figure 7.2, these two dimensions generate nine alternative options, depending upon the degree to which the firm is going to challenge convention.

The lowest level of risk presented in Figure 7.2 is to change neither function nor form convention. There is also minimal risk in repositioning product function whilst leaving the product form unchanged. Changing product form involves a certain degree of risk because of the need for the small firm to physically alter the product form. To develop a completely new product form is clearly much more risky. Possibly the safest option in this situation is not to change product functionality, because the new product can then simply be marketed as a product form replacement. Finally the highest risk proposition

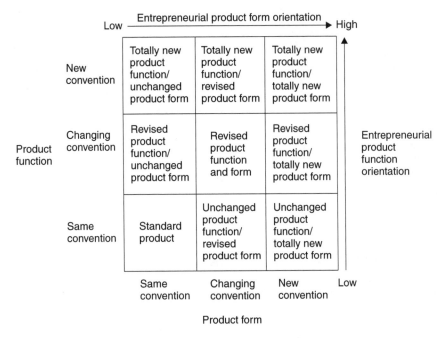

Low — Entrepreneurial product form orientation → High

		Same convention	Changing convention	New convention
Product function	New convention	Totally new product function/ unchanged product form	Totally new product function/ revised product form	Totally new product function/ totally new product form
	Changing convention	Revised product function/ unchanged product form	Revised product function and form	Revised product function/ totally new product form
	Same convention	Standard product	Unchanged product function/ revised product form	Unchanged product function/ totally new product form

Same convention   Changing convention   New convention   Low

Product form

Entrepreneurial product function orientation

Figure 7.2 A product function/form planning matrix

is to introduce both a new product form and seek new users (a 'new to the world product').

PRODUCT PORTFOLIO MANAGEMENT

Small firms must accept that all their products and service have a finite life in a market. This concept provides the basis of a theoretical paradigm known as the Product Life Cycle (PLC) curve (Figure 7.3) which proposes that products and service pass through the four phases of introduction, growth, maturity and decline (Heldey 1977). In recognition of the risks associated with a small firm depending upon a single product which has a finite life, the more successful small firms will have a number of products positioned at different stages on the life cycle curve. The objective is that such a portfolio will ensure long term revenue stability.

The Boston Consulting Group (BCG) originated the idea of a decision matrix based around the two dimensions of market share and rate of market growth. The theories underlying the BCG matrix are that (a) high market share products generate large profits and (b) the earlier a product achieves market domination, the more likely it is that this share will be retained as the

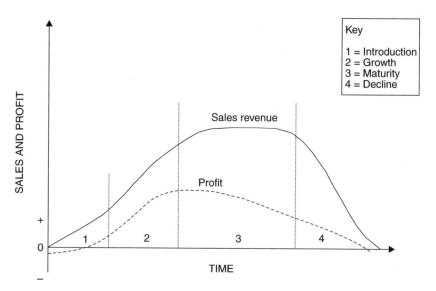

Figure 7.3   The product life cycle curve

market moves into maturity phase on the PLC. Although evolved by the Boston Group as a tool for assisting their large firm clients more effectively manage their portfolio of products, the concept has potential for application in the SME sector.

The BCG model exhibits the potential weaknesses that (a) market share may be a somewhat crude assessment of performance and (b) market growth rate may be an inadequate description of overall industry attractiveness (Doyle 1998). To handle the criticism about using share of market, Slywotzky (1996) suggested that firms should assess sales revenue of a product relative to proportionate share of the total financial value of all firms contained within a market sector.

The problem of market growth rate being an inadequate description of overall industry attractiveness can be overcome by replacing market growth in the BCG matrix with the new dimension of product uncertainty (Chaston 1999). As suggested in Figure 7.4, it is then possible to determine appropriate marketing strategies for a product portfolio which is more reflective of the objectives of value maximisation and management of risk.

During the introduction and growth phases of the PLC, uncertainty is high because suppliers need to convince customers that adopting their specific product is the correct decision. By the time a market moves into the maturity phase, most customers have become loyal to a specific product and their level of confidence is high. If a small firm's product has achieved a dominant share of total market value by the time the market has reached maturity then,

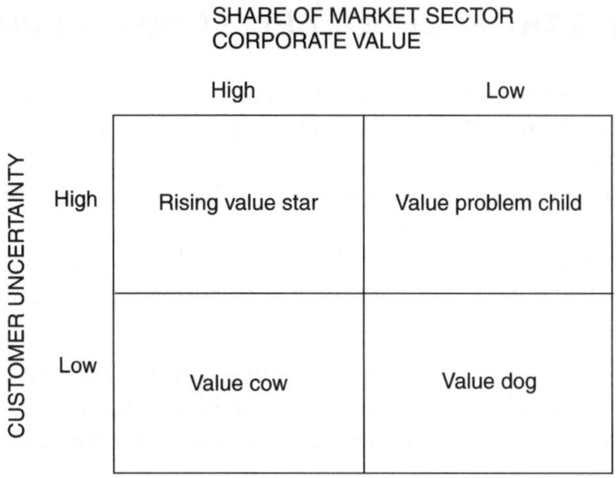

SHARE OF MARKET SECTOR
CORPORATE VALUE

		High	Low
CUSTOMER UNCERTAINTY	High	Rising value star	Value problem child
	Low	Value cow	Value dog

Figure 7.4   An alternative product portfolio matrix

because customers are extremely confident about their purchase choice, the firm will only have to expend limited funds as a percentage of sales on promotional activity to sustain market position. Hence this product, the 'value cow', will contribute a significant proportion of the company's total value. In contrast the 'value dog' product is in the unenviable position that (a) low value generation by the product will depress the company's financial value and (b) the profits needed to increase the company value can only come from stealing sales from a market leader. Because this latter firm's customers are now highly certain about the correctness of their product choice, the company with a value dog product will have to expend a massive level of funds and/or dramatically reduce price in order to stimulate switching by eroding customer loyalty. In most cases this strategy is not financially viable, which is why value dog products are rarely able to overthrow value cows in most markets.

If a small firm owns a low value share product during a high market uncertainty phase, a 'value problem child', then this is the most appropriate time to act, for it is when customers are still at the stage of finalising their decision about which supplier offers the best proposition. Consequently small firms with a low value share product are well advised to assess whether, while customer uncertainty is still high, a more entrepreneurial approach to new product development might result in an unconventional proposition capable of effectively attacking the 'rising value stars'. An example of this approach was the decision by ex-IBM employees to start the new small business Compaq Corporation to market a PC with a specification equivalent to IBM products but which could be offered at a much reduced price.

OPTIMISING THE PRODUCT DEVELOPMENT PROCESS

A number of authors have undertaken research to identify factors influencing the success and failure of new products. One of the most prolific writers in this area, Professor Robert Cooper (1975, 1986, 1988, 1990), has conducted numerous cross-sectional and longitudinal studies of Canadian firms. Application of factor analysis has permitted the development of his Newprod computer-based evaluation tool. The factors which form the basis of the Newprod predictive assessment of probable performance of a new product are:

- *product superiority/quality* – how product features, benefits, uniqueness and/or overall quality contribute to competitive advantage;
- *economic value* – whether the new product offers greater value than existing product(s);
- *overall fit* – whether the product development project is compatible with the organisation's existing areas of production and marketing expertise;
- *technological compatibility* – whether the product is compatible with the organisation's existing areas of technological capability;
- *familiarity to firm* – whether the firm can draw upon existing expertise or will be forced to learn completely new operational skills;
- *market opportunity* – the nature of market need, size of market and market growth trend;
- *competitive situation* – how easy it will be to penetrate the market and cope with any competitive threats;
- *defined opportunity* – whether the product fits into a well defined category as opposed to being a truly innovative idea providing the basis for a completely new market sector;
- *project definition* – how well the product development project is defined and understood within the organisation.

A research project (Rothwell 1976, 1979) concluded that there were a number of common causes for failure within UK firms. These were either market related (for example, no market existed, insufficient information on the market/competition, inadequate marketing skills and product did not offer any real benefit), or of a technical/managerial nature (for example, poor overall management, limited resources, poor R&D and inadequate communication/control systems).

Growing recognition of the costs of failure has resulted in the development of various systems to manage the new product development process. These models were originally evolved for use in the large firm sector, but many small firm advisors utilise very similar process models when providing guidance on innovation management to SME sector businesses. Traditionally these systems are of a linear sequential nature of the type illustrated in Figure 7.5.

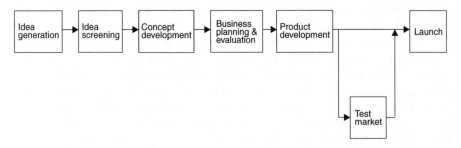

Figure 7.5 A traditional linear new product process management model

The entry point for this type of process is idea generation, with the ultimate aim being to launch only those products for which success is guaranteed. As the small firm moves through the process, at each stage the question is posed whether the product under development should be progressed or terminated. Costs associated with development increase at almost an exponential rate while the product is being progressed from idea stage through to market launch. Hence the earlier the small firm reaches a project termination decision, the greater will be the savings made.

The objective of the idea generation stage is to maximise the number of ideas available for consideration. This is achieved by involving as many sources as possible such as the customer, intermediaries, the sales force, employees from all areas of organisation, the R&D department, and suppliers; and by identifying weaknesses in competitors' products.

At the idea screening stage, the objective is to progress only those ideas which appear to have genuine potential for success. The ideas approved for development then enter the concept development phase. New ideas are usually framed around phrases and descriptions used by individuals within an industrial sector, many of which are often not understood by the customer. Hence the first step in the concept development phase is to redefine ideas into statements of customer-orientated benefit and product attributes. The resultant concept statements can then be tested with possible target audiences using techniques such as focus group meetings and one to one interviews.

Data from focus groups and interviews permit the small firm to assess purchase probability, appeal of product benefit and customer price expectations. These data provide the basis from which to forecast sales and to then evolve a business plan for the new product. The sales forecast, when linked with estimates of cost of goods, marketing expenditure, operating overheads and fixed asset requirements, permits estimation of expected profits and return on investment for the project.

Understanding of specified customer benefits identified during the concept development stage, when linked to forecasted production costs in the business plan, permits the creation of a detailed specification for use during the product development phase. Once prototypes have been produced, market research can commence to determine whether the actual product is capable of fulfilling customer needs. In consumer goods markets, this research is often based on activities such as blind side-by-side comparisons and in-home placement tests. In industrial markets, firms often involve potential customers in the evaluation activity through a technique known as Beta-site testing. In this situation, customers are kept closely involved in all aspects of the prototype development programme. Through usage of the test product in their organisations, they are able to provide detailed feedback about possible significant modifications to improve the final product.

In industrial markets the relatively small number of customers, the high unit value of purchase per customer, and the use of one to one personal selling as the primary promotional vehicle usually mean that following successful completion of the prototype development phase, the new product can immediately be launched. Virtually none of the market research undertaken during all of the new product development phases will, however, answer the question of whether a new product will survive in the self service environment characteristic of many consumer goods markets. This means that prior to the launch decision, many consumer goods are further evaluated through the medium of a test market.

The objectives of the test market are, in a geographically restricted area, to assess the performance of the product when placed alongside competitive offerings in end user outlets. During the test, research studies are undertaken to measure variables such as product awareness, trial rate, repeat purchase rate, market share attainment, achieved level of in-store distribution and behaviour of competition. Measurement of this latter variable is necessary in order to determine whether competitors are behaving normally or mounting a specific response to the test market which they would never duplicate in a national situation (such as doubling promotional spend or offering 'buy one, get one free' sales promotions).

There are four possible outcomes of a test market, each of which has different implications. Outcome 1, high trial/high repeat, will usually mean the test market has been successful and the product should be launched immediately. Outcome 2, low trial/high repeat, would require further investigation. The high trial/low repeat associated with outcome 3 is a little more worrying because it usually implies that having tried the product, consumers remain unconvinced of the merits of adding the item to their 'shopping basket' of regularly purchased goods. The worst scenario is outcome 4, where both trial and repeat rates are low. Here one must assume that fundamental organisational problems exist and, therefore, serious questions need to be posed of the project team to find out what exactly has been going on at all stages in the new product development process.

ACCELERATING THE INNOVATION MANAGEMENT PROCESS

Linear product development models of the type shown in Figure 7.5 are essentially orientated towards minimising mistakes. Hence owner/managers should raise questions of any external advisors who propose this type of new product process management approach. Assuming that the small firm is prepared to take risks then a possible alternative approach to innovation is to revisit the classic 'stage gate' process described in Figure 7.4 and to recognise that this is essentially a linear system which can lead to rigid and inflexible decision making within the firm.

Cooper (1994) has proposed that greater creativity within the stage gate process can be achieved by permitting progression to the next stage in the development even though certain issues may still require further investigation. Essentially what drives Cooper's new vision is a fact repeatedly validated by Japanese corporations: that organisations must find ways of reducing the time taken from idea generation through to product launch. In an increasingly competitive world, when seeking to reduce time to market owner/managers will have to balance the risks of not proceeding to the next phase until key information becomes available against being pre-empted by a more entrepreneurially orientated competitor.

An extremely important tool for reducing new product development times is the process known as concurrent engineering (Hartley 1992). This involves crossfunctional teams using available information to initiate parallel activities possibly even while the concept is still at the preliminary idea stage. For example the manufacturing team begins to design a new production line; suppliers commence work on the development of machine tools to manufacture components that will be required by the new product: and the advertising agency begins to evolve an appropriate promotional campaign.

Although concurrent engineering is an intuitively appealing concept, effective implementation is often found to be extremely difficult. Dickson (1995), in a study of high-growth, high-profit companies, concluded that senior managers often felt that they have not effectively managed the transition from sequential to concurrent engineering. Identified problems include testing the validity of manufacturing process prior to adoption, accurate cost estimation, and waiting too long before involving suppliers and/or customers in the development process.

The modern computer has made an almost immeasurable impact on accelerating time to market. Designers can now use computer aided design (CAD) systems to develop and evaluate virtual reality prototypes. By linking these systems to computer aided manufacturing (CAM) systems, engineers can often assess the feasibility of manufacturing a new product prior to construction of a new production line. Furthermore if the manufacturer is willing to overcome reservations about project confidentiality, the small firm can provide potential suppliers with real time data links. These permit suppliers to remain totally informed about all new product projects as they progress from idea through to manufacture of early prototypes.

An extremely important issue in enhancing innovation management is to optimise the organisational structure and lines of authority for managing the new product development process. The more autocratic owner/manager will tend to retain total control over new product development. Unfortunately time pressures and other managerial responsibilities often mean that new product projects in many small firms are severely delayed. The solution is for the owner/manager to delegate new products to an individual with both sufficient experience and authority to make things happen. This individual will typically operate independently of the established product marketing operation, acquire access to resources across the entire organisation, and usually create a cross-functional team that reports directly to the main board of the company.

An important impact of this alternative approach is that new products are no longer seen to be aligned with any single department, but are now the responsibility of all employees within the organisation. This increases the breadth of sources from which ideas can be drawn and avoids development delays because all employees are recognised as having a critical role to play in the management of innovation. Furthermore because emphasis is placed on effective intra-organisational communication, inappropriate decisions are avoided which might cause problems at a later date. For example, design staff work in partnership with manufacturing staff to overcome potential product assembly problems; procurement staff validate the availability of key raw materials; and the views of service engineers are sought to avoid design features that would cause maintenance problems when the product is on-site at a customer location.

Once an organisation has accepted that the goal of 'delighting the customer' should drive the innovation process, then the next step is abandon the classic 'not invented here' syndrome and widen the search for ideas to encompass sources outside the firm. Relationship orientated firms have the advantage over their transactional counterparts because the former can turn to suppliers and/or customers to identify new opportunities for innovation.

Over the last twenty years, as more research has been undertaken on the factors influencing the performance of firms, some theorists have suggested that senior management need to pay greater attention to the nature of the prevailing culture within their organisations. Unfortunately these various writers rarely appear to agree on exactly what they mean by the concept of culture. Hence for the purposes of the following discussion it is assumed that culture is a reflection of the dominant attitudes and values exhibited by the majority of the workforce.

Large multinational companies usually offer superior value, standardised goods across a diverse range of transactionally orientated markets around the world. It is perhaps understandable, therefore, that many of these firms find that the most effective operational culture is one based on closely defined employee job roles, permitting minimal variation in personnel policies between departments and using detailed, performance indicator-type monitoring systems to rapidly identify financial variances. Unfortunately this type of culture also seems to appeal to the more autocratic owner/managers in the SME sector.

The risk with highly regimented internal environments in both large and small firms is that employees cease to exhibit creativity and flexibility in responding to new situations. Hence many firms have found that as markets have become more competitive there is a need to become more entrepreneurial, but that implementing a culture shift of this magnitude is no easy task.

Although a large firm exemplar, 3M Corporation provides some effective guidelines for stimulating innovative behaviour in any size of firm. The cornerstone of its success is to strive to retain an entrepreneurial culture directed towards new ways of delivering customer satisfaction. Rigid operating policies are kept to a minimum, salaries are tied to the success of new products and employees are encouraged to be inventive. The 25 per cent rule requires that a quarter of a division's sales must come from products introduced within the last five years. Any barriers to success such as turf fights between departments are kept to a minimum and the 'not invented here' syndrome is actively discouraged.

At 3M, staying close to the customer is an ingrained cultural trait. Researchers, marketers and manufacturing personnel are actively encouraged to spend time in the field and customers are routinely invited to join brainstorming sessions organised by 3M. Once an employee comes up with an idea, they are encouraged to participate in a multidisciplinary action team to progress the new concept through to market launch. To give people thinking time, there is a 15 per cent rule which permits virtually anybody to spend up to that proportion of their working week engaged in an activity of their choosing as long as this is associated with product development or improvement.

ORGANISATIONAL STYLE AND THE FOCUS OF INNOVATION

Major new-to-the world innovation typically occurs because a highly entrepreneurial individual in a small firm decides to break free from existing customer satisfaction conventions and to offer a radically new solution. This type of innovation is somewhat difficult to achieve in large firms serving established markets because internal orientation is towards discovering new ways of improving the quality/value mix for existing products through emphasis on process-orientated innovation. For the small originator firm, however, it is critical for the owner/manager to understand whether the firm's marketing style is compatible with the owner/manager's aspirations.

As illustrated by the innovation ownership matrix in Figure 7.6 (Chaston 1999), once a new-to-the world concept has been launched, there are two possible life cycle pathways which can occur. Which pathway becomes a dominant influence within an industrial sector will be determined by the two factors of product technology complexity and market penetration. In those cases where the technological complexity is relatively low, as the product gains acceptance within a market the originating small entrepreneurial-transactional firm usually faces the choice of (a) retaining ownership through the late growth/maturity stages of the product life cycle by revising the firm's operational style or (b) accepting that over time, product ownership will shift into the hands of conservative-transactional, usually larger, firms who are more competent at producing standardised products offering a superior price/quality/value combination. Whether the new product originator changes style or ownership moves to larger firms, the focus of innovation within the market sector will tend to shift away from product performance towards being focussed on using upgraded process technologies to further enhance product value.

In many of today's industrial markets, once a scientific breakthrough has been made, the complexity of technology is on such a scale that to be successful the entrepreneurial originator will need to form partnerships with other organisations. This step is necessary in order to gain access to the additional expertise required to create a product which offers genuine performance benefits to the customer. An example of this approach is provided

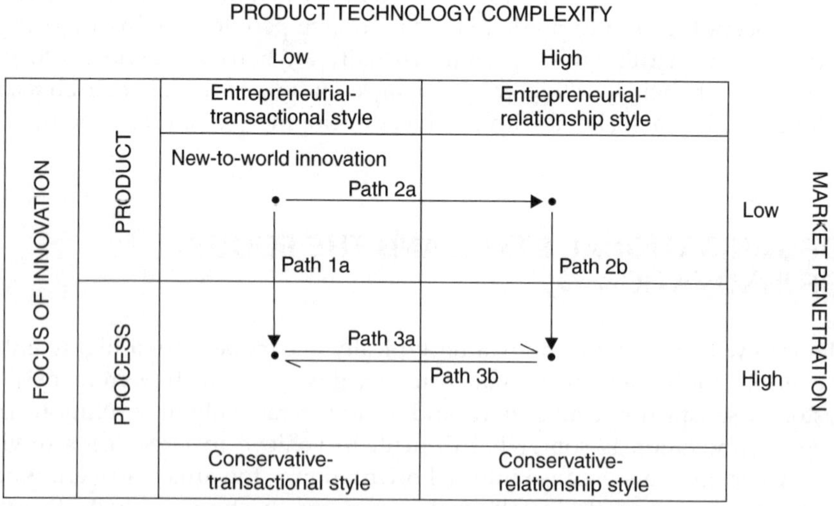

Figure 7.6 Innovation ownership matrix

by a strategic partnership between Elite.com, a leading provider of web-based time/expense tracking and invoicing services, and Employee Matters, which specialises in providing outsourcing solutions to firms lacking the skills to operate an in-house employee administration systems (PR Newswire 2000). The alliance means that together the two firms can now offer an entire suite of accounting, administrative and human resources management services that permit professional service firms to streamline their business operations.

Having entered the late growth/maturity phase of the life cycle, as shown in Figure 7.6, effective process innovation may involve switching between transactional and relationship marketing styles. It is posited that path 3a may occur because members of a supply chain recognise that to exploit new technologies it is necessary to work in much closer partnership with others. This trend is most noticeable in manufacturing industry where original equipment manufacturers are increasingly seeking assistance from their smaller suppliers and using project teams constituted of employees from different firms within the supply chain.

It is also suggested by path 3b in Figure 7.6 that once a technology is widely understood and price becomes the dominant influencer in the purchase decision, small firms will find their place in the market taken from them by large firms. These latter organisations, which are extremely competent at conservative-transactional process innovation, may become the major players in a market sector.

DISCUSSION QUESTIONS

1. Discuss how decisions over changes to both product functionality and product form can influence the innovation process.
2. Present a detailed review of the application of the linear, sequential new product management model.
3. Discuss what techniques exist for minimising time to market during execution of the new product development process.

REFERENCES

Chaston, I. (1999), *New Marketing Strategies*, Sage Publications, London.

Cooper, R.G. (1975), 'Why new industrial products fail', *Industrial Marketing Management*, Vol. 4, pp. 315–26.

Cooper, R.G. (1986), *Winning at New Products*, Wesley, Reading, Mass.

Cooper, R.G. (1988), 'The new product process: a decision guide for managers', *Journal of Marketing Management*, Vol. 3, No. 3, pp. 235–55.

Cooper, R.G. (1990), 'Stage-gate systems: a new tool for managing new products', *Business Horizons*, Vol. 33, No. 3, pp. 44–54.

Cooper, R.G. (1994), 'Third-generation new product processes', *Journal of Product Innovation Management*, Vol. 11, pp. 3–14.

Dickson, P. (1995), 'Managing design in small high-growth companies', *Journal of Product Innovation Management*, Vol. 12, pp. 406–14.

Doyle, P. (1998), *Marketing Management and Strategy*, Prentice-Hall, Hertfordshire.

Hartley, J.R. (1992), *Concurrent Engineering*, Productivity Press, Cambridge, Mass.

Heldey, B. (1977), 'Strategy and the business portfolio', *Long Range Planning*, February, pp. 1–14.

Innovation Awards (1999), www.awards.abfl.co.uk

PR Newswire (2000), 'Offer web-based employee benefits and HR administrative services', PR Newswire California, 14 June, 12.00 am.

Rothwell, R. (1976), 'Marketing – a success factor in industrial innovation', *Management Decision*, Vol. 14, No. 1, pp. 43–54.

Rothwell, R. (1979), 'The characteristics of successful innovation and technically progressive firms', *R&D Management*, Vol. 17, No. 3, pp. 191–206.

Slywotzky, A.J. (1996), *Value Migration: How to Think Several Moves Ahead of the Competition*, Harvard Business School Press, Boston, Mass.

PROMOTION

LEARNING OBJECTIVES

After studying this chapter you should be able to understand:

1. how buyer behaviour can be influenced by promotion;
2. the various options available for delivering promotional information;
3. the influence of customer behaviour and position in the product life cycle on promotional decisions;
4. promotional options in industrial versus consumer markets;
5. the implications of using the Internet as a promotional platform;
6. some problems associated with measuring the activity of online customers;
7. the potential benefits of participation in promotional networks.

CHAPTER SUMMARY

Buyer behaviour models demonstrate the role of information in the purchase decision process. One source of required information is the promotional messages delivered by the supplier. There are a large variety of promotional delivery mechanisms available to the firm. These include advertising, personal selling and PR. Given limited resources within most small firms, many owner/managers acquire their promotional expertise through a process of trial and error.

Selection of promotional tools is influenced by both customer behaviour and position of the product in the product life cycle. Additionally the nature of the market influences the tool selection process. Industrial markets tend to use personal selling, whereas advertising is the more dominant technique in consumer markets. The advent of the Internet has changed the promotional options available to firms. There are, however, some problems with measuring the actual nature of online behaviours exhibited by customers. In addition to the Internet, another effective promotional option available to the small firm is participation in promotional networks.

INTRODUCTION

The ultimate objective of the marketing process is to persuade the customer to select a firm's products or services in preference to offerings being made by competitors. An effective tool for gaining insights into the purchase decision process is a buyer behaviour model. Although these models can be of varying complexity depending upon market circumstances, in many cases the basic process can be visually described by a five phase model of the type shown in Figure 8.1.

The model entry point is the customer's recognition of need. This is followed by the customer progressing through the subsequent phases of acquisition of information, evaluation of alternatives and the purchase decision. While progressing through these phases, the customer is acquiring expectations about product performance. These expectations are tested against actual experience of using the product or service during the post-purchase evaluation phase.

As shown in Figure 8.1, at every phase within the model the customer is acquiring and processing information from two sources, internal and external. Internal information comes from those sources not under the control of suppliers. These sources can include personal product usage experience and

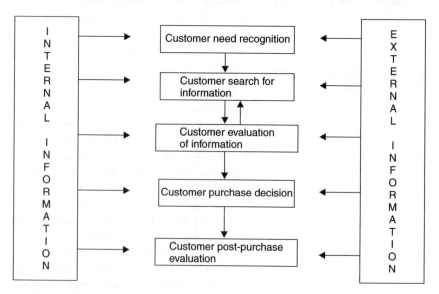

Figure 8.1 Five phase purchase process model

inputs from of respected sources. In consumer markets these latter sources include other family members, relatives and friends. In business to business (B2B) markets these sources can be colleagues within the same firm, contacts in other firms or professional advisors such as accountants. The primary sources of external information are data made available by suppliers' promotional activities. Promotion can be defined as all of the activities of the small firm associated with communicating information about a product or service to the customer. Marketers have a variety of alternative information delivery systems available to them that can be used to construct an appropriate 'promotional mix strategy'. These include (Kotler 1997):

- *advertising* which permits the delivery of a non-personal message through the action of renting time and/or space within an advertising channel (radio, television, cinema, newspapers, magazines and billboards);
- *collateral promotion* which covers a variety of message delivery approaches including brochures, packaging, merchandising materials, logos/company information on delivery vehicles, layout of office areas where service providers have contact with the customer, and the corporate clothing worn by company personnel;
- *direct marketing* which exploits advances in technology to create an ever increasing portfolio of techniques to interact with the customer (such as mail shots, telemarketing, e-mail, fax, voice mail and Internet home pages);
- *personal selling* which involves one to one interaction between the customer and the producer's sales force (and/or the sales staff of intermediaries) within the marketing channel;
- *public relations and publicity* which is constituted of a broad range of activities designed to promote the organisation and/or the organisation's products (for example, an article about the organisation in a trade magazine; sponsorship of a local football team by paying for the team strip);
- *sales promotions* which involve activities that offer the customer some form of temporary, increased value (for example, a coupon good on next purchase; an offer of 'buy one, get one free').

Many small firms have limited financial resources and thus face restrictions on the scale of their promotional activities. Hence successful small firms recognise the critical importance of seeking to persuade third party sources to act as internal sources of information. This behaviour is known as 'word of mouth advertising' or 'customer referrals'. The process offers two major advantages over any other way of seeking to influence customers. Firstly most people place greater trust in recommendations from satisfied customers than in any other source of market information. Secondly word of mouth advertising requires no expenditure on the part of the supplier. Hence it is no coincidence that small firms work very hard on seeking to satisfy existing customers, because owner/managers recognise that such individuals can act as promotional emissaries for the firm in terms of directing new customers to the organisation.

For many small firms one of the critical factors influencing the effective communication of promotional messages is the ability of employees to act as providers of information to customers. In the case of small hotels, for example, advertising in a tourism brochure probably has much less impact than factors such as the friendliness and efficiency of their reception staff. Hence in an increasingly competitive world, especially where there are minimal tangible differences between the small firm's product offering and those of competitors, owner/managers must be cognisant of the fact that all contacts between the organisation and the customer should be considered as a critical component of the promotional process.

Recognition of the potential negative impact on a small firm's market image of employees 'behaving badly' requires that the promotional process should be perceived as any activity associated with the provision of information that may influence the customer at any time during the purchase behaviour process cycle. This situation demands, therefore, careful management of all customer/employee interactions, starting with initial customer need recognition and sustained throughout all phases of the customer purchase decision and consumption process.

Promotional information which might influence customer perceptions can be that that which has been communicated (a) during the purchase transaction process (such as an answer provided by a sales person) or (b) by staff working in back office environments (such as a member of the accounting staff contacting customers about overdue invoices). In view of this broader perspective on the nature of the promotional process, it should be apparent that although planning a promotional strategy may remain the responsibility of the owner/ manager or the firm's marketing manager, implementation of process will involve every employee within the organisation (Garvin 1987; Peters 1987).

EXAMPLE: FIGHTING FOR SURVIVAL

In the USA, as in most countries in the Western world, over the last 40 years small retailers have faced a series of market changes that have threatened their survival (Lowry 2000). These have included the emergence of giant, multi-outlet discount retailers such as K-Mart and Wal-Mart, the construction of out-of-town shopping malls, manufacturing firms opening factory outlets, the growth of direct mail catalogue selling, and now most recently the Internet. Despite all of these adverse trends, 40 per cent of all retail sales within the USA are still generated by small independent retailers.

One advantage that these small firms enjoy is the fact that they tend to occupy locations where rents are low. Additionally labour costs can often be kept to a minimum by employing part time staff. To survive, however, it is critical that these small retail firms are able to establish an effective market positioning that can then be communicated through appropriate forms of low cost promotional activity. The commonest market positioning is that of being a local firm which is part of the community, both socially and economically, orientated towards delivering an individualised, relationship orientated range of retail products. To succeed this positioning must be communicated in any advertising campaigns and confirmed during customers' shopping experience. This latter activity will usually require that the owner/manager be involved in continually dialoguing with customers to determine their specific shopping needs and to ensure that the store is responsive to requests for additional products or services. Thus, for example, CB's Boat and Tackle store in Sarasota, Florida, in addition to selling fishing equipment, also provides seminars on fishing techniques and has linked up with local charter fishermen to offer discounted fishing trips to customers.

Although small retailers rely heavily on building close relationships with customers to generate repeat sales and word-of-mouth recommendations to generate new customers, where there is intense market competition there is usually the need to also execute promotional campaigns to build awareness of the outlet's existence. The problem confronting the owner/manager is that exposure in media such as newspapers or local radio is often expensive. One solution in this situation is to form a collaborative relationship with other independent retailers and to pool limited resources to increase the size of the promotional budget. An example of this approach is provided by six independent computer dealers in Baltimore, Maryland. They all trade under the same brand name of MicroAge, which is featured in their jointly funded promotional campaigns. A similar approach has been adopted by six marine products dealers in Arizona. These firms trade under the common brand name of Dockside Rudder.

Another approach to establishing a common brand identity is for a group of small retailers to form a voluntary group linked to a major wholesaler. This approach provides sufficient scale to obtain supplies at competitive prices and also permits trading under a common brand name. One example is small lawn and garden centres across the USA trading under the brand name of Growise. Another is the voluntary group True Value hardware stores, all members of which purchase their products from the wholesaler TrueServ Corporation.

EXAMPLE: RANDOM WALK PROMOTIONS

Although small firm promotional spending is dwarfed by the activities of large firms, in many cases supporting a promotional campaign can often be a smaller firm's single greatest item of annual expenditure. Thus it would seem advisable for owner/mangers to undertake detailed cost/benefit analyses of opportunities when determining how best to allocate promotional funds. The reality, however, as with other aspects of the managerial process in the SME sector, is that many small firms implement promotional decisions on the basis of 'learning by doing'. The outcome of this situation is that as long as any promotional decision error does not irretrievably damage the small firm, owner/managers acquire their promotional management expertise by intuitively learning how to select the most effective alternative promotional action plan.

Two Chinese-American sisters, Susan and Yan Lee, illustrate the application of this promotional philosophy (Chaplin 2000). These two individuals recognised that in the USA, there existed few cosmetic products specifically designed to suit the facial coloration needs of Asian women. The company was launched as a direct mail, catalogue order business based in the two sisters' houses. New customers were attracted via the medium of advertising in Asian language weekly newspapers.

One of their advertisements attracted the interest of the department store Nordstrom, which in 1995 offered the sisters the promotional opportunity of establishing a counter in their Bellevue, Washington store. Unfortunately although sales were high, the costs of this operation were only slightly less than the revenues being generated. In seeking another promotional channel, the sisters created their own website. This move attracted the attention of a merchandiser at another major retailer, JC Penney. In 1996, this company offered the sisters the chance to open outlets in 33 store locations. As expected, accepting this offer caused Nordstrom to terminate its relationship with the firm.

By 2000, the company had expanded into 47 JC Penney locations. In the same year, again due to somewhat fortuitous circumstances, a new opportunity arose: gaining distribution in eight Navy and Airforce exchanges, which provide access to the US military personnel market. The sisters also decided that cyberspace marketing offers new opportunities and hence in May 2000 they added an online order facility to the firm's existing website.

PROMOTIONAL MIX

Over time customer understanding deepens through the purchase and consumption of products or services. This scenario means that the role of promotion can be expected to change over time depending upon the product's position on the product life cycle (PLC) curve (Wasson 1978). In the early stages of the PLC, generic promotional activity will need to be directed towards both educating the customer about the new product and building market awareness. As the product enters the growth phase, promotional activity, although still aimed at generating trial among new customers, now also has the concurrent role of stimulating repeat purchase. Maturity is typically the most competitive period during the life of the product, with promotional activity very much concerned with defending the product against competition. Usually this will require a promotional strategy stressing the nature of the benefit superiority offered to the customer. Once the product enters the decline phase, price usually becomes the dominant factor influencing demand, and therefore promotional activity is usually drastically reduced.

Where the small firm wishes to offer increased value to customers but wishes to avoid using lower prices to deliver this promise, then sales promotion can provide the solution (for example, a coupon offering money off the next purchase). As such, sales promotion management is as much concerned with providing a tool to supplement the product pricing strategy, as it is a mechanism for communicating information to customers. The variable of price becomes a more dominant influencer on customer purchase behaviour the further the product progresses through the PLC. This means that sales promotion is likely to become a dominant feature of the promotional mix during both the maturity and decline stages of the cycle. For example a small tourist hotel seeking to generate revenue during seasonal periods of low occupancy might run a sales promotion offering low price 'bargain weekend breaks'.

Promotional campaigns can be considered as a process whereby information about the organisation's product or service is encoded into a message for delivery to the customer (Ray 1982; Crowley and Hoyer 1994). This concept is illustrated in Figure 8.2. It is proposed that upon message delivery, a possible feedback response may be initiated by the customer; namely a request for additional knowledge prior to reaching a purchase decision, or after purchase, on how to utilise the product effectively. In those cases where

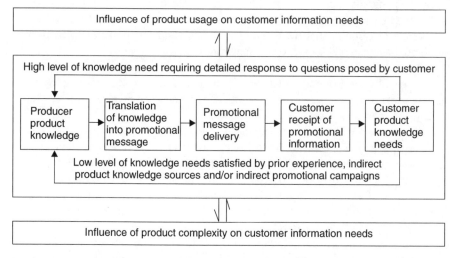

Figure 8.2 Information needs and information flows

customers need to be provided with a high level of knowledge, it is very probable that the customer will seek more information from the supplier. This scenario would apply, for example, in the case of a company wishing to purchase a new networked office computer system from a local, small office equipment distributor. As dialogue is possibly the most effective form of communication, the small distributor will rely heavily upon the use of a sales person to deliver the majority of the promotional message.

Unfortunately personal selling is an expensive method for delivering information to individual customers (Anderson 1994). Hence although many small firms would probably like to include a larger sales force in their promotional portfolio, it only becomes cost effective where the average unit of purchase per customer is very high. Consequently where the small firm is servicing a highly concentrated market containing few customers each buying a large proportion of the organisation's total output (such as a small manufacturer producing components for large original equipment manufacturers), the dominant promotional tool will be personal selling. In many cases a significant proportion of this role is undertaken by the owner/manager because over time, they have developed an in-depth understanding of the needs of the firm's key customers. Where the market is constituted of numerous customers each purchasing a very limited percentage of output, personal selling will tend to be replaced by other information delivery systems such as advertising or sales promotion.

EXAMPLE: SALES FORCE MANAGEMENT

The use of personal selling to drive the promotional process can be illustrated by the New Zealand case of The Clean Green Shirt Company (Stockport 1994). Started by two entrepreneurs, its launch idea was based upon making available a range of clothing that from raw materials, through manufacturing to packaging, have minimal impact on the environment.

To develop a market for the product the company recognised the need to gain distribution in retail outlets across the country. This was achieved by the very usual process in new startup companies; namely the owner/managers 'hitting the road and knocking on retail doors'. Fortunately one of their first retail approvals was in the Three Bears store in Newmarket. The owner of this store, Kevin Malle, is well known in the New Zealand fashion scene. He was so impressed with the product line that he took samples to other retailers while travelling around the country. The outcome of this type of customer referral, plus the endeavours of both the owner/managers and their sales staff was that in less than two years, The Clean Green Shirt company's products were stocked in over 70 retail outlets across New Zealand.

The high costs associated with the operation of a sales force have caused large firms to create highly sophisticated, often computer based management systems to assess and direct the activities of their sales personnel. The prevailing view of small firms in the academic literature is that they tend to adopt a somewhat informal approach to guiding all employees in the effective execution of task roles. This implies that a similar level of informality can be expected to be encountered in owner/managers' approach to the management of their sales force operations. Among the few researchers who have attempted to test the validity of this assumption are Shipley and Jobber (1994).

These researchers examined the sales management practices of small, independent, owner-managed industrial distributors. As a mechanism to direct the activities of their sales force, most large firms include a significant commission element in their remuneration package. This commission is usually calculated on the basis of achieved sales revenue generated by the individual sales person. In contrast, the researchers found that only a minority of the small distributors studied had adopted this approach. Instead the majority pay a salary and additionally at year-end, a bonus linked to total firm profitability. Shipley and Jobber feel this latter situation reflects the fact that the small firm owner/manager, being directly involved in the selling process, is able to direct the activities of a relatively limited number of other sales personnel without having to rely on commission payments to motivate these individuals. Furthermore they believe that utilising a year-end bonus based on profitability as a sales force incentive reflects the greater importance owner/managers place on profitability. This can be contrasted with large firms who tend to adopt a business objective concerned with maximising the sales revenue generated by their sales force.

The other key difference reported by the researchers in comparing large versus small firms, is the former's greater emphasis on utilising detailed quantitative sales performance analysis tools. These include activities such as measuring sales volume per call, orders per call, average cost per call and the volume of customer complaints, to assess sales force performance. In contrast, most small firms seem to rely on more simple analysis tools that examine current versus past performance in relation to issues such as number of accounts gained or lost and sales volume per account. The researchers' explanation of this situation is that small size of a sales force permits the owner/manager to hold a more accurate mental map of each individual's performance. Hence unlike large firms, there is no need for a structured, formalised system to keep management informed of each sales person's achievements.

In most consumer markets, where each customer makes a purchase which represents only a very small proportion of the small firm's total output, the promotional mix will often tend to be biased towards the use of advertising as the mechanism to build market awareness of the firm's products or services. As most small firms have extremely limited financial resources, they are rarely in a position to utilise the mass media promotional channels such as television advertising that are popular with fast moving consumer goods (FMCG) companies. Typically emphasis in the smaller firm will be on lower cost, often regional, media such as local newspapers and Yellow Pages advertisements.

Van Auken *et al*. (1992) undertook a study of advertising practices of small Iowa firms. They found that in descending order of importance, referrals, newspapers and Yellow Pages were the top three promotional tools utilised by respondent firms. Small retailers also used radio advertising and in a small number of cases, these organisations also included television advertising in their promotional mix. Few respondents had created any formal mechanisms through which to quantitatively assess the cost/benefit relationships offered by different media channels. Instead owner/managers tended to use their own perceptions of effectiveness based upon which media seemed to have greatest impact in terms of influencing customer behaviour. The researchers identified some differences between the perceptions of retailers and other small firms concerning relative channel effectiveness. Although all small firms considered referrals as the most important influencer of customer behaviour, retailers rated radio ahead of newspapers and the Yellow Pages. In all other market sectors, respondents considered that for their businesses, newspapers and Yellow Pages were more effective than radio.

In many countries small professional businesses such as those of accountants, doctors, dentists and lawyers constitute a significant component of the SME sector. Their behaviour is often affected by the fact that their own national professional bodies have placed constraints on what are considered ethical forms of marketing activity. Although professional bodies are beginning to relax their control over their members, in some countries it can still be the case, for example, that the only permitted form of advertising is via telephone directories and the Yellow Pages.

Given the importance of Yellow Pages one would expect small professional practices to have evolved an in-depth understanding of how to maximise the impact of their advertisement. Research by Sanchez (1988) on the use of the Yellow Pages by dentists in the USA suggests, however, that this is not the case. He demonstrated that consumers' response to Yellow Page insertions is heavily influenced by the provision of information on service attributes offered, such as areas of expertise, office hours, emergency services and the professional qualifications of the staff. Yet his analysis of page content revealed that the vast majority of dentists did not bother to purchase a display advertisement, but instead relied upon a single line insertion describing just their practice address and telephone number.

FORMALISING THE PLANNING PROCESS

Given the financial risks of making an incorrect promotional decision, it would seem reasonable to propose that small firms could possibly learn from their large firm counterparts and introduce somewhat more formalised planning systems. In making this suggestion, it is necessary to recognise there are two important reasons why large firms have established such systems. Firstly it is the only way to keep track of the diversified range of activities associated with employing a large workforce. Secondly such behaviours are necessary to meet the demands of shareholders for stable, sustained growth of share values and declared dividends (Peel and Wilson 1996).

As the majority of very small firms have less than ten employees and do not have to worry about the demands of shareholders, it is perhaps not surprising that the owner/managers in such operations can rarely be persuaded of the merits of establishing formalised promotional planning systems. However, Flushing *et al.* (1993) found that as the number of employees begins to rise or external stakeholders acquire an equity position, small firms do appear to begin to adopt a more formalised approach to forecasting the impact of their marketing decisions.

These researchers found that in small firms with ten or more employees, the owner/manager still retains responsibility for analysing and forecasting future performance. The usual approach that is adopted is to rely on personal intuition and inputs provided by sales staff. If available, the firm will also make use of data provided by industry trade associations of specialist government agencies. Small manufacturing firms appear to undertake more frequent, quantitative analyses of market trends than service sector firms. This is presumably because for the former, adverse estimates of future sales trends can have a major impact on production schedules and levels of on-hand finished goods. In contrast small service firms commit fewer resources to the forecasting process and in many cases rely upon qualitative, intuitive estimates of expected future performance trends.

The researchers also found that in both the large and small firm sectors, consumer goods firms use a more diversified source of data and undertake formalised market research studies to acquire understanding of customer trends. This contrasts with B2B markets where small firms rely more heavily on the views of their sales force and data issued by external agencies concerning forecasted trends in total industry sector sales.

For the owner/manager who decides that prevailing organisational circumstance merits the need to adopt a more formalised approach to promotional planning, then an advisable start point is to specify objectives for current marketing activities. In doing so, it is critical that relevant data can either be extracted from company records or generated by feasible, low cost market research. Possible objectives might be proportion of customers attracted via various promotional activities (data for this analysis can be obtained by a simple customer survey), average customer order size, per cent distribution among market intermediaries, and the costs of information delivery for each area of promotional activity.

Once these goals have been established, it then becomes feasible to determine whether current promotional activities appear to be supportive of them.

Knowledge of the strengths and weaknesses of current promotional activities can also be utilised in the formulation of future promotional campaigns. For example, the future promotional budget for a personal selling operation can be developed by calculating the optimal size for the sales force based upon data concerning the number of customers to be contacted and the required call frequency per customer. Similarly small firms which participate in trade shows can specify the number of new customer contacts required to cover the costs of participating in such an event and then, by tracking post-show outcomes, determine if promotional spending breakeven has been achieved.

Determining quantitative relationships between advertising expenditure and market impact is an activity which even large firms find extremely difficult. Hence the small firm is advised to keep this type of analysis relatively simple. For example, if the number of new customer contacts per advertising medium are adequate, then possibly not making any changes in the level of advertising expenditure is a reasonable decision. If, however, a higher level of customer response is required, it will probably only be possible to adopt a 'learning by action' approach. This could involve increasing advertising expenditure by 25 per cent for a defined period and then monitoring any changes in the rate of new customer attraction or the average total value of purchases by individual customers.

One of the issues associated with small firm promotional planning is the degree to which the activity is done in-house versus delegating some aspects to an external supplier. For example if the small firm is planning to allocate a significant level of funds to advertising, it may be advisable to assign to an advertising agency the responsibility for developing advertising campaigns and recommending appropriate media channels for message delivery. Having finalised the promotional plan, it is critical that the owner/manager ensures that prior to programme implementation, systems are in place to assess actual versus planned performance. This means that should variance relative to plan become apparent, the small firm is in a position to immediately instigate effective remedial action. Thus, for example, a small firm manufacturing catering equipment may have planned to attend three trade shows. The promotional planning assumption is that each trade show will generate at least ten new customer contacts, and in order to cover trade show attendance costs, incremental sales of at least £5000 from this new customer base. Then if after the first show, this aim does not appear likely to be achieved, the owner/ manager can immediately examine whether it would be advisable to cancel attendance at the two subsequent trade shows.

Owner/managers, like most line managers in a large organisation, normally prefer to minimise the number of control systems utilised to monitor actual performance versus plan (Chaston 1993). Hence there is a tendency for most small firms to adopt simplistic control systems. Unfortunately these are only capable of providing a very limited assessment of actual events (such as a quarterly review of sales by total sales achieved, without any breakdown by product category). The fundamental flaw in this approach is that the consolidated nature of the data yields very little information, and also some months will have passed before anybody realises that a promotional problem may be developing.

Small firms which realise the importance of responding to adverse situations before they develop into a major problem tend to adopt the view that survival in today's highly competitive world mandates that their marketing operation can benefit from regular, frequent monitoring of events (Peters 1987). Even as far back as ten years ago, Raymond (1992) concluded that although still in the minority, some small firms had already recognised that computerised accounting systems permit them to capture and evaluate sales revenue on a daily basis. This author posits that small firms which have adopted a computer-based information management orientation to the marketing process can be expected to have a much higher survival rate than their counterparts which perceive little benefit in establishing formalised performance assessment systems.

Nash (1995) articulated a similar view in relation to the use of computer-based analysis of customer response by small firms engaged in direct marketing. He concluded that small firms which track customer order patterns and collect data on which promotional device prompted customer response, are in a position to rapidly assess the effectiveness of the various promotional activities in relation to specific customer target groups. Additionally this in-depth knowledge of customer behaviour permits these small firms to be able more accurately to forecast future short term demand patterns for the range of items that constitute their often highly diversified product portfolio.

EXAMPLE: LIVING WITH CHANGE

Most small firms are aware of the risks associated with changing customer needs. Fewer it would seem, however, recognise it is just as critical to appreciate that new information delivery can impact market trend (Van Auken *et al.* 1992). Thus to survive, the small firm needs to consider that promotional programme execution is a dynamic process which must be continually adapted to suit identified changing circumstances in the external market environment.

An example of the risks associated with incorrect reliance on an unchanging promotional philosophy is provided by the regional beer brewer Genesse Brewing of Rochester, New York (Holdren 2000). In 1932, Louis Wahle purchased a failing brewery and almost single handedly rebuilt the business. His secret weapon was to recruit people who wanted to become beer distributors. Many of these people drove their own trucks to the brewery and ran their sales and delivery routes from their homes. By the 1960s, the promotional model of Genesse's sales staff calling upon independent bars to open new accounts, linked to a committed distributor network to service existing accounts, had created a business with annual sales in excess of one million barrels.

In 1964, the son of the founder, Jack Wahle, was appointed CEO. He recognised the need to build brand awareness and added a limited amount of television advertising to the promotional mix. Action was also taken to update the product range with the launch of Genesse Cream, a darker, slightly sweeter lager. Traditionally the US regional beer brands had survived by offering products at a lower price that national beer brands. By the 1960s, however, the national brewers such as Anhauser Busch and Millers were using sophisticated market research to formulate products capable of meeting clearly identified customer drinking habits, supporting their brands with heavy promotional spending and reducing prices so that these were similar to those of their regional competitors. The role of a sales force linked to a loyal distributor network began to become less critical because bars began to base their purchase decisions mainly upon which brands were being heavily promoted on television.

As Genesse sales began to decline in the face of price competition and the massive promotional onslaught of the national beer brands, the company responded by launching new products such as Irish Amber and Honey Brown lager. Little or no market research was undertaken, with formulation decisions being based upon what personally appealed to senior managers. The primary promotional support for new products continued to be reliance upon the sales force organising tasting events in bars and offering in-premise sales promotions such as giving away glasses. Only modest levels of television and radio advertising were used to support these new products.

In the face of price competition and a market where consumer purchase decisions were strongly determined by the scale of national advertising, there could only be one outcome of Genesse's insistence on relying upon an outmoded promotional philosophy. By the late 1990s, sales had declined dramatically. Sadly by the end of the millennium, the parent company, Genesse Corporation, announced plans to exit the brewing industry and concentrate on its commercial interests in the food processing and real estate sectors.

TRENDS IN PROMOTIONAL INFORMATION INTERCHANGE

In the case of small firms operating in classic conservative-transactional marketing environments, the customer is typically seeking to purchase the lowest priced, standardised goods which can fulfil their well defined product usage parameters. Configuration of information interchange channels in this type of environment is likely to be of a highly formalised nature: for example the customer contacts the sales department to confirm the quoted price and to place an order (Van De Ven 1976).

In B2B markets, as organisations move towards a relationship marketing orientation, the tendency is for the number of inter-organisational contact sources to increase as both parties promote the concept of maximising the number of communications links between employees in each other's organisations. Typically this change in the nature of the organisational relationship is also accompanied by a sharp rise in the overall volume of data exchange. As both parties begin to acquire mutual trust in each other the relationship deepens to the point where commercial confidentialities can be exchanged with each other. Thus a very usual pattern in such markets is for the supplier to 'open up' their organisation and make it easier for the customer to make immediate contact with the relevant department which can service their needs for information at specific points in the purchase decision and usage cycle. Again, as in other areas of promotional management, computer technology has made a major contribution to permitting more complex information interchange than was even thought possible just a few years ago.

Some firms offer an automated routing system where, upon making an initial telephone contact, the customer is instructed to press one of various number combinations to reach the department with which they wish to make contact. Accompanying the front end system is a 'behind the scenes' online response system. This latter element is critical in order to ensure the customer receives an appropriate response. It is usually based around an integrated, computerised, customer database system which permits the responding employee both to validate the background on the customer and to record actions which have been initiated in response to each enquiry.

Originally these automated arrangements relied heavily upon using electronic data interchange (EDI) to link together the computer systems within each organisation (thus a supermarket can link its store level stock movement analyser to its order replenishment system, which in turn is linked online to small suppliers' ordering and production scheduling systems). More recently linkages have been made even more effective through the creation of inter-firm Extranets. These can be linked with groupware systems such as Lotus Notes which can be programmed to automatically copy all individuals in both supplier and customer organisations who might wish be remain updated on any changes in supplier–buyer decisions initiated by an individual working elsewhere in their respective organisations.

THE INTERNET AND THE COMMUNICATIONS MIX

The Internet offers a whole new range of promotional opportunities to both large and small firms. An important dimension of the Internet is that the medium combines the features of both broadcast and publishing to facilitate two way communication with customers. Leong *et al.* (1998) sought the views of Australian marketing practitioners about where the Internet fits in relation to other media. With respect to small firms' early usage of the technology, most practitioners consider these organisations are using the Internet in a way which is very similar to direct mail. This is because many small firm websites in their early stages of development are essentially online catalogues. Like direct mail, the Internet has the ability to provide information that may precipitate the action of causing the visitor to make a purchase. An important advantage that the Internet offers the small firm, however, is that when compared to traditional forms of direct marketing, the costs of reaching target markets are much lower.

Most marketing practitioners do not see the Internet as replacing other media. Instead they feel that it complements other channels such as television or magazine advertising. Hence the recommended promotional philosophy is for small firms to adopt the approach of considering the Internet in relation to the range of other, more traditional channel options which may exist. In this way a move onto the Internet should only be considered if this decision delivers the most cost effective approach for achieving the aims which have been specified for a promotional campaign.

Berthon *et al.* (1996) suggest the Internet can be used to generate awareness, passively provide information, demonstrate the product and if required by the customer, support interactive dialogue. Acceptance of this perspective suggests it is feasible to perceive the Internet as being capable of fulfilling the role of guiding the customer through all phases of the purchase transaction process. When the Internet first became available, some academics perceived that the medium would also introduce a new level of promotional democracy into world markets. The authors proposed that the medium offered small firms the unique characteristics of:

- a medium which is relatively easy and inexpensive to access;
- compared to other media, access opportunities which are the same for all firms, no matter their size;
- uniform share of voice – no firm can drown out others;
- initial setup costs which mean that there are virtually no barriers to entry.

Small upmarket pottery firms in South West England have always faced the constraint that revenue is often limited to that which can be generated by operating their own outlet and/or by gaining distribution in retail craft shops in their local area. Although their owner/managers are sometimes successful in achieving retail distribution in major cities such as London, the high level of time commitment and sales management costs associated with sustaining a relationship with city retailers often prohibits effective exploitation of this channel of distribution. The advent of the Internet has dramatically changed this situation. Owner/managers recognise the unique attributes of the new technology and have created online pottery stores. The outcome is that many have attracted new customers, not just in the UK, but from consumers elsewhere in the world using the Internet to locate new sources of unusual craft goods.

For small firms considering an entry into cyberpsace marketing, it is necessary to point out that as large companies have come to understand the potential offered by the Internet, they have initiated various actions to ensure that they, not small firms, can dominate this new marketing channel. The first important event in this trend was the realisation by the major portals such as Yahoo and AOL that their visitors were a valuable asset for which they could charge other firms money. Along with this realisation came the 'banner advertisement'. These Internet advertisements, the first of which was sold by HotWired Inc. in 1994, usually take the form of a small insertion on a web page, communicating a brand name, a simple benefit message and/or web address.

Briggs and Hollis (1997) found that for creating brand awareness, banners compare favourably with both television and magazines. Large firms were not slow to appreciate the potential offered by banner advertisements. In 1995, only $312 million was expended on online advertising. By 1997, this had risen to $906.5 million and exceeded $5.0 billion early in the new millennium (Drez and Zufryden 1998). A Forrestor research study estimates that by 2004, Internet advertising expenditure will rise to $33 billion, 33 per cent of which will be outside the USA. The prime reason for this situation is that long established brands such as Ford and IBM and the large firm, online retailers are all committing large budgets to online advertising. One example of this activity is Amazon.com, which signed a $19 million contract to rent banner advertising space for three years on AOL's home page (www.aol.com). In the face of such levels of expenditure on this new medium, it is not surprising that most small firm advertisers can no longer afford the costs associated with being featured on the major Internet portals.

In the early years of the Internet, when the number of websites was still relatively small, companies could often rely on the search engines such as Netscape and Alta Vista to bring new customers to their sites. Now, however, the global explosion in the total number of websites means that most firms are being forced to use massive terrestrial promotional campaigns to build market awareness for their online operations. For example in 1999, E*Trade (www.etrade.com), an online discount stockbroker, spent $200 million communicating its website address. CNet, an online publisher (www.cnet.com) has spent $100 million and the toy maker Mattel $90 million. The outcome of this spending spiral is that over the period 1997 to 1999, the offline cost of establishing an e-commerce brand is estimated to have risen from $5–10 million to somewhere in the region of $50–100 million (Alexander 1999). Thus as this trend is expected to continue, it will become increasingly difficult for small firms to merely depend upon being identified in an online search by potential customers as a way to establish a viable new online business.

McLuhan (2000) has also identified another problem that small firms face in cyberspace markets, namely increased price competition. He believes that because many companies have not evolved Internet strategies capable of differentiating their offering from competition or building long term online relationships with customers, many consumers are just switching between websites looking for the lowest possible price. Already in the US, almost 80 per cent of online shoppers admit that price is the main motivator in causing them to revisit a website. To overcome this problem, McLuhan believes small firms must develop online offerings which are more personalised and of real interest to their customers. This can sometimes be achieved by using the Internet to offer specialist knowledge to specific customer groups. This situation has, for example, already resulted in some small firms establishing editorial advertising campaigns based around pages containing detailed information about product usage.

INTERNET MEASUREMENT ISSUES

Website servers have an amazing ability to collect data about visitor numbers, time spent on-site and information viewed by the visitor. Hence when the small firm rents web space on an Internet service provider (ISP), this host organisation is able to supply data that can be used to gain greater understanding of site visitor behaviour and demographics. For example, website servers have the ability to measure the number of pages requested, how much time is spent in each page, and what types of computers made the page requests. The implications of the ability of the ISP to record such information mean that small firms can use the analytical ratios of the type shown in Figure 8.3 to rapidly gain insights into online customer behaviour and thereby evolve even more effective online promotional campaigns.

It is necessary to register that the level of accuracy of such measurements to a certain degree may be questionable. This is due to the problems of identifying site visitors and the way the visitor's PC stores (or 'caches') data locally (Drez and Zufryden 1998). In the traditional media, surveys and panel studies permit the unique identification of customer by name, telephone number or address. On the Internet, the tendency of many ISP firms is to avoid investing in expensive audits to track customer behaviour. Instead they use the visitors' Internet protocol (IP) addresses to build their files, which measure visitor traffic and site usage patterns. Unfortunately one drawback is that these IP addresses may not be unique to a specific visitor. Several users may be assigned the same IP in multi-user systems such as AOL. Additionally visitors who use an ISP which operates a dynamic IP allocation system, may have a different IP assigned to them each time they connect with the ISP. Then as if this were not a large enough problem, if the ISP is using a 'multiple proxy

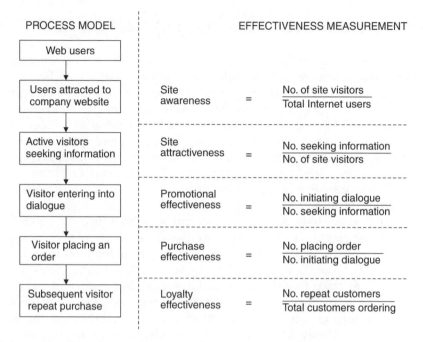

Figure 8.3 Website promotional effectiveness assessment

server' system, site visitors can be assigned multiple addresses by an ISP even during a single session.

Another important variable in the assessment of website effectiveness is the number of pages requested by the site visitor. If a visitor requests a page, the displayed page will usually have links to other pages. Should the visitor, having requested a second page, then use the 'back button' to return to the first page, the website will not record the second exposure to the first page. The reason for this is that the user's PC will have cached the first page on its hard drive. Hence upon clicking the back button, the PC will not return to the website, but instead retrieve the page from its own cache. Under these circumstances the website statistics will underestimate exposure frequency for the pages read by the site visitor.

A third issue is the reliability of reported measures in terms of whether the requested page is actually received by the reader and if received, actually read. For example, the user may request a page, decide it is taking too long to download and terminate their computer session. The issue of whether the downloaded page is actually read is, however, no different to the problems faced by the traditional media. People may have their television on, but there is no guarantee anybody is watching. Similarly a person may buy a magazine, but only look at certain pages, thereby never being exposed to advertisements on the unread pages.

165

PROMOTIONAL DELIVERY THROUGH NETWORKS

A common constraint facing many small firms is their inability to fund promotional activity on a scale sufficient to achieve parity with larger competitors. One way of overcoming this obstacle is to form an alliance with other firms through the formation of a business network. Early evidence on the utilisation of promotional networks came from studies in Sweden of the behaviour of firms entering overseas markets. Subsequently other researchers have identified similar behaviour in other countries. For example Holmlund and Kock (1998) found that the majority of small firms in Finland form vertical relationships with customers or horizontal relationships with other firms as a mechanism for entering new overseas markets.

Similar findings have emerged in the context of how successful high technology firms execute a growth strategy based upon internationalisation of their operations. Jones (1999) surveyed small American high technology firms and concluded that those involved in overseas markets could be classified as reluctant developers (not that interested in export sales), conventional developers (firms gradually expanding overseas), rapid developers (conventional firms beginning to enjoy a significant increase in export sales) and international entrepreneurs. This latter group has high growth aspirations from day one of the firm's creation. To achieve these goals they recognise the need to rapidly gain market penetration in both their domestic and foreign markets. They recognise that achievement of this latter goal is unlikely to occur by relying solely on their own resources. Hence their owner/managers actively seek to form formal cooperation agreements with overseas firms. Areas where cooperation is agreed usually include sharing marketing resources and technological data exchange.

In the development of a marketing strategy for a small business network, there are two dimensions which determine the focus of the selected promotional campaign. One is the customer target dimension. The choices along this dimension are, first, that of sharing of promotional resources directed towards increasing sales to current customers, gaining access to new customers in existing markets, or entering completely new markets. The second dimension is which product form will be supported in the planned promotional activity. The three choices here are to focus on existing products, combine together the product offering from network members to offer an enhanced proposition, or develop an entirely new range of products.

By combining these two dimensions, as demonstrated in Figure 8.4, one can generate the following nine different pathways from which firms can then select the best option for using collaborative promotional campaigns to enhance market performance:

- *Cell 1* – sales of existing products to existing customers are increased by a pooling of promotional resources;

- *Cell 2* – pooling of promotional resources permits access to new customers for existing products;
- *Cell 3* – sales of existing products can be increased by pooling of promotional resources to permit entry into a new market sector;
- *Cell 4* – combining together the different products from network members and pooling promotional resources permit the marketing of an enhanced product proposition to current customers;
- *Cell 5* – combining together the different products from network members and pooling promotional resources lead to the creation of an enhanced product proposition which can be marketed to new customers in the existing market sector;
- *Cell 6* – combining together the different products from network members and pooling promotional resources to enhance an existing product portfolio make entry into a new market sector an affordable option;
- *Cell 7* – the pooling of product development and promotional resources permits the creation of a new product marketed to existing customers;
- *Cell 8* – pooling product development and promotional resources permits the marketing of a new product to new customers in an existing market;
- *Cell 9* – pooling product development and promotional resources leads to the development of a new product to create access to a new market sector.

Market / Product	Existing market sector		New market sector
	Existing customers	New customers	New customers
Existing product	(1) Sharing promotional resources to increase existing customer sales	(2) Sharing promotional resources to gain access to new customers	(3) Sharing promotional resources to execute new market entry strategy
Merged product and promotional resources	(4) Increased sales to existing customers by offering an enhanced product proposition supported by joint promotions	(5) Access to new customers through offering an enhanced product proposition supported by joint promotions	(6) Gaining access to new markets through offering an enhanced product proposition supported by joint promotions
New product and shared promotional resources	(7) New sales to existing customers through launching new product and promotional campaign	(8) Gaining access to new customers by launching new product and promotional campaign	(9) Gaining access to new markets through offering new product and promotional campaign

Figure 8.4 A promotional network options matrix

Table 8.1 Changing processes to support the move to network-based promotional activities*

Managerial process	Autonomous small firm	Network organisation
Control	Functional roles driven by owner/manager	Structure determined by information acquisition and flow processes
Employee involvement	Sales and marketing staff	Individuals from across all areas of the member firms and/or the customer organisations
Promotional objective	Maximising the number of successful sales transactions	Building strong inter-organisational bonds with the ultimate aim of maximising customer loyalty
Promotional claims	Based on communicating superiority across areas of perceived customer need	Based upon confirming the network's ability to fulfill the needs and expectations communicated by customers
Communication process	Primarily one way from supplier to customer	Emphasis on two way interactive dialogue between both network members and customer groups
Advertising media	Preference for using media channels seen as traditionally appropriate within sector	Adoption of diverse, customer specific messages delivered by a multiplicity of different innovative media channels
Use of IT	Restricted to monitoring of financial performance	Recognised as providing the only effective way through which to manage network member and customer information flow interactions and often the capability to offer a path differentiating the network from competition

*Data acquired by authors during observations and analysis of small business networks in Australia, Europe and New Zealand

In proposing the opportunities associated with the formation of small firm promotional networks it is necessary to accept that although this sounds like an intuitively good idea, in practice obstacles to concept execution must be expected. Variables such as differing company cultures, variation in business objectives and lack of trust all combine to make network creation and operation a very difficult task (Chaston 1999). Furthermore having formed promotional networks, many of the participants rapidly encounter the problem of having to manage information flows, not just with customers, but now also with other members within the new collaborative trading entity. This situation is clearly exacerbated in those cases where the network members, as owner/managers in their own organisations, tend to (a) prefer retaining absolute control over information and (b) often exhibit a bias towards a transactional orientation in the execution of promotional activities.

As shown in Table 8.1, for owner/managers in SME sector firms to enter and then operate successfully within networks designed to enhance promotional programme effectiveness, pressure begins to grow for a whole range of fundamental shifts in operating philosophies and practices. Typically the first phase in this process shift will be in the area of revising promotional claims and adding to the diversity of media channels used to communicate with customers. As the network members begin to recognise the benefits of sharing information between both themselves and their customers, more open relationships begin to emerge during which all parties begin to perceive that there are genuinely mutual advantages from working more closely together. This outcome causes a rapid expansion of both the volume of information interchange and the number of individuals involved in the promotional process. In the face of this almost exponential rise in the volume of inter-organisational communication, the network will typically begin to move towards adopting flatter, more organic structures and concurrently investigating how investment in IT can assist in further enhancing the strength of relationships both within the network and with the network's customers.

DISCUSSION QUESTIONS

1. Compare and contrast the various techniques available for delivering promotional information to customers.
2. How does the Internet represent a new mechanism through which to deliver promotional information?
3. Why is the acquisition of information critical in determining the effectiveness of promotional campaigns? What types of problems confront the firm seeking to acquire information about the behaviour of online customers?

REFERENCES

Alexander, G. (1999), 'Advertising fever grips e-commerce', *The Sunday Times*, Business Section, London, 21 November, p. 9.

Anderson, R. (1994), *Essentials of Personal Selling: The New Professionalism*, Prentice Hall, Englewood Cliffs, New Jersey.

Berthon, P., Pitt, L. and Watson, R. (1996), *The World Wide Web as an Industrial Marketing Communication Tool: Models for the Identification and Assessment of Opportunities*, Henley Management Centre, Henley, Oxfordshire, Working Paper series.

Briggs, R. and Hollis, N. (1997), 'Advertising on the Web: is there response before click-through?' *Journal of Advertising Research*, Vol. 37, No. 2, pp. 33–46.

Chaplin, H. (2000), 'How the Yee sisters fly in the face of conventional wisdom', *Fortune*, 7 February, pp. 13–17.

Chaston, I. (1993), *Customer-Focused Marketing*, McGraw-Hill, Maidenhead.

Chaston, I. (1999), *New Marketing Strategies*, Sage, London.

Crowley, A.E. and Hoyer, W.D. (1994), 'An integrative framework for understanding two-sided persuasion', *Journal of Consumer Research*, March, pp. 44–55.

Drez, X. and Zufryden, F. (1998), 'Is Internet advertising ready for prime time?', *Journal of Advertising Research*, May–June, pp. 31–46.

Flushing, S., Herbig, P.J. and Golden, J.E. (1993), 'Forecasting: who, what, when and how', *Journal of Business Forecasting Methods and Systems*, Vol. 12, No. 2, pp. 16–27.

Garvin, D.A. (1987), 'Competing on the eight dimensions of quality', *Harvard Business Review*, Nov.–Dec., pp. 101–9.

Holdren, M.W. (2000), 'Saying so long to Genny', *Brandweek*, 15 May, pp. 50–8.

Holmlund, M. and Kock, S. (1998), 'Relationships and the internationalisation of Finnish small companies', *International Small Business Journal*, Vol. 16, No. 4, pp. 46–63.

Jones, M. (1999), 'The internationalisation of high-technology firms', *Journal of International Marketing*, Vol. 7, No. 4, pp. 15–41.

Leong, E.K.F., Huang, X. and Stanner, P.J. (1998), 'Comparing the effectiveness of the web site with traditional media', *Journal of Advertising Research*, Vol. 38, No. 5, pp. 44–53.

Lowry, J.R. (2000), 'The fight for survival by independent retailers', *US Today*, July 2000, pp. 22–5.

McLuhan, R. (2000), 'A lesson in online brand promotion', *Marketing*, 23 March, pp. 31–2.

Nash, R. (1994), *How to Transform Marketing Through IT*, Management Today Publications, London.

Peel, M.J. and Wilson, N. (1996), 'Working capital and financial management practices in the small firm sector', *International Small Business Journal*, Vol. 14, No. 2, pp. 52–61.

Peters, T. (1987), *Thriving On Chaos*, Alfred Knopf, New York.

Ray, M.L. (1982), *Advertising and Communications Management*, Prentice-Hall, Saddle River, New Jersey.

Raymond, L. (1992), 'Computerisation as a factor in the development of entrepreneurial firms', *International Small Business Journal*, Vol. 11, No. 1, pp. 23–32.

Sanchez, P.M. (1988), 'Professional dental services: the Yellow Pages advertising decision', *Health Marketing Quarterly*, Vol. 15, No. 3, pp. 95–104.

Shipley, D. and Jobber, D. (1994), 'Size effects on sales management practices in small firms: a study of industrial distributors', *The Journal of Personal Selling & Sales Management*, Vol. 14, No. 1, pp. 31–44.

Stockport, G. (1994), 'Greening your shirt: The Clean Green Shirt company', *New Zealand Strategic Management*, Vol. 1, No. 1, pp. 54–69.

Van Auken, H.E., Doran, B.M. and Rittenburg, T.L. (1992), 'An empirical analysis of small business advertising', *Journal of Small Business Management*, Vol. 30, No. 2, pp. 87–101.

Van De Ven, A. (1976), 'On the nature, formation and maintenance of relations among organisations', *Academy of Management Review*, Oct., pp. 24–36.

Wasson, C.R. (1978), *Dynamic Competitive Strategy and Product Life Cycles*, Austin Press, Austin, Texas.

9

PRICING AND DISTRIBUTION

LEARNING OBJECTIVES
....

After studying this chapter you should be able to understand:

1. the critical role of pricing in determining market performance;
2. how customer attitudes can influence pricing strategies;
3. how price can be used to support a product quality positioning decision;
4. the role of the Internet in influencing pricing behaviour;
5. the new opportunities created by online auctions;
6. the issues associated with determining an appropriate distribution strategy;
7. how TQM and JIT have influenced distribution theory;
8. the role of logistics is supporting company image;
9. how the Internet is changing the structure of many distribution systems.

CHAPTER SUMMARY
....

Price is a critical determinant in influencing market performance. A number of factors can influence the pricing decision. Customer attitudes determine whether prices will receive market acceptance. Transactional customers typically expect to pay lower prices for conventional goods. A key internal issue is how price will be used to support a firm's product quality positioning decision. The Internet may be a potential source of threat because the technology has the potential to drive down prices and reduce customer loyalty. The Internet, however, has also created a new opportunity, the online auction market.

Distribution decisions are influenced by factors such as the nature of the product and the conventions which exist with specific market channels. Selection of an intermediary can be a critical determinant of market success. Philosophies such as TQM and JIT have influenced distribution decisions. Logistics is now recognised as an opportunity to further influence customers' perceptions of products and services. One solution to optimise the logistics process is to participate in distribution networks. Just as with price, the Internet is also impacting distribution activities. Firms have the options of sustaining their traditional strategy or of using the technology to radically alter their management of the way the organisation links with end user markets.

INTRODUCTION

Pricing management can appear to be one of the simpler aspects of small business management. As long as the firm's products or services can be sold for a price that exceeds costs, the objective of profit generation will be achieved. Furthermore in most markets, demand curves, which are constructed by plotting quantity sold against price, slope downwards. Hence if a small firm wants to generate more sales this can usually be achieved by lowering the price.

Unfortunately in the real world there are some very critical factors which influence whether these simple rules about pricing management can be utilised. Firstly it is necessary that all parties involved in the transaction are fully informed. In many markets, however, customers may have very limited access to the data required to reach a 'fully informed' purchase decision. Secondly customers may reject a quoted price if they perceive there are tangible differences between goods being sold by a small firm and those being offered by competitors. Thirdly it is usually a requirement that to generate a sale the small firm, having quoted a price, does not face the situation of other suppliers being willing to offer the equivalent items at a much lower price. The fourth necessity is that all suppliers have adopted similar decisions concerning other marketing mix variables such as promotion expenditure and distribution.

In view of the need to add all of these market factor caveats, when it comes to the subject of price management it is necessary to accept that 'real life' pricing is often a somewhat complex affair. One approach to determining small firm pricing policies is to recognise the influence of the variables illustrated in Figure 9.1. This diagram presents visually the idea that market price is an outcome heavily influenced by complex interactions between prevailing industrial, organisational and customer circumstances.

CUSTOMER ATTITUDES

Two driving forces influencing customer attitudes are perceptions about the economic circumstances confronting these individuals, and the way their expectations over pricing levels have evolved from prior usage of the product

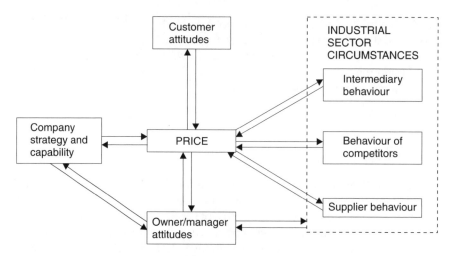

Figure 9.1 Factors influencing the determination of price

or service. Economic circumstances can have an adverse influence in consumer goods markets when individuals feel they are likely to face financial uncertainty in the future. This will cause them to want to buy lower priced goods or services. For example, in the second half of the year 2000, New Zealanders faced a 30 per cent decline in the value of their dollar in relation to other world currencies. The weaker dollar did not just reduce overseas travel; many domestic small tourism businesses also faced the problem that many New Zealanders moved to purchase lower price vacation options even in their own country. Similar customer attitudes also prevail in industrial markets when firms perceive a potential worsening in future trading conditions. Small printers are well aware that during an economic downturn, customers may wish to purchase lower cost printed materials and will also seek a number of quotes before issuing a contract for a print job.

Reverse scenarios are, however, just as valid; thus rising optimism among customers about economic conditions will be reflected in a willingness to pay a higher price. Thus in the year 2000, while the New Zealand travel industry was impacted by a falling currency, in the UK, the strength of the pound sterling resulted in small travel agents enjoying a business upswing. This was because more people opted for more expensive holidays and wished to travel to exotic overseas locations.

In relation to usage experience, product life cycle theory contends that prices tend to fall as the market approaches maturity (Day 1981). An underlying force affecting this situation is that when inflationary pressures are low, then the longer a product stays in the market, the greater are customer expectations that generic category prices will gradually decline. In the face of such expectations, firms wishing to retain current prices often find this aim can only be achieved by regularly making available product improvements that are perceived as adding value to their market offering.

For the small business seeking to determine what price is acceptable to customers, it is necessary firstly to determine the product value expectations of the customer. One way of approaching this analysis is to create a value map to determine interactions between customer requirements and price (Rangan *et al.* 1992). Typically the vertical dimension in a value map is the price customers are willing to pay for the core product. Customers who seek a 'no frills' product will be willing to pay a low price, whereas customers who require that the product be augmented in some way are willing to pay a higher price. For example an accounting practice offering a basic year end audit service to price conscious small business clients can offer to complement this service with financial management and tax planning services to slightly larger firms, who are then willing to pay a higher fee.

A possible horizontal axis for a value map is the degree to which the customer seeks a relationship with the supplier. As shown in Figure 9.2, combining the two dimensions generates four alternative pricing scenarios. Conservative-transactionally orientated customers are those who are seeking to pay a low price, will accept a standard product and have minimal expectations of the supplier being prepared to become involved in activities such as adding pre- and/or post-support services. An example of this type of small business is the operator of a chain of mobile ice cream vans.

Conservative-relationship orientated customers also expect to pay a relatively low price for the core product. In this case, however, if the supplier is able to offer additional, value added services, then this type of customer is willing to pay a higher price for an augmented product offering in those cases where they seek to build long term relationships with suppliers. An example of this marketing style would be a small office furniture distributor who in addition to selling standard products, also offers to provide an office layout design

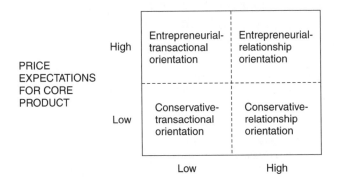

Figure 9.2 A value-relationship price matrix

service and an ability to structurally modify furniture to fit unusually shaped rooms. The supplier must recognise that in some cases, however, especially where there is intense competition between suppliers, the customer will expect an augmented product offering, but will not tolerate being charged a higher price.

In an entrepreneurial-transactionally orientated market sector, the supplier will exploit innovation to offer new, truly superior products, and because (a) competitors are unable to match the offering and/or (b) customers are not expecting service augmentation from the supplier, a high price can be commanded for the core product proposition. An example of this type of small firm is a software house that develops sector specific software packages marketed as downloadable products on the world wide web. This is in contrast with the entrepreneurial-relationship orientated sector, where although customers are willing to pay a high price, they also expect the supplier to work closely with them through offering augmented propositions such as collaborative R&D support. An example of this marketing style is provided by a company that develops customised website and automated, e-commerce, back-office transaction systems for clients.

COMPANY CIRCUMSTANCES

Price must reflect, and thereby support, a small firm's business strategy. As shown in Figure 9.3, there are a number of pricing alternatives depending

RELATIVE PRICE

	High	Average	Low	
PRODUCT PERFORMANCE POSITIONING	Premium price	Penetration pricing	Challenging convention	High
	Skimming	Average price	Sale price	Average
	Zero customer loyalty	Limited customer loyalty	Economy pricing	Low

Figure 9.3 A price/product positioning matrix

upon which strategic position the small firm wishes to adopt within a market sector. Small firms that are positioned on the basis of offering superior product performance have three alternative pricing strategies that can be considered. Premium pricing involves charging a high price to support the claim that the customer is being offered the highest possible product performance. Penetration pricing involves offering product at a price lower than is usually expected by customers. It is used by firms wishing to rapidly build market share through aggressive pricing. Successful application of this strategy requires being able to offer the customer a reason why the price is below that normally offered for this level of product performance. Typically this is achieved by gaining high market share over the longer term, because this will permit the supplier to reduce costs by exploiting economies of scale. As small firms are rarely able to enjoy scale benefits compared to large firms, penetration pricing is not frequently encountered in the SME sector. Offering a low price on a superior product usually involves the risk that the customer, applying the adage of 'you get what you pay for', is suspicious of the validity of the performance claim. Hence small firms considering this approach must first be assured that they have created sufficient trust in the market that they are able to safely challenge convention.

A skimming strategy involves the customer deciding there is benefit in paying a high price for what they clearly recognise are only average quality goods. Antique detailers in London, for example, have found that private collectors from overseas are willing to pay a price somewhat higher than that charged for an equivalent item offered by an antique dealer in their home country. Average pricing is used by small firms servicing the needs of the majority of customers who seek average performance from products being purchased. Sale pricing is used by small firms (such as discount retailers) serving the needs of the more price sensitive customer wishing to purchase average performance goods but at lower than usual prices.

A policy of low quality and high price clearly cannot sustain any degree of long term customer loyalty. Those small firms which use this strategy usually can only survive if customers whom the firm loses after a single purchase are easily replaced by new buyers entering the market segment. Similarly small firms using a low performance/average price strategy can only survive in those markets where customers who change their loyalty after two or three purchases are regularly replaced by an influx of new, less informed customers. Economy pricing involves offering low but acceptable quality goods at highly competitive prices to customers whose price sensitivity is usually a reflection of limited financial means. It can be an extremely successful market position, but the low margin per unit of sales does mean the small firm has to sustain a very high level of customer transactions in order to achieve an adequate level of overall profit.

In the selection of a price positioning compatible with overall strategy, the owner/manager must also consider whether their firm has the internal capabilities to support the selected marketing positioning. If, for example, a small electronic components producer is to compete on low price, then the manufacturing operation must have the ability to produce low cost output. Similarly a small furniture manufacturer charging a premium price must employ craftsmen with the skills required to produce high quality products.

INDUSTRIAL SECTOR CIRCUMSTANCES

Small firms are rarely able to make pricing decisions without considering the conditions prevailing within the industrial sector in which they operate. Within most markets, the small firm will be surrounded by competitors who may or may not share a common view about the degree to which price should feature as a lead variable within the marketing mix. Garda and Marn (1993), for example, believe that using price wars to achieve business growth is a destructive philosophy which rarely results in a satisfactory outcome for the supplier. They feel the approach should be avoided because as profits are extremely sensitive to price falls, any advantage gained is usually short lived and the activity can distort customer expectations. Guiltinan and Gundlach (1996) adopt a somewhat different perspective. Their view is that if a firm, through a strong market position or access to appropriate resources, feels there is long term benefit in using low price to drive competitors from a market, then such a strategy should be considered as a viable operational option. Small firms, however, are rarely in a position to adopt such a predatory pricing strategy. In fact they are often the organisations who are on the receiving end of such attacks by large firm competitors. Should the small firm fall foul of predatory pricing the most feasible response is to seek to avoid the confrontation and attempt to retreat to a more profitable market niche or channel of distribution.

The degree to which upstream and/or downstream circumstances will influence prevailing prices will depend upon the power that various organisations exert within a specific market system. If, for example, upstream suppliers wish to generate higher absolute revenue by increasing total output, the creation of a 'supply glut' may subsequently be followed by a period of falling prices. Alternatively if these same producers wish to obtain a higher price per unit of sales, they may decide to withhold supplies from the market. An upward movement in prices will reflect the created scarcity. This latter situation has prevailed for most of the new millennium because the OPEC oil producers have sought to drive up world prices by restricting output. The resultant increase in energy costs has severely impacted both large and small firms across virtually every sector of industry around the world.

In those markets where a small number of downstream market system members have strong control over the flow of goods and/or services, then again their behaviour may have a dominant influence on prices within a market sector. This situation, for example, has prevailed for many years within the UK supermarket sector, where four major chains control almost 80 per cent of all grocery products sold in Great Britain. These firms prefer to purchase goods from large suppliers who can offer a full product line, competitively priced goods and will assist in-store movement by funding massive advertising campaigns. Small firms are not in a position to match such behaviour and as a result many of them are severely constrained from being able to gain distribution in sufficient retail outlets to generate a high level of sales from the UK consumer goods sector.

OWNER/MANAGER BEHAVIOUR

There is a tendency for small business academics to assume that small firms act rationally. Consequently one may encounter articles in which owner/managers are taken to task for not following conventional business practices. Livesay (1989), however is one of the first writers to acknowledge the importance of recognising the influence of social and cultural factors in reviewing the viability of a business decision within a small business. He suggests that when examining activities such as the determination of price, for example, one must accept that decisions are made by individuals, not anonymous organisations. Hence in the small firms sector, the personalities of owner/managers can have a decisive influence on the strategic actions that might be implemented.

Curran *et al.* (1997) have examined the issue of rational decision making in the specific context of price setting in the SME sector. They point out that most small business research assumes that owner/managers exhibit 'instrumental rationality'. Consequently traditional pricing theory would propose that their behaviour is driven by an attempt to make sound economic decisions such as seeking to maximise profit. Curran *et al.* applied a grounded theory approach to ask owner/managers to describe the rationale behind their pricing decisions. What emerged was evidence that the respondents were heavily influenced by their perceived social role within their business system, and this resulted in prices being determined by a diverse range of 'non-economic' factors.

Owner/managers are aware that within their market there exists a 'price window' or a price range within which sufficient demand exists to ensure business viability. Inside the boundaries determined by the window, different behaviours are found to exist. One individual, for example, always charges wealthy customers a higher price because he perceives they can afford it. Less

179

wealthy individuals are quoted lower prices. Another owner/manager expressed concerned about sustaining the success of customers' businesses and will hold back on a price increase if this would have an adverse effect upon customer business operations. Another perspective presented by a number of respondents is that the price quoted is designed to generate sufficient sales that they can avoid having to lay off staff or make anybody redundant.

In reviewing these results the authors make the important observation that business advisory services should cease to offer prescriptive guidance involving pricing theories associated with economic objectives. Instead there is a need for guidance which is rooted in the real world and acknowledges that in determining price, owner/managers should draw upon their own mental maps of the world and include non-economic variables when determining the optimum price to be quoted to customers.

EXAMPLE: FACING BIG FIRM COMPETITION

Operating in manufacturing sectors where (a) the customer is seeking a standard product and (b) economies of scale are available to large firms, will usually mean that small firms are faced with some challenging operational problems. The conventional wisdom is that the small firm should avoid attempting to compete on price and instead differentiate the business relative to larger firms in the market by occupying a specialist niche. Any attempt to try and replicate large firm behaviour usually only proves feasible if these latter organisations opt to utilise their scale advantage to generate higher than average profits, not compete on price as a route to maximising market share.

In 1932, Frank Sieberling founded the Sieberling Rubber Company manufacturing car tyres in a small plant in Barbeton, Ohio (French 1993). The US tyre business even at that time could be divided into two sectors, one supplying the big car manufacturers and the second selling renewal or replacement tyres to vehicle owners. The big tyre companies such as Goodyear and Firestone dominated the car manufacturer sector because they could exploit their economies of scale and thereby offer very competitively priced products to car makers such as Ford and General Motors.

The smaller tyre firms concentrated on the replacement market, selling to independent tyre dealers, service stations and department stores such as Sears Roebuck. Sieberling's marketing strategy was that of offering a superior quality, replacement tyre at a premium price to independent dealers. The company avoided involvement in selling lower priced private brand products to national petrol companies or department stores.

After the Second World War, the big tyre manufacturers made a concerted effort to enter the tyre renewal market. They exploited their economies of scale to obtain private brand business and in some cases even opened their own retail outlets. These large firms also sought to further reduce operating costs by relocating their factories away from the Midwest where employees were highly unionised. In building new factories the large firms took this opportunity to introduce automated production processes. These firms were also the leaders in industry innovation in relation to actions such as introducing new synthetic raw materials into the industry.

Sieberling continued to operate a unionised plant in Ohio, did not invest in automating production and was slow to adopt new materials in its tyre designs. Through the early 1950s this situation was not seen as a problem because the large firms appeared more interested in using their scale advantage to maximise profits and apparently saw little benefit in lowering prices to acquire higher brand shares. A problem which did begin to hurt Sieberling, however, was that the car industry moved towards offering a wider range of car designs. This meant all tyre manufacturers were forced to expand the range of tyre sizes that they produced and then held in finished goods inventories. By the mid 1950s Sieberling was producing a diverse range of tyres, but in the face of large firm innovation was finding increasing difficulties in sustaining its upmarket position. Its tyres were only slightly less expensive than national brands, but more expensive than private brands or similar quality brands being offered by other small manufacturers.

After intense pressure from line management, in 1960 the Sieberling family accepted the perspective that possibly the prevailing market conditions demanded a strategy change. Its solution was to approve the launch of a range of low price tyres sold under the Holiday brand name. This product was sold through independent tyre dealers, although the company also established its own retail outlets by leasing space in department stores.

In the mid 1950s the large manufacturers in the tyre industry moved from profit maximising to using aggressive pricing to build share of sales in the replace-ment tyre market sector. With price now dominating the renewal market, plus Sieberling's lack of action in areas such as plant automation or product innov-ation, it soon emerged that the Holiday brand move proved to be an inadequate response to the market conditions confronting the firm. Financial performance continued to worsen. Life for the Sieberling family was made even more difficult because they had to face the highly vocal criticism of an entrepreneur, Edward Lamb, who had purchased a significant shareholding in the company.

Eventually in 1962 Lamb acquired majority control and the Sieberling family was forced to accept a loss of managerial influence within the business. Lamb believed the only viable future was to compete on the basis of price. The number of premium tyre lines was reduced, the Holiday brand line expanded and efforts made to obtain private brand business. These actions proved to be 'too little, too late'. In the face of mounting losses, in 1967 the tyre business was sold to Firestone.

THE INTERNET THREAT

It is becoming increasingly evident that the primary reason individuals utilise the Internet in their search for products and services is that they perceive the technology will permit them to purchase lower priced goods. The fact that Internet customers are more price conscious than their terrestrial counterparts has some worrying implications for the small firm. Sinha (2000) has reviewed the potential impact of the Internet on the future level of prices that can be commanded for goods and services. He points out that it is in the seller's best interest to keep costs opaque because this permits companies to claim unique benefits for their brands and thereby command premium prices in the market-place. Prior to the arrival of the Internet, sellers were assisted in this objective because customers encountered severe problems if seeking to acquire detailed information on competitive offerings prior to reaching a purchase decision.

The advent of the Internet means that consumers can use sites such as www.pricescan.com and online shopping agents such as www.bottom dollar.com to rapidly compare prices and features on thousands of products. They can also visit sites such as www.epinions.com to read about the purchasing experience of others and through sites such as www.travelocity.com, gain access to information that was once only accessible to travel agents. Similar scenarios are also emerging in business-to-business markets. For example, textile manufacturers can visit the site www.alibaba.com to gain free access to a directory of over 35 000 companies.

The outcome of this situation, in both consumer and industrial markets, is that small firms are beginning to find that their pricing strategies are becoming much more transparent to potential customers. The outcomes for the small firm are a reduced ability to command a premium, a tendency for products to become commodities and a weakening in customer loyalty. In view of these potential implications, small firms need to examine how new online strategies can protect the business from being forced into cutting prices. Sinha has proposed that there are a number of strategic options available to organisations to achieve this goal. One is to seek to offer improved benefits and superior services to those available from competition. Another approach is to bundle products together such that it is more difficult for buyers to determine the cost of any single item. A third approach is to invest in innovation that leads to the launch of new and distinctive products.

AN INTERNET OPPORTUNITY

As with most business scenarios, what may pose a threat to one individual may be seen by somebody else as an opportunity. Such is the case with the

Internet's ability to rapidly communicate pricing information as the basis for stimulating sales. An entrepreneur who recognised the potential opportunity associated with Internet price transparency was Pierre Omidyar. He realised that the Internet offers a new way of creating markets, namely establishing an online auction site where buyers and sellers can negotiate transactions. His business model was highly profitable from the start because his operation, www.eBay.com, avoids the costs associated with handling inventory or distributing goods. All eBay does is to take a commission on sales (Anon. 1999).

The appeal of cyberauctions is demonstrated by the fact that in 1999, it was estimated that online auctions accounted for the majority of goods sold being traded online. Currently the top selling auction category is computers, but it is expected that in a few years this volume of trade will be matched by other categories such as those of airline tickets, hotel rooms, cars and clothing. To attract participants to a cyberauction, most sites have followed the eBay model. The visitor fills out a registration form. Access is then granted to a list of available items and information is provided on the highest previous bid. Some auctions also make available data on bidding history, number of bids, bid amounts and the cybernames of the bidders.

Although consumer-to-consumer cyberauctions were the first to gain popularity on the Internet, they were soon followed by the creation of B2B sites. Many of these sites have followed the eBay model, with the site owners taking a commission on sales. Gerry Haller, the founder of FastParts (www.century.fastparts.com), for example, became aware that electronics firms frequently face the problem of having too many or too few spare parts, but are unwilling to trade with other firms which they perceive as business rivals. FastParts offers the opportunity for the anonymous auctioning of parts via a trusted intermediary. Over 2500 electronics firms now use the site's thrice-weekly auctions as a mechanism for improving their spare part stock levels (Anon. 1997).

EXAMPLE: AUCTION BASED BUSINESSES

The launch of eBay on 5 September 1995 soon caused some people to realise that starting online auction businesses represented a new small business opportunity (Knol 2000). Currently eBay has ten million users of whom, based on their usage patterns, approximately 20 000 are operating full time, auction based operations. Collectors who have turned their hobby into an online business started many of these enterprises.

Lori Frankel in New Jersey was an avid stamp collector as a child. Her hobby is now an online auction operation. In an average week she runs 150 to 200 auctions which generate about 250 orders. Revenue is currently heading towards $10 000 a month. Mike Hakala in Wisconsin uses eBay as a platform for his coin business. Working from home he and his wife, plus a part-time assistant, run 20 to 50 auctions a day, respond to over 200 e-mails and mail out product. Currently they are generating around $25 000 a month from their operation.

AVOIDING ONLINE PRICE COMPETITION

Anandarajan *et al.* (1998) concluded that many firms who were early entrants into business-to-business cyberspace marketing exhibited a transactional marketing orientation, because they were committed to using the technology to reduce costs across all aspects of the transaction process from initial enquiry through to post-purchase product usage support. In their study of Extranet based systems, they identified a number of cost saving opportunities when using the Internet to manage business-to-business supply chains. Across inbound logistics, online data integration reduces costs through consolidation of the total numbers of suppliers utilised and reduction in time taken over the administration of delivery processes. Inside the buying organisation, cost savings occur in relation to reducing the time taken by employees involved in administering the scheduling of manufacturing activities and the operation of production processes. Outbound logistic efficiencies are also improved, resulting in cost savings for both absolute expenditure on freight services and management of the delivery documentation process. Furthermore, with suppliers and customers in direct contact via an electronic medium, time is saved in terms of both discussions about orders in progress and the resolution of transaction errors. Additionally, with suppliers communicating promotional information via the Internet, customers can access these data at a workstation in their office. This ensures customers can take the maximum benefit offered by price discounts being made available by suppliers in support of their product lines.

Gummesson (1997), one of the originators of the concept of relationship marketing, identified the potential conceptual links between marketers avoiding price competition by using communities or networks to build relationships, and the similar motives exhibited by the original designers of the Internet. He noted that electronic relationships are rarely discussed within the marketing literature. This led to his proposal that effective exploitation of the Internet to avoid price competition would only occur once marketers (a) ceased viewing the technology as a mechanism for supporting transactional marketing and (b) recognised that electronic information provides a foundation stone upon which to build closer relationships with customers. Speckman *et al.*'s (1997) research on collaboration in business-to-business markets was supportive of this view. These authors noted, however, that successful electronic relationships demanded the active participation of both the seller and the buyer, with both parties willing to proactively share information with each other. This perspective is reflected by Chaston (2000) who posits that in online relationship markets, customers will seek to purchase specific, customised products and seek close, frequent interactions with their suppliers. In response, suppliers will be able to sustain current pricing by utilising the Internet to acquire detailed understanding of specific customer needs and be orientated towards using innovation to evolve highly customised product and services. Without information sharing as the basis for evolving a customer-supplier partnership, relationship marketing would be an extremely difficult process to effectively manage. Pine *et al.* (1995) concluded that electronic technology has a critical role in sustaining partnerships because IT provides the basis for building stronger relationships with customers by exploiting the additional knowledge that is gained from recording every customer-supplier interaction. All phases of the interaction, from customers seeking information, to making a purchase and requesting post-purchase services, can contribute to the expansion of the firm's databases. These can subsequently be interrogated during the development of future services capable of further deepening the customer-supplier relationship and thereby increasing long term customer loyalty. All these data also create a switching barrier as customers would have to spend time educating a competitor before the latter could offer a similar level of service responsiveness (Grant and Schlesinger 1995). Moreover as the supplier gains a detailed understanding of customer need, this knowledge can provide the basis for electronically communicating to customers additional products and service offers which have a high probability of being of interest to the customer. In this way the firm is able to able to sustain current pricing levels without risking the probability of customers defecting to the competition.

Zineldin (2000) has posited that recent advances in the application of IT to support more effective information interchange now mean that entrepreneurial-relationship orientated marketing offers the most effective path through which firms can achieve a differential advantage over less technologically sophisticated, transactionally orientated competitors. This can occur because the Internet permits the supplier to consider customers more as individuals and then to evolve products customised to meet specific needs. Furthermore the low cost of information exchange using IT means that entrepreneurial-relationship orientated firms are able to enjoy the benefits of having to spend significantly less money on promotional activities to sustain customer loyalty than their more transactionally orientated counterparts.

Zineldin (2000) also posits the importance of employees sharing information when seeking to service the needs of online customers. He notes that relationship orientated firms have been assisted in this objective by technology such as that of Intranets which permits the rapid sharing of both knowledge of customer behaviour and of activities undertaken to respond to customers' placement of online orders. In seeking to determine whether an orientation of internal data sharing is beneficial to online operations, Barua *et al.* (2000) undertook a survey of over 4000 firms across all areas of the US economy. They concluded that a common attribute exhibited by firms involved in e-commerce which have achieved above average financial performance is a strong commitment to employees sharing information and actively collaborating with each other when seeking to resolve customer problems.

Additional support for the importance of a company-wide orientation to customer relationship management is provided by research undertaken by the consulting firm Arthur Andersen (2001). Their study of over 100 senior executives involved in online operations in major US companies revealed that 20 per cent of respondents already have a company-wide customer relationship management system in operation and that a further 45 per cent are in the process of embedding this type of systems orientation across their entire organisation.

In relation to perceptions about customers and marketing activities, recent research (Chaston, in press) on small UK firms operating in online B2B markets indicates that firms exhibiting an entrepreneurial marketing style, when compared with their transactional, more price orientated counterparts, have differing perceptions in relation to these five factors:

- Customers are more aware of competitor offerings.
- The Internet provides more knowledge about customers.
- The Internet requires closer integration of internal activities.
- The Internet means market niches are easier to identify.
- The Internet means the firm can develop closer customer relationships.

This research also indicated that in every area concerned with the management of information, firms exhibiting an entrepreneurial marketing style differ from their transactionally, more price orientated counterparts. Within the former organisations greater emphasis is given to activities such as maintaining detailed records, integration of databases and providing employees with immediate access to relevant customer information.

The results provide empirical support for the views expressed by Gummesson (1997) and Zineldin (2000) about the importance of effective management of internal information systems in order that employees are able to effectively react to the needs of online customers. It is necessary to note, however, that the research study could not determine if entrepreneurial small firms had already developed such systems to service the needs of customers in terrestrial markets, or whether these systems were specifically evolved to support an entry into cyberspace trading.

Data were also acquired which indicated that in every area concerned with the management of internal organisational processes, small entrepreneurial firms adopt a different philosophy than that of firms operating in transactionally, more price orientated market sectors. Research data suggest that entrepreneurial small firms place greater emphasis on activities such as dialoguing with customers, team based activities, expectations over employee behaviour, focus of appraisal systems, and customisation of products, prices and promotional activities.

Although both transactional price orientated and entrepreneurial firms in the author's research study reported similar levels of involvement in adopting e-commerce technologies, what the data could not resolve is why differences exist between these two types of small firms in respect of their use of information and the management of internal processes. One possibility is that transactional firms are aware that visitors to their websites are expecting their suppliers to exploit the capability of the technology to offer highly competitive prices, convenience and rapid response. If this is the case, it seems reasonable to suggest that transactional firms will perceive minimal benefit in upgrading IT systems or reorientating employee behaviour because their customers do not perceive close relationships with their supplier as an important factor in the execution of purchase transaction activities.

DISTRIBUTION MANAGEMENT

Marketers have tended to consider 'place' to be the least exciting variable within the marketing mix because essentially it is perceived as being concerned with minimising the cost of moving goods from a producer to the point of final consumption within a market system. Distribution systems are usually presented as vertical systems where responsibility for goods being shipped is transferred from one level to the next. An example of a small computer manufacturer's distribution system is provided in Figure 9.4.

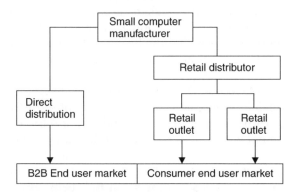

Figure 9.4 Alternative distribution systems

The supplier has the choice of working directly with customers or alternatively involving one or more distributors. Direct supplier-customer distribution tends to occur where each end user purchases a large proportion of total output, and/or goods are highly perishable, and/or the complex nature of the goods requires a close working relationship between supplier and final customer. This scenario stills prevails in many B2B markets.

In those markets where an indirect distribution system is perceived as being more cost effective, then one or more distributors will become involved in the distribution process. These distributors will typically receive a truck-load size shipment which they break down into smaller lot sizes. These are sold to an end user outlet that will be responsible for managing both the purchase transaction and any customer post-purchase service needs.

In terms of issues impacting an owner/manager's distribution management decisions, Stern and El-Ansary (1988) have proposed that the following factors will need to be considered in the selection of an appropriate system:

- the capability of intermediaries in the logistics role of sorting goods, aggregating products from a variety of sources and breaking down bulk shipments into saleable lot sizes;
- the capability of intermediaries in routinising transactions to minimise costs (such as a store selling a variety of shoe designs to consumers);
- the capability of intermediaries in minimising customer search costs (such as a computer store having available information and demonstration models of computers from a range of different suppliers).

Multi-layered distribution systems were a feature of Western nation consumer goods markets in the 19th century. They remain the predominant system in most developing nations and also in many of the Pacific Rim nation economies. A common occurrence in Western nation economies during the 20th century has been that of retailers perceiving scale benefits in purchasing directly from suppliers. In these cases, the outcome is usually that of 'cutting out the middleman' with the retailers establishing vertically integrated procurement, warehousing, distribution and retailing operations. Exploitation of this opportunity provided the basis for the successful establishment of trading dynasties such as Sears Roebuck in America and Marks & Spencers in the UK.

Authors such as Mayo *et al*. (1998) present models describing how intermediaries, by consolidating purchases from a number of sources, could concurrently reduce the number of transactions and increase the variety of choice offered to customers within a market system. In these writings, the owner/manager is warned about the possibility of power imbalances within indirect distribution systems that can be to their disadvantage during price negotiations and ultimately may lead to the small firm being displaced from the market system entirely.

EXAMPLE: SMALL FIRM DISTRIBUTION IN IRELAND

The agri-food sector is an important element of the Irish economy, representing 14 per cent of GDP and 12 per cent of all exports (McDonagh and Cummins 1999). For many years the fragmented nature of the country's infrastructure meant that producers of food staples such as bread and cheese were small producers who distributed their goods directly to small retailers in towns and villages near to the location of the producer business. Suppliers and customers developed close, personal relationships and the supplier typically was totally responsible for managing all aspects of the product delivery system.

Economic growth and the associated urbanisation of the Irish economy were seen as an opportunity for the big UK supermarket chains to enter the Irish market. These companies now control well over 70 per cent of all grocery product sales in Ireland and hence are in a strong position to dictate the behaviour required of suppliers. Distribution has been centralised, logistic systems computerised and suppliers expected to make available a full range of products. The impact of this situation is that many small producers of standard staple goods have been forced out of business as the supermarkets have opted to purchase their products from major national and multinational branded goods food manufacturers.

Survival for the small food producer has necessitated a move into sectors where distribution can remain direct and local, or can go through the few remaining independent retailers left in the major urban areas. To achieve this goal, these small producers have turned to the speciality food market across categories such as farmhouse cheeses, smoked fish, confectionery, preserves, fresh herbs and meats. The growth in the speciality food market has been influenced by three factors: more affluent consumers seeking greater product choice, consumer preferences being altered by foreign travel, and a major expansion in the number of foreign visitors holidaying in Ireland. Selection of distribution channel is influenced by factors such as ability to supply and the sector of the market being targeted. Some producers choose to market their products direct to local consumers or through local retail or catering outlets. Others have opted to access the more affluent consumers who live in cities. This usually involves forming a relationship with a distributor who can handle both the selling of products to specialist outlets in urban areas and manage the logistics of moving goods from point of production to location of final sale. As output is small and many of these producers are based in remote areas of Ireland, developing an effective relationship with a distributor is not easy. Furthermore some producers find that the intervention of a distributor means it is much more difficult to obtain market intelligence than is the case when the producer sells directly to an end user outlet. Despite these obstacles some small firms are so satisfied with involving intermediaries that they have opted to develop additional sales by linking up with food distributors based in overseas markets. Additionally some firms are now experimenting with the Internet as a system for adding global reach to their operations.

A recent trend in Irish SME sector food production has been the move towards producing organic foods. This small business sector is very much at an emergent stage. This means that distribution channels are still not well developed. Some producers focus on satisfying local demand by selling direct to consumers using a box delivery system and to local catering outlets. As output has begun to rise, some organic producers are moving to form networks to sell consolidated output through cooperative shops and market stalls. Few small organic producers are interested in marketing their output through supermarket chains even though these outlets have expressed interest in their products. The view of the small producer is that supermarket loyalty to their suppliers is low and that as other supply chain sources for organic food become available (such as multi-acre organic farms coming on stream in Spain), small Irish producers would be dropped as a supply source.

THE CHANGING FACE OF DISTRIBUTION

A potential error in many of the early theories concerning channel management was that by focussing on the issue of minimising distribution costs, small firms were often unaware of the concurrent, critical issue of sustaining customer satisfaction. During the 1980s, however, some small firms began to discover that effective management of distribution channels can actually provide additional opportunities to gain advantage over competition.

Recognition of the concept of increasing customer satisfaction through effective channel management was initially prompted by lessons learned during the implementation of a Just In Time (JIT) operating philosophy. As small firms began to make smarter decisions about effective management of raw materials on hand, work in progress and finished goods inventories, they also began to realise that an important side effect was an enhanced ability to more rapidly respond to changing customer needs. In the world of manufacturing, adoption of the principles of JIT and automation of production processes led to recognition of the benefits of flexible (or 'lean') manufacturing systems (McKenna 1991). The service sector also provides examples of where increasing intensity of competition is causing small firms to re-examine how their management of distribution channels and the exploitation of advances in IT might offer new ways of delivering customer satisfaction. Howcroft (1992) posits that the effective management of distribution channels will be the central issue in the future development of appropriate marketing management processes within services industries well into the 21st century.

Small firms that perceive distribution as a mechanism for enhancing customer satisfaction must be capable of always fulfilling their promises of offering on-time delivery. This issue has become even more important in the world of e-commerce, because it is very apparent that online customers expect much higher levels of distribution efficiency than their terrestrial counterparts. By adopting and modifying the analysis of factors contributing to a market image of being capable at logistics management presented by Kumar and Sharman (1992) it is possible to suggest that the following five possible gaps can lead to customer dissatisfaction:

- Gap 1 – the customer and the supplier have different views of the factors influencing customer satisfaction. For example, the customer may assume the quoted time for delivery is the time from order placement until the goods arrive. The supplier may believe the quoted time relates to the period between when goods are manufactured and arrival at the customer destination.
- Gap 2 – the small firm managers have failed to develop specified standards against which delivery performance can be assessed. These can be variables such as the allowable time between order placement and delivery, ensuring specified high percentage of orders being shipped without any missing goods, and speed of response to customer complaints about shipping errors.
- Gap 3 – within the small firm the operational systems, equipment and staff skills are inadequate for meeting the distribution performance standards which have been specified. For example employees may not have been trained in the use of the computer based order entry system and hence errors are being made at time of order acceptance.
- Gap 4 – there are incorrect information flows either in external communications between employees and the customer or in internal communications between staff within the organisation.
- Gap 5 – the combined effect of Gaps 1 through 4 on the actual quality of distribution experienced by the customer. Where this experience is poorer than the customer's expectations, then customer dissatisfaction can lead to the loss of future orders.

The interaction of gaps in the distribution process is summarised in Figure 9.5. Closure of identified gaps is critical to the success of the small firm. To achieve this aim the owner/manager will need to dialogue with customers to determine their expectations over achievement of distribution targets. This knowledge can be used to establish clear standards of performance for the small firm. An audit of internal operations will be required to ensure employees are able to meet the specified performance standards. Finally a communications audit will be necessary to determine whether there are effective information flows between the firm and customers, and between all employees inside the firm.

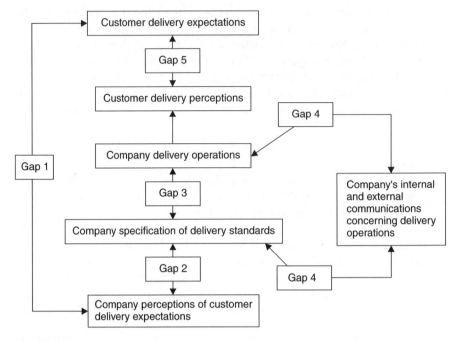

Figure 9.5   A distribution gap model

CHANNEL INTEGRATION

Another important force in the changing world of channel management has been the move by some distributors to examine how competitive advantage can be gained by changing operational strategies. Massey (1992) has examined how in the world of computers, sales channels are changing as a result of falling prices and shifts in customer attitude. Some small computer distributors recognised that their specialist knowledge of their clients' complex sector specific problems, and the tendency of some larger manufacturers to sustain a mass marketing approach of offering low price, standard solutions to all, represented a new market opportunity. Their response was to become value-added resellers (VARs) by acting as systems integrators bringing together appropriate hardware and software from various sources to satisfy market need. Those dealers who continued to act in the traditional role of acting as the link between supplier and customer encountered the problem of surviving in the face of a growing number of direct marketing operations entering their market offering similar hardware at significantly lower prices.

Rangan *et al.* (1993), in commenting upon the strategic implications of new approaches to channel management, have suggested that firms must carefully review the future flow of goods and services in a market sector. During this review they should seek to resolve the questions of whether channels can (a) serve to create competitive entry barriers, (b) enhance product differentiation and (c) enable greater customer intimacy. These authors propose that it is necessary to 'unbundle' the channel functions of information provision, order generation, physical distribution and after sales service. The next step is then to determine how customer needs can best be met by channel members working together as a team of channel partners each performing those tasks at which they excel.

Moriaty and Moran (1990) have referred to these new, more customer orientated approaches to channel management as 'hybrid marketing systems'. They present the example of firms moving from a single channel based around their own sales force, to expanding into a hybrid operation involving dealers, VARs, a catalogue selling operation, direct mail and telemarketing. Moriaty and Moran's view is that the two forces driving this type of change have been (a) the need to expand market coverage and (b) the concurrent requirement to contain costs by improving the efficiency of channel members.

EXAMPLE: THE NEW ZEALAND WAY

New Zealand small manufacturing firms perceive exporting as a mechanism to increase profitability, spread risk and provide impetus for further innovation (Osborne 1996). This author's research reveals that these firms perceive there are numerous alternative channel options available through which to achieve an integrated approach to managing overseas market distribution. The lowest level of integration is to use either agents or distributors. Even in these two channels, however, success is often influenced by the degree to which the small firm develops a close relationship with these overseas representatives. Degree of commitment to the relationship is often reflected in the small firm investing time and resources in training the staff in these market channels.

A higher level of channel integration can be achieved through involvement in granting licences, forming joint ventures or establishing an overseas subsidiary. Osborne's study revealed that the small firms would select the nature of channel integration in relation to the factors of market volatility and product complexity. In volatile markets, such as those where there is political unrest, the usual approach is to rely on agents or distributors. Only in highly stable overseas markets were these small firms prepared to become involved in joint ventures or creation of a subsidiary. Typically, more complex products usually require the provision of pre- and post-purchase services. Where this was a characteristic of the product portfolio, again the tendency was to utilise highly integrated channel solutions.

DISTRIBUTION NETWORKS

The growing recognition of the potential benefits of moving from an adversarial to a cooperative orientation in the management of the flow of goods from supplier to final customer has prompted a number of writers to promote the advantages of creating vertical distribution networks. A significant influence on this area of marketing theory was Williamson's (1975) work on markets and hierarchies in which he used a transaction cost analysis approach to analyse buyer-seller relationships. He concluded that new interdependent organisational forms are necessary if firms are to remain able to sustain a flexible response to rapidly changing customer needs.

The new form of vertical distribution network is a system where there is close collaboration between members. In traditional vertical systems each member fulfilled their own role, retained all knowledge specific to that role and sought to adopt an autonomous position within the system. Within the new networks, participants share data with the aim that through active collaboration the entire system is significantly more efficient and more able to rapidly respond to changing market conditions. In many of these new vertical systems a critical infrastructure component to support collaboration is the use of interactive, linked computer systems which allow network members to share real time data on how goods and services are flowing through the system.

The post-Fordist landscapes painted by writers such as Piore and Sable (1984), of relationship orientated suppliers and downstream channel members working together in complete harmony to achieve the joint aim of absolute customer satisfaction, are aesthetically pleasing. However, it should possibly be recognised that these idyllic scenarios may reflect a lack of appreciation of real world circumstance. For as demonstrated by researchers such as Ford (1990) and Håkansson (1982), the small firm would be well advised to carefully analyse the orientation of the various parties who may constitute a specific channel situation prior to opting for involvement in a vertical network.

Nevertheless around the world examples can be found of small firms collaborating with channel members to create collaborative, mutually beneficial distribution systems. Vertical distribution networks are usually only likely to be an outcome in those cases where both supplier and downstream channel members perceive mutual advantage in the creation of this type of relationship as the most effective basis for linking final customer with sources of supply. One of the best known examples of a small firm/large firm vertical network is the Italian fashion goods company, Benetton. This organisation acts as a manufacturing and marketing hub, complementing products manufactured by the company with others drawn in from small Italian clothing firms. Benetton also provides support to small firms within the network in areas such as the purchase of new machines, and guidance on new fashion trends in the retail clothing industry that the firm acquires through operating retail outlets in various parts of the world. The success of this type of supply relationship is heavily influenced by the fact that although Benetton has the power to act as are directive monopolist, the firm chooses to adopt a philosophy of maintaining a close collaborative relationship with all participants in the network which they have created. A similar approach to marketing management is utilised by the Swedish furniture retailer IKEA which is strongly committed to working in partnership with the small manufacturing firms which supply the majority of the retailer's product line.

E-COMMERCE DISTRIBUTION

The advent of e-commerce is causing small firms to have to reassess their approach to utilising distribution systems to acquire and sustain competitive advantage. One approach to determining the best strategy for selecting an optimal e-commerce distribution channel is to assume that there are two critical dimensions influencing the decision: whether to retain control or delegate responsibility for transaction management, and whether to retain control or delegate responsibility for logistics management. This concept can be visualised in the form of an e-commerce channel option matrix of the type shown in Figure 9.6.

An example of an e-commerce market sector where the suppliers retain control over both distribution dimensions is the provision of specialist computer consultancy services, where the small firms wish to retain absolute control over both the transaction and delivery processes. The case of the e-commerce transaction being delegated, but delivery responsibility retained, is provided by a small, regional airline marketing flights through online travel agents.

Possibly the most frequently encountered e-commerce distribution model is that of retaining control over transactions and delegating distribution. It is the standard model that is in use among most online retailers. These firms,

Figure 9.6 An e-commerce distribution option matrix

having successfully sold a product to a website visitor, will use the global distribution capabilities of organisations such as FedEx or UPS to manage all aspects of distribution logistics.

In the majority of offline, consumer goods markets, the commonest distribution model is to delegate both transaction and logistics processes (for example, a manufacturer of designer swimwear marketing its products through upmarket fashion boutiques). This can be contrasted with the online world where absolute delegation of all processes is still a somewhat rarer event. The reason for this situation is that many small firms, having decided that e-commerce offers an opportunity for revising distribution management practices, perceive cyberspace as an way to regain control over transactions by cutting out intermediaries and selling direct to their end user customers. This process, in which traditional intermediaries may be squeezed out of channels, is usually referred to as 'disintermediation.'

To assist in the assessment of viable e-commerce distribution strategies, Pitt *et al.* (1999) have proposed that small firms should recognise that the technology has the following implications:

- distance ceases to be a cost influencer because online delivery of information is substantially the same no matter the destination of the delivery;
- business location becomes an irrelevance because the e-commerce corporation can be based anywhere in the world;
- the technology permits continuous trading, 24 hours a day, 365 days a year.

By combining these implications with the basic roles of intermediaries (assortment management, transaction routinisation and minimisation of customer search activities), Pitt *et al.* have evolved an e-commerce strategic distribution options matrix of the type shown in Figure 9.7. It is recommended that the

SUPPLIER ORIENTATION

	Directive monopolists	Transactional orientation	Relationship orientation	
DOWNSTREAM CHANNEL MEMBER(S) ORIENTATION	Outcome Negotiated compromise	Outcome Buyers' market	Outcome Potential impasse	Directive monopolists
	Outcome Sellers' market	Outcome Price competitive market	Outcome Potential impasse	Transactional orientation
	Outcome Potential impasse	Outcome Potential impasse	Outcome Distribution network market	Relationship orientation

Figure 9.7 Distribution strategic options matrix

owner/manager use this type of matrix to identify potential competitive threats caused by other actors within a market system exploiting e-commerce technology to enhance the distribution process.

A characteristic of offline distribution channels is the difficulty that smaller firms face in persuading intermediaries (such as supermarket chains) to stock their goods. This scenario is less applicable in the world of e-commerce. Firms of any size face a relatively easy task in establishing an online presence. Market coverage can then be extended by developing trading alliances based upon offering to pay commission to other online traders who attract new customers to the company's website. This ease of entry variable will reduce the occurrence of small firms' marketing effort being frustrated because they are unable to gain the support of intermediaries in traditional distribution channels. Eventually e-commerce may lead to a major increase in the total number of firms offering products and services across world markets. As this occurs, markets will become more efficient, and many products will be perceived as commodities with the consequent outcome that average prices will decline.

DISCUSSION QUESTIONS

1. How can firms use price to support their product quality positioning decisions?
2. Why does the Internet represent both a source of opportunity and a threat in relation to pricing decisions?
3. How is the Internet changing the face of distribution decisions in many market systems?

REFERENCES

Anandarajan, M., Anandarajan, A. and Wen, H.J. (1998), 'Extranets: tools for cost control in a value chain framework', *Industrial and Management Systems*, Vol. 98, No. 3, pp. 29–38.

Anon. (1997), 'Going, going , gone . . . on-line auctions', *The Economist*, 31 May, pp. 61–2.

Anon. (1999), 'Going, going, gone', *Business Week*, 12 April, pp. 30–1.

Arthur Andersen (2001), *Executive Business Panel: Customer Strategies and Channels*, www.andersen.com/MarketOfferingseBusinessResourcesExecutivePanel/Customer Relationships.

Barua, A., Konana, P., Whinston, A. and Yin, F. (2000), 'Making e-business pay: eight drivers for operational success', *IT Pro*, November/December, pp. 2–8.

Chaston, I. (2000), *E-Marketing Strategy*, McGraw-Hill, Maidenhead.

Chaston, I. (in press), 'Relationship marketing in online B2B markets', *European Journal of Marketing*.

Curran, J., Jarvis, R., Kitching, R. and Lightfoot, J. (1997), 'The pricing decision in small firms: complexities and the deprioritising of economic determinants', *International Small Business Journal*, Vol. 15, No. 2, pp. 17–32.

Day, G.S. (1981), 'The product life cycle: analysis and applications issues', *Journal of Marketing*, Vol. 45, Fall, pp. 60–70.

Ford, I.D. (1990), *Understanding Business Markets*, Academic Press, San Diego, California.

French, M. (1993), 'Structure, personality and business strategy in the US tire industry', *Business History Review*, Vol. 67, No. 2, pp. 246–67.

Garda, R.A. and Marn, M.V. (1993), 'Price wars', *The McKinsey Quarterly*, No. 3, p. 83.

Grant, A.W.H. and Schlesinger, L.A. (1995), 'Realize your customers' full profit potential', *Harvard Business Review*, September–October, pp. 59–72.

Guiltinan, J.P. and Gundlach, G.T. (1996), 'Aggressive and predatory pricing: a framework for analysis', *Journal of Marketing*, Vol. 60, No. 3, pp. 87–105.

Gummesson, E. (1997), 'Relationship marketing as a paradigm shift', *Management Decision*, Vol. 35, No. 3–4, pp. 267–73.

Håkansson, H. (1982), *International Marketing and Purchasing of Industrial Goods*, Wiley, New York.

Howcroft, B. (1992), 'Contemporary issues in UK bank delivery systems', *International Journal of Service Industry Management*, Vol. 3, No. 1, pp. 39–51.

Knol, A.S. (2000), 'Take this job and love it', *eBay Magazine*, April, pp. 47–50.

Kumar, A. and Sharman, G. (1992), 'We love the product, but where is it?' *Sloan Management Review*, Vol. 33, No. 2, pp. 93–107.

Livesay, H.C. (1989), 'Entrepreneurial dominance in businesses large and small, past and present', *Business History Review*, Vol. 63, Spring, pp. 1–21.

McDonagh, P. and Cummins, P. (1999), 'Food chains, small-scale enterprises and rural developmennt', *International Planning Studies*, Vol. 4, No. 3, pp. 349–71.

McKenna, R. (1991), 'Marketing is everything', *Harvard Business Review*, Jan.–Feb., pp. 65–79.

Massey, J. (1992), 'Distribution: changing channels', *Computer Weekly*, 28 May, pp. 28–31.

Mayo, D.T., Richardson, L.D. and Simpson, T. (1998), 'The differential effects of the uses of power sources and influence strategies on channel satisfaction', *Journal of Marketing Theory and Practice*, Vol. 6, No. 2, pp. 16–25.

Moriaty, R.W. and Moran, U. (1990), 'Managing hybrid marketing systems', *Harvard Business Review*, Nov.–Dec., pp. 146–55.

Osborne, K. (1996), 'The channel integration decision for small manufacturing exporters', *International Small Business Journal*, Vol. 14, No. 3, pp. 40–54.

Pine, B.J., Peppers, D. and Rogers, M. (1995), 'Do you want to keep your customers for ever?', *Harvard Business Review*, March–April, pp. 103–14.

Piore, M. and Sabel, C. (1984), *The Second Industrial Divide*, Basic Books, New York.

Pitt, L., Berthon, P. and Berthon, J. (1999), 'Changing channels: the impact of the Internet on distribution strategy', *Business Horizons*, Vol. 42, No. 2, pp. 19–34.

Rangan, V.K., Moriaty, R.T. and Swartz, G. (1992), 'Segmenting customers in mature industrial markets', *Journal of Marketing*, Vol. 56, October, pp. 72–82.

Rangan, V.K., Moriaty, R.T. and Swartz, G. (1993), 'Transaction cost theory: inferences from field research on downstream vertical integration', *Organization Science*, Vol. 4, No. 3, pp. 454–77.

Sinha, I. (2000), 'Cost transparency: the Net's real threat to prices and brands', *Harvard Business Review*, March–April, pp. 43–52.

Speckman, R.E., Salmond, D.J. and Lambe, C.J. (1997), 'Consensus and collaboration: norm-regulated behaviour in industrial markets', *European Journal of Marketing*, Vol. 31, No. 11–12, pp. 832–47.

Stern, L.W. and El-Ansary, A.I. (1988), *Marketing Channels*, 3rd edn, Prentice-Hall, Englewood Cliffs, N.J.

Williamson, O. (1975), *Markets and Hierarchies*, Free Press, New York.

Zineldin, M. (2000), 'Beyond relationship marketing: technologicalship marketing', *Marketing Intelligence & Planning*, Vol. 18, No. 1, pp. 9–23.

10 INFORMATION AND OPERATIONS

LEARNING OBJECTIVES

After studying this chapter you should be able to understand:

1. the issue about the degree to which small firms need to be effective managers of information;
2. whether a contingency approach to information management is the most appropriate philosophy for small firms;
3. how learning theory and knowledge management style will influence the effective operation of information systems;
4. the impact of electronic data interchange on information management attitudes within smaller firms;
5. how enterprise resource planning systems are influencing attitudes to information management;
6. the significant impact that the advent of the Internet is having on small firm information management systems;
7. the behavioural antecedents necessary to effectively exploit Internet-driven information systems.

CHAPTER SUMMARY

Small firms tend be poor at managing information. The conventional view based on large firm experience is that even small firms would gain from using formalised management information systems to manage internal operations. Actual research on the validity of this perspective raises doubts whether all small firms would benefit from formalising their information systems. An alternative perspective is that a contingency approach reflecting the specific circumstances facing the small firm may be more appropriate. The way in which small firms handle knowledge will influence the effectiveness of information interchange within the firm. Adoption of a 'just in time' operating philosophy tends to enhance information management capabilities. In recent years small firms have been forced by large customers to accept new technologies such as electronic data interchange and the Internet as platforms through which to manage all aspects of the transaction process. The Internet is possibly the most dramatic technological change ever to confront the small firm because the organisation will need to move to a real time utilisation of data flows. Execution of an effective information strategy normally requires the small firm to be customer driven, accept total quality management/just in time working and to be competent in information technology.

INTRODUCTION

An area where owner/managers have faced criticism over the years is over their approach to the acquisition, storage and utilisation of information to support decision making within their organisations. Accountants complain about startup firms that store their financial records in shoeboxes or plastic shopping bags. They also express frustration over the fact that even long established small firms will not develop management accounting systems capable of assisting the determination and resolution of business problems. Similarly academics interested in issues such as information or marketing management have strongly articulated the view that an investment in the creation of a management information system (MIS) significantly improves the operational performance of a small firm.

Malone (1985) proposed that an MIS acts as a core resource that can enhance the activities of analysis, planning, plan implementation and control. Furthermore this researcher concluded that an information system (IS) can improve the quality of decision making in small firms. The declining costs of computer hardware and software have caused many academics to strongly support the view that a small firm can gain additional benefits from investing in the development of a computer based MIS to guide future operations.

Bergeron and Raymond (1992) are confident that computer based information systems will give small firms a new source of competitive advantage. They describe a structured process that small firms should adopt which appears to be based upon a classic large firm strategic management approach. Owner/managers are urged to form a project team, analyse the entire organisation, identify opportunities and develop a structured information management strategic plan. Pollard and Hayne (1998) concluded that because a large firm can acquire a competitive advantage from a computerised MIS, then small firms should also exploit information technology (IT) to achieve the same strategic goal. They also believe that the failure of some small firms to exploit IT reflects the influence of factors such as the autocratic attitudes of owner/managers who do not understand the benefits of adopting new technologies, inadequate IT skills within many small firms and poor project management capabilities.

Examining some of these research findings in more depth can lead to the emergence of some potentially worrying methodological issues. For example a number of writers seem to rely upon qualitative data from a single case example as the basis for extrapolating to the perspective that all small firms should invest in acquiring more computing power. Thus a management expert might propose that small manufacturing firms should use computer based scheduling systems. The basis for this proposal is the case evidence that this proved beneficial to a kitchen cabinet manufacturer whose position in the supply chain demanded an improved response involving adoption of a computer aided design system.

Positivist researchers (that is, those who believe that research produces evidence of real-world facts) have used survey data to prove that a relationship exists between use of computer based decision tools and market performance. Yet when one examines their research design, it is not unusual to find that the selected sample frame is dominated by medium sized firms that employ between 100 and 250 staff. In relation to this latter research design problem, it is interesting to find that when the researchers specifically focus on smaller firms, they often have much more trouble proving their hypotheses concerning a positive correlation between the exploitation of IT and the enhancement of management practices within SME sector firms. Loadi (1998) provides an interesting example of this scenario in which he encountered real difficulties when seeking to validate the hypotheses that in small firms, the effectiveness of information processing activities is influenced by factors such as structural organicity, functional differentiation between departments and stability of the external operational environment.

TOWARDS AN ALTERNATIVE PERSPECTIVE

Durham Business School in the UK has championed the perspective that in evolving SME sector management theories one should avoid drawing upon large firms as the exemplars of practice. Instead this academic organisation believes it is critical that evolution of SME sector theories be based upon observing 'good practice' in real-world small businesses. Over the years, one of the Durham team, Ted Fuller, has made some important contributions to the field of information management within the small firms sector.

For example, Fuller (1996) made the observation that owner/managers are critical influencers of the managerial practices adopted within their organisation. Furthermore he posited that the effectiveness of owner/manager decision making is influenced both by (a) their business vision and (b) their willingness to promote learning within their organisation to acquire the new knowledge required to ensure achievement of the firm's performance goals. Additionally Fuller believes that in adopting new advances in IT systems, the situation is complicated by the behaviours and interactions which occur between the actors both inside the small firm and between the organisations which constitute the surrounding supply chain.

Fuller's perspective, as summarised in Figure 10.1, is that in considering the effective operation of information systems one must take into account the interaction between actors in the business system. The owner/manager has a key role because it is this individual's business vision and ideas that will strongly influence the degree to which the firm uses a formalised, computer based decision support system. This individual will also tend to work closely with the firm's employees in the creation and operation of new IT systems. How the owner/manager acquires the knowledge about information systems depends upon the attitudes and behaviours within the business system. Many small firms prefer to rely upon trusted sources and hence will turn to their social and business networks for guidance. It is very probable that external support sources such as vendors and consultants will be able to offer more up-to-date knowledge than many social or business network sources. Nevertheless the small firm's utilisation of external support sources will be heavily dependant upon whether the small firm perceives that guidance from such sources can be trusted.

Until recently the major suppliers of computer hardware and software such as IBM or Microsoft have tended to use intermediaries to service the

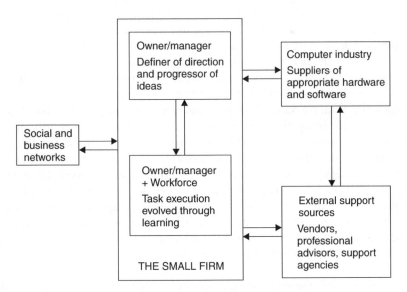

Figure 10.1   Actors in the IT knowledge acquisition process

needs of their SME sector customers. Recognition of the growing importance of the sector as a source of potential business, however, has resulted in these major producers beginning to work directly with small firms. The degree to which they are successful will be determined by whether such firms have acquired an adequate understanding of the differences that exist between the data processing needs in the large and small firm sectors. For only if this has occurred will these large suppliers avoid the common mistake of assuming that the IT systems which they have developed for large firm customers can be also be utilised, without making any product modifications, by SME sector organisations.

Another common error made by both computer industry producers and their market intermediaries is to assume that the SME sector is homogeneous and that most small firms have common information management needs. The reality, however, is that there are huge variations between the types of problems confronting small firms and consequently, their needs in terms of access to appropriate information. Dodge and Robbins (1992) have suggested that one approach to understanding the needs of small firms is to assume that the development of these organisations can be captured by the following four phase model:

1. *business formation*, during which the owner/manager is converting an idea into a business entity. Priority issues confronting the business are those such as gaining customer acceptance, being able to produce the first generation product and gaining access to external borrowing;
2. *early growth*, during which sales are rising rapidly and commercial viability is being validated. Priority issues confronting the firm are those such as ensuring an ability to expand production capacity to meet market demand, sustaining product quality, cash flow management and beginning to formalise the firm's organisational structure;
3. *later growth*, during which sales growth begins to slow due to factors such as entry of competitors into the market sector, or the gap between actual sales and total market sector potential sales beginning to narrow. Priority issues confronting the firm are sustaining profitability, identifying new market opportunities and the creation of control systems for the more formalised monitoring of all aspects of the firm's internal operations;
4. *business stability* emerges when the owner/manager has been able to create an operation where capacity and market demand are in balance and internal systems are in place than can ensure employee performance is optimal. Priority issues are those such as succession planning, delegation of managerial tasks, adopting a team based management philosophy and minimising internal operating inefficiencies.

In the real world, the evolutionary path individual small firms actually follow will often be at variance with the proposed four phase conceptual development model. Nevertheless the underlying concept is useful because the existence of different managerial priorities in each phase does permit the suggestion that information management should be considered as a contingency issue. In this way determination of an appropriate information management system will be heavily influenced by which stage of development the firm is engaged in managing.

Writers who promote the advantages of formalised information management systems are also making another critical assumption, namely that owner/managers will exhibit the characteristics of being rational decision makers. The strategic management literature contains numerous articles that set out to present a convincing case that the performance of organisations can be enhanced through managers acting rationally. Dean and Sharfman (1996), for example, proposed that effective rational decision making involves (a) a strong orientation towards achieving appropriate organisational goals, (b) basing decisions on accurate, detailed information that permits assessment of alternative actions and (c) having an in-depth appreciation of the environmental constraints facing the firm.

In an attempt to determine whether a relationship exists between rational decision making and organisational performance, these researchers interviewed executives in 24 firms ranging in size from annual turnover of $1.5 million and 50 employees to annual turnover of $3 billion and over 6000 employees. Unfortunately the researchers did not present data on how variation in the size of firm influenced their results. What they did find, however, was a positive relationship between the performance of firms and rational decision making in those cases where (a) market conditions are perceived as highly stable and (b) the nature of the industrial sector is such that managers have access to detailed information about environmental trends. A similar relationship could not be validated where markets are unstable or minimal data are available on market trends. The researchers proposed that this latter scenario required more work in order to gain a better understanding of effective decision making by managers facing this type of operational disadvantage. What the researchers did not mention, however, is that this is exactly the type of scenario that is faced by many small firms. Hence one interpretation of their findings is that rational decision making may not be the most effective approach in many SME sector markets. Under these circumstances it might be necessary for owner/managers who have access to a limited market to reach decisions based upon exploiting prior experience and a willingness to act intuitively.

A CONTINGENCY APPROACH

Owner/managers' preference for autocracy and their scepticism about the validity of guidance espoused in management textbooks means that prescriptive statements about the need for formalised information management systems are very likely to be ignored. Possibly a more practical approach is to persuade the owner/manager to reconsider their approach to information management by getting them to review how their firm recently handled the process of resolving a significant operational problem. One way this can be achieved is to ask them to consider how the issues described in Figure 10.2 are relevant to the problem solving process within their organisation.

The first issue is whether, by involving others within the firm, the problem solving activity might have been enhanced. This is an important issue because as a small firm moves from the startup phase of being a micro-enterprise employing one or two people to a growth business employing ten or more individuals, owner/managers should possibly delegate more problem solving to others inside the organisation. The next issue is whether the problem was resolved using existing knowledge and experience or by adding to existing experience by drawing upon new sources of knowledge. The former approach has been labelled as a single loop learning style, and the latter a double loop learning style (Cyert and March 1963). The differences between these two learning styles are illustrated in Figure 10.3. Single loop learning is probably appropriate when the problem being confronted is amenable to resolution by applying well established, proven organisational processes. Where the problem is complex, or the problem involves issues about which

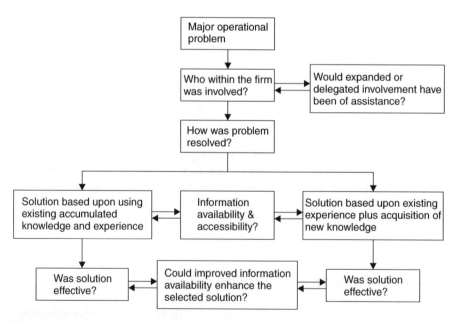

Figure 10.2   A problem solving flow diagram

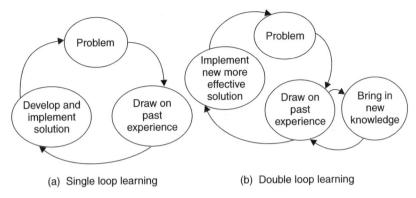

(a) Single loop learning   (b) Double loop learning

Figure 10.3 Alternative learning styles

the firm has limited experience, then a double loop approach of bringing in new knowledge might be found to be more effective.

Linked to the learning style question is the issue of how the availability and accessibility of information contributes to the formulation of an appropriate solution. This issue of information management is also revisited at the solution assessment phase because it is usually feasible to persuade the owner/manager to consider whether the problem/solution process might be enhanced by upgrading their firm's information management practices.

Nonaka (1991) has proposed that within organisations, information is available in two forms. *Implicit information* is those data that are stored in peoples minds and only accessible through dialogue. *Explicit information* is those data which are formally stored within the firm's record system. The advantage of explicit information is that the stored format means the data are accessible to anybody who is authorised to access the relevant files. Evidence would tend to suggest that implicit information is the dominant data storage approach within small firms that are at an early stage of development. This scenario means that when employees need to seek out knowledge they are forced to rely on the availability of the relevant employee in order to acquire information. Once small firms begin to grow, often accompanied by a rising number of employees, implicitly stored information can act as a barrier to operational efficiency. Research on this issue would seem to suggest that where owner/managers desire to sustain operational performance during growth, then a move to a more formalised, explicit information system of the type shown in Figure 10.4 might be an advisable action (Chaston 2000).

It should be recognised that construction of an explicit information system of the type shown in Figure 10.4 will usually take several years to achieve. The guidance to an owner/manager seeking to initiate an information formalisation process is to determine which area of the firm's operations should be given priority. In most cases the selected priority will be the small firm's financial management system. Actions here might involve moving to

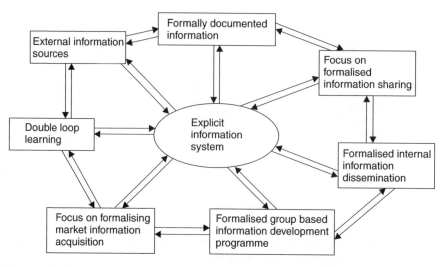

Figure 10.4   Components of an explicit information system

a computerised financial reporting system using standard software from suppliers such as Sage or Pegasus. Over time other systems can be added such as production and procurement, marketing and human resources management. Figure 10.5 provides a visual description of the integrated information system utilised by the Candle Company, which is the basis of the free computer

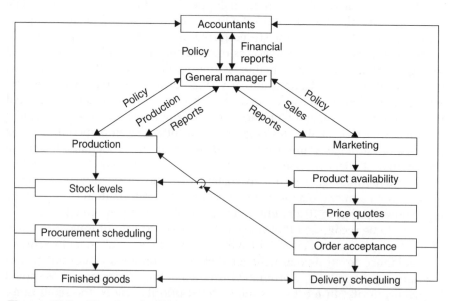

Figure 10.5   The Candle Company management information system

simulation accompanying this text. This system permits the production, marketing and accounting staff to use data available from the various areas of departmental responsibility as the basis for optimising their decision making. The general manager can also use the same system to monitor actual performance versus those aims they have specified for the firm's performance.

There are real benefits in the small firm creating integrated systems such that data from a number of sources can easily be incorporated into activities associated with analysing complex problems. For example integrating the marketing and accounting systems in the Candle Company will permit assessment of the relative profitability of sales of different products. Nevertheless it is necessary to caution owner/managers about assuming systems integration is an easy process. For although software firms such as Microsoft and Oracle have worked hard to improve the ease with which data can be exchanged between operating platforms, an integrated system of the type shown in Figure 10.5 often demands upgrading of one of more of the firm's software packages. Furthermore, in many cases the purchase of one or more new file servers will be necessary in order to create a system which has sufficient capacity to permit rapid electronic information interchange between databases.

ACCELERATED DECISION MAKING

In the 1980s, leading Japanese manufacturing firms questioned the industrial convention that cost optimisation could be achieved by scheduling long runs of individual products based upon output volumes determined by using a mathematical model to calculate Economic Order Quantities (EOQs). The Japanese's alternative approach was to investigate the potential for only scheduling production to match on-hand orders from customers. Subsequently their outstanding achievements in this area have become better known as a 'just in time' (JIT) manufacturing philosophy.

By the 1990s, JIT manufacturing principles had become accepted not just by large manufacturers, but also by small firms seeking to optimise production costs. Storey (1994) recommends that any firm, no matter the size, in order to be effective in utilising a JIT approach must:

- carefully monitor customer order patterns;
- respond very rapidly to orders received and have the capability to acquire cost effectively sufficient raw materials for the next scheduled production run;
- minimise machine tool setup times;
- have a highly proactive, responsive workforce;
- establish logistics systems capable of economically delivering smaller order quantities to customers;

- operate real time information capture systems capable of immediately diagnosing the cause of any emerging procurement, production scheduling or delivery problems.

Initially proponents of a JIT philosophy perceived the concept as a mechanism to enhance financial performance. Within a short period of time, however, it was also realised that JIT had massive implications in the areas of delivering customer satisfaction and the development of new products. Davis (1987) proposed that in today's society, customers will increasingly be seeking 24 hour service, seven days a week, 365 days of the year. He believes that this change in customer demand necessitates that all firms should adopt the vision of *zero based time*, which has the ultimate goal of never keeping the customer waiting.

Tucker (1991) has expressed similar views. He also believes the number one driving force for any size firm seeking to survive in increasingly competitive markets is to revise organisational processes to improve the speed with which the organisation can respond to customer needs. He suggests there are the following eight steps which permit exploitation of the 'speed imperative':

1. assess the importance of speed to the customer;
2. challenge every time based convention which exists within the firm;
3. involve the customer in both identifying their waiting time dissatisfaction and generating ideas to reduce response times;
4. continuously monitor time savings achieved as new initiatives are implemented with the goal of eventually identifying new, incremental actions to further reduce response times;
5. clearly promote the nature of your speed imperative philosophy to the market;
6. reflect the costs of outstanding speed in the pricing of products and services;
7. reward employees for finding new, entrepreneurial ways of saving time;
8. having achieved a high speed response, build this achievement into your customer guarantee system.

Writings on the strategic implications associated with time and process revision usually propose that many of the opportunities for delivering greater customer satisfaction can only be achieved by the entire organisation focussing upon new approaches that can influence factors such as build quality, delivery time and lower prices. In the manufacturing sector achievement of such goals by small firms has in many cases been a requirement specified by a manufacturer during negotiations over rating the small firm as an approved supplier. Fulfilling such customer demands, as many owner/managers have discovered, will usually require the creation of a fully integrated, computer based information system.

Implementation of a JIT operating philosophy will typically reveal that to be effective, it needs to be extended outside of the firm in order to encompass all of the components which constitute a supply chain within an industrial sector. This is because organisations within a supply chain need to be orientated towards minimising time and resource wastage during the handling and storage of products (Anon. 1998). The growing awareness of the waste contained within many supply chains has caused a diversity of different industries to revisit the basic conventions that determined supplier-customer relationships for most of the 20th century. Recognition has gradually dawned amongst the players that there is a need for all parties to begin to move away from traditional, adversarial relationships. Instead they should adopt a philosophy based upon cooperative partnerships with the mutual aim of finding new ways of building more efficient supply chain systems (Buzzell and Ortmeyer 1995). The incentive which drove many Western firms to adopt a more cooperative orientation was the recognition that without such change, costs would continue to rise and ability to rapidly respond to changing market circumstances would become increasingly inadequate. The outcome is that in many industrial sectors large manufacturers such as GE, Ford, DuPont, General Motors, IBM and Xerox have moved towards adopting the concept of working in partnership with their large and small firm component suppliers.

What both sales staff from suppliers and customer firm procurement personnel soon discover when adopting a cooperative orientation, however, is that without effective information management systems, aspirations of optimising supply chain performance can rarely be fulfilled. Firms of all sizes aiming to exploit JIT have sought to find ways of improving the speed and accuracy of data interchange. This has caused attention to be focussed upon how electronic data exchange could permit firms to more effectively manage both their internal operations and their interactions with other organisations within their market system.

Initially the approach promoted by large firms was a technique known as electronic data interchange (EDI) which, when linked to use as bar coding to label products, permits real time electronic exchange of data between customer and supplier. Having adopted EDI as the medium for communication, supplier and customer are then in a position to be able to examine opportunities to reduce administrative burdens through actions such as minimisation of purchase orders, inventory holdings, credit notes, invoices, delivery documentation and returned goods (MacGrath 1996). Small firms, however, who have adopted the technology can expect to encounter problems such as (a) variation between manufacturers as to which EDI software their suppliers should purchase and (b) technological obstacles encountered when attempting to integrate an EDI package into the small firm's existing computer system.

Chen and Williams (1998) empirically investigated the impact of EDI on UK SME sector firms. The majority of the respondents had been required to adopt the technology by one or more of their key large firm customers. Having made the investment, many small firms found that the number of transactions remained minimal with order frequency being so low that it would have been quite feasible to retain the pre-EDI approach of having customers submit their orders by mail or fax. Respondents also indicated their large firm customers wanted the EDI system to encompass both order submission and automated invoice generation. The implication of this latter request is for the EDI software to be integrated into the small firm's existing computer based information system. Having investigated this scenario, however, most small firms will opt to run their EDI system on a standalone, dedicated PC and to avoid the probable complications of attempting to integrate EDI software with other databases within the organisation. The researchers' overall impression was that small firms in the UK had reactively installed an EDI system at the request of the large customers, and apart from wishing to avoid alienating these customers, did not perceive any real benefits had been gained from the adoption of this technology.

EXAMPLE: EARLY MOVERS IN ELECTRONIC INTERCHANGE

In 1993, the Custom Clothing Technology Corporation (CCTC) was launched by Sung Park in Boston (Bianchi 1993). The company offers consumers the opportunity to be individually measured for designer jeans in selected retail stores. The store transmits the data electronically to CCTC. The firm forwards the data to its small manufacturing operation in Texas from where the customised product is shipped directly to the customer's home. A company called Second Skin Swimwear based in Florida developed a similar concept for customised swimwear. Again the customer's measurements are taken in store and the company uses the data to manufacture a made-to-measure swimming costume.

Another firm which has also adopted this approach is the clothing manufacturer Satisfied Sport. Based in Seattle, it produces clothing carrying the logos and brand names of consumer service market firms such as restaurant chains. Upon receipt of an order, Satisfied Sport uses computer aided design to create the garment patterns and these data are transmitted electronically via a modem to contract clothing manufacturers in Los Angeles.

SHOULD SMALL FIRMS GO LEAN?

Many large manufacturing firms which adopted JIT to achieve a more flexible, faster response to customers within their supply chain system have found it necessary to totally redesign their internal production processes. The concept, known as flexible manufacturing systems (FMS), involves revising engineering design and production processes by exploiting the technological benefits offered by equipment such as robots, flexible machining centres and automated assembly machines (Goldhar and Lei 1995). Traditional mass production factories are based around exploiting economies of scale to optimise productivity. Having adopted an FMS philosophy, firms are able to shift to much lower unit production runs. It then becomes cost effective to both offer a more diverse of products and rapidly respond to fluctuations in market demand. Having completed the computer based integration of internal processes, organisations can begin to consider building automated response systems for electronically linking the firm to customers.

The initial response of small firms when first exposed to the concept of flexible manufacturing is that (a) this is not applicable to their business because they already have extensive batch production and (b) the investment in new technology is unaffordable. In an attempt to determine the validity of this perspective Luria (1996) used the Industrial Technology Institute benchmarking database to examine the performance of 116 small metal forming engineering companies. His analysis utilised three scales. 'Systematic' rated firms by their ability to track orders, level of faulty product, machine setup time and response to machine breakdowns. 'Modern' measured investment in hardware and software for use in process automation. 'Distinctive' assessed the ownership of proprietary or design-intensive products and/or an ability to perform sophisticated procedures such as ultra high tolerance machining. Luria determined it was possible to classify the sample firms into the following three types:

1. *Low-roaders* score poorly on all three scales. They are firms which operate in the bottom of the market, use outmoded technology, unskilled labour and compete purely on the basis of lowest possible price for standard components. These firms constitute about 50 per cent of the sample.
2. *High-roaders* score well on 'modern' and 'distinctive' but show variable scores on 'systematic'. These firms, which represent 25 per cent of the sample, invest heavily in new technology, are committed to employee training and seek to differentiate their output from competition. Their market survival is dependant upon sufficient customers seeking highly distinctive product. If large manufacturers move towards more standardisation in their procurement, these firms may be placed in a vulnerable position.
3. *Lean commodity firms* score high on 'systematic' but not that high on 'modern' and 'distinctive'. These firms, which represent about 25 per cent of the sample, are actively involved in adopting flexible manufacturing as a path to producing high quality products at a competitive price. They focus on activities such as minimising waste, being faster at machine setup and minimising machine downtimes by utilising preventive maintenance.

The conclusion reached in the study is that over time low-roaders will face the need to replace ageing machinery, and rising labour costs. Their lack of focus on actions to sustain productivity will mean that they will be unable to compete with small firms located in developing nations. In contrast the lean commodity group of firms are exploiting the philosophy of flexible manufacturing to continually achieve productivity gains within their operations. This achievement when linked to their product quality standards means that they can expect to meet the needs of their manufacturer customers and will not be threatened by competition from overseas producers.

THE ADVENT OF ENTERPRISE RESOURCE PLANNING

Since the 1980s, very large firms with highly diversified product ranges and retailers stocking a vast selection of goods have both been searching for better ways to manage information interchange that would optimise decisions related to issues such as production scheduling, inventory control and supply chain linkages. The first attempt to solve this problem was a software product known as materials requirement planning (MRP). This evolved into manufacturing resource planning (MRP II) which analysed all aspects of the materials associated with procurement and manufacturing activities. In some cases, adopters of MRP and MRP II reported operational difficulties because these organisations were operating a number of incompatible hardware and software systems. To overcome this major problem, firms such as SAP, PeopleSoft and Oracle developed fully integrated software known generically as enterprise resource planning or ERP. This system claims to link together all databases from marketing, logistics, manufacturing, procurement, accounting and so on to permit real time analysis of activities in progress across the entire organisation (Zuckerman 1999).

Utilised properly, ERP offers the benefits of optimising profits, customer service and capacity utilisation. Hewlett-Packard, for example, faced the problem that over the last decade there has been intense price competition in the computer printer market. To survive the firm needed a way to upgrade and optimise internal operational processes. By using ERP to map data flows Hewlett-Packard was able to determine how organisational processes, systems and structures could be improved. The outcomes included a move from 65 per cent to 95 per cent on-time delivery whilst concurrently finished goods inventory levels were reduced by 10 per cent (Trunick 1999).

Initially these systems were perceived as providing the route to optimising usage of resources inside organisations. Over time, however, the systems have been extended outwards as a way of more closely linking together firms within entire supply chains. Colgate-Palmolive, for example, utilised a SAP-based ERP system to link together all elements of its global operation to cut order-to-shipment cycle times in half and dramatically reduce finished goods inventory levels. They have now provided their large and small firm suppliers with access to ERP information so that they can take over responsibility for managing raw material inventories (Moad 1997).

Just as in the earlier situation with EDI, once large firms had installed ERP they began to express a desire that all their suppliers, both large and small, should consider adoption of the same technology to improve information interchange within their respective supply chains. The initial reaction of many owner/managers, when informed of the huge cost of installing an ERP system, was less than positive. Furthermore, although the business press contained case materials about the success of ERP, small firms began to hear about major names such as Hershey Foods and Whirlpool, having spent millions establishing their systems, who were less than happy about the outcome. Allied Waste Industries, a waste management company based in Arizona dumped a $130 million SAP installation on the grounds that the cost of maintaining the software and the constraints the software placed on decision making meant that retention of the system could no longer be justified. Another SAP customer, W.W. Grainger in Illinois, a $4.3 billion distributor of maintenance, repair and operating supplies, reported trading losses which they attributed to bugs in their ERP package (Gilbert 1999).

An important reason why some large firms encountered these problems is that ERP vendors' approach to product development had been to analyse business processes in numerous firms to develop database structures that incorporated a vast range of identified process variations. This design strategy makes these systems enormously complicated (Unitec 2000). Companies purchasing the software may have to make a huge time commitment and abandon existing business processes in order to develop an effective ERP solution. Furthermore in some cases, successful operation of the ERP system may necessitate a complete re-engineering of fundamental organisational processes.

More recently both small firms and software developers have come to realise that large firm ERP solutions are probably totally inappropriate for the SME sector. Hence a number of new players have entered the ERP market, offering lower cost, modular systems that are seen as offering a more flexible, simplified approach to data management than the very large systems marketed by firms such as SAP, Baan and J.D. Edwards. These simpler, lower cost ERP systems are perceived as affordable by SME sector firms. ACE Controls in Michigan provides an example of this simpler, lower cost approach (Chalmers 1999). The company makes industrial shock absorbers for applications such as decelerating loads in amusement park rides around the world. As the business grew, problems emerged using the existing IT systems to manage tasks such as scheduling and interdepartmental communication over product availability. The company purchased a low cost ERP system known as Resource Planner. The system runs on a Microsoft Excel platform using NT to permit multiterminal usage within the firm. On the system is a master scheduler which permits employees to interrogate the manufacturing schedule, determine capacity constraints and undertake 'what if' exercises to assess how scheduling changes might impact delivery dates. The primary demand on staff time during the installation of the system was in taking a more disciplined approach to activities such as part numbering, work centre definitions, bills of material and production cycle times.

Another vendor of ERP systems for SMEs is Alliance/MFG for Windows (Meikle 1997). This company identified market resistance among small firms to the ERP prices being quoted by the large software houses. Their low cost solution has a Job Master core module that creates, maintains and tracks all job costs. Linkage to sales orders, purchases and work orders means the firm can monitor manufacturing performance. A critical design feature is that the system provides an automatic link to the leading PC-based accounting packages used by small firms. ICDA, a US firm which manufactures infra red night visioning systems, adopted the system to manage its new contractual relationship with Texas Instruments. Another US firm, Electronic Assemblers, a wire harness subcontractor, purchased the software to resolve the problem that in the face of rapid business growth, it was becoming impossible to manage its procurement, production scheduling and logistics system using the existing IT facilities.

ENTER THE INTERNET

The two sectors which pioneered the use of EDI in the automation of supply chains were banking and large manufacturers. Their perspective was that EDI permitted fast, secure delivery of information. Nevertheless many organisations, especially in the SME sector, remained less than totally committed to the technology because of the high installation and operating costs. EDI systems are typically proprietary software systems offered to users by operators of value added networks (VANs). These VAN suppliers usually charge a very high up-front connection fee and the users face heavy ongoing costs based upon the volume of data being transmitted.

The advent of the Internet, using the TCP/IP protocol, offered an open, non-proprietary data exchange for transmitting data between users. The initial reaction among firms with well developed EDI systems was that the Internet was unreliable and open to the risk of databases being accessed by hackers. Hence in these organisation there were two initial reactions to proposals about moving to an Internet based supply chain system. The first was that the technology is totally unsuitable for commercial operations. The second perspective was that although the Internet might be utilised as an adjunct communications system, the core of the supply chain management must be based around EDI because this is the only way to effectively and reliably handle the volume of transactions (Dyck 1997).

Other, more enlightened organisations, however, saw the Internet as a low cost platform, which meant that even the smallest of firms within their supply chain could now afford to become involved in computer based data interchange. Additionally, in response to concerns over security, software developers began to evolve virtual private networks (VPNs) which could operate over the Internet but only permit access by approved users. The usual form of VPN adopted by most organisations has been that of establishing Extranets. These are simply Internet systems with controlled user access. Software developers also created Intranets. These are computer systems for use within firms to permit rapid electronic communication between all employees. Because Extranets and Intranets operate on a common platform, the move to permit secure electronic communication with individuals outside the organisation is technically a relative simple task (Urbaczewski *et al.* 1998).

EXAMPLE: EXTRANETS
....

An early entrant into the use of the Internet to improve supply chain management was the US home improvement retailer, Home Depot Inc. For a number of years the company has used an EDI system to manage its purchasing activities with large company suppliers. Home Depot, like all large retailers, is continually seeking ways to achieve increased transaction speeds, more efficient logistic systems and operational cost reductions. The problem facing Home Depot was how to achieve these goals by improving its procurement operation when working with the firm's 300 overseas SME suppliers. Located in Asia and South America, these firms lacked the capability to utilise EDI and consequently order placement was by telephone, fax or mail. To improve the procurement process Home Depot has established a website for use by low volume suppliers. Vendors receive an electronic purchase order which the supplier uses to confirm prices and product availability. These data also provide the basis for the automatic submission of an electronic invoice when the goods have been shipped to Home Depot (Chabrow 2000).

Stride Rite Corporation, a major US retailer of athletic and casual footwear, has also adopted an Internet solution to handle its links with small overseas suppliers. Having closed down its own manufacturing operations the firm now contracts with independently owned footwear manufacturers in China. Their online system has been beneficial both to the company and to its suppliers: it has been able to reduce trans-Pacific transportation costs by 30 per cent and increased inventory turnover rates by 25 per cent.

Once a large retailer has created a hub site for managing relationships with suppliers, this same technology can be utilised for building stronger links with business-to-business customers further downstream in the supply chain. One such firm that has moved to exploit this opportunity is the online clothing operation Land's End (Rabon 2000). The company's corporate sales division sells business casual apparel, often carrying customised embroidered corporate logos to a diversified group of B2B customers in America. Its e-commerce system permits customers to access its own specific Extranet to review product designs, check availability and place orders. For SME customers the company has created Lands' End Live, a real time customer assistance application that allows a customer service representative to share a browser with the client. The two parties can communicate by telephone to resolve any problems that the customer is encountering during the transaction process.

Boise Cascade Office Products Corporation (www.bcop.com) is a $2 billion operation based in Itasca, Illinois. The company acts as a hub in a supply chain comprising 1200 suppliers and 17 000 customers, many of whom are SME sector businesses. For some years the company has been using EDI to manage transactions with its larger suppliers and larger customers. It recognised, however, that the cost of installing and operating EDI systems was perceived as prohibitively expensive by smaller firms within their supply chain (Aragon 1997). The company used in-house developed e-commerce software linked to ECXpert, an integrator package supplied by Actra Business Systems of California. ECXPert permits the company to translate Internet order information into an EDI protocol, which is understood by the firm's mainframe. This approach is known as Electronic Data Interchange Internet (EDIINT) and permits transmission of data across the Internet with the same security that previously was only available through an EDI VAN system. The overwhelming advantage of EDIINT is that data transmission costs have been reduced by 20 per cent and users do not need to invest in specialist computer equipment in order to gain access to the system. Customers access the system via Boise's public homepage and then enter the order site using a user ID. They can peruse an online catalogue containing over 10 000 products. 'Easy order forms' assist the ordering process and payments can be made using standard credit cards. In the first year of operation, Boise saved over $1 million by reducing the time customer service representatives spend taking orders by telephone. On the supplier side the firm is exploiting the Internet to reduce paperwork, improve warehouse receiving procedures and reduce inventory management activities.

ASSEMBLING SUCCESSFUL SYSTEMS

Owner/managers seeking information on the design and operation of e-commerce systems will soon find that the same large company case examples such as Dell and Cisco seem to be featured in virtually every business magazine article and book. Repeated mention of the same company examples is no coincidence. It is a reflection of the fact that to date, even in the large firm sector, very few organisations have been successful in creating effective, totally integrated, automated systems. One of the reasons underlying this situation is that even before considering a move into e-commerce, firms, no matter their size, need to already exhibit all of the following three attributes: be customer driven; have a longstanding commitment to JIT and TQM; and have expertise in IT based supply chain management. These are explained in more detail in the three subsections below.

Customer driven

When using an automated information provision and purchasing system, frustrated customers can move to an alternative supplier at the 'click of a button'. Hence creating a customer friendly interface between the market and the organisation can only be achieved if the company has already developed a total commitment to delivering customer satisfaction. For it is only by being highly market orientated that an organisation can acquire the in-depth understanding of customer needs that provides the template around which the e-commerce system can be constructed.

Long established commitment to JIT and TQM

In both offline and online markets, the primary focus of marketing effort should be on seeking to retain the loyalty of existing customers. The pragmatic reason for this philosophy is that the marketing costs of acquiring a new customer are at least ten times higher than those of generating additional sales from an existing customer. Loyal customers introduced to the idea of using e-commerce to communicate with their suppliers have an expectation that events will happen more rapidly online when compared to buying the same product in an offline world. Fulfilment of this requirement can only occur if the supplier is already committed to using JIT to minimise order to delivery cycle times.

When small firms first become involved in e-commerce they usually have a website which generates e-mails describing online orders which have been received. Servicing these orders is typically undertaken using the firm's existing accounting, production and delivery systems which support the firm's terrestrial trading activities. As the small firm's online operation becomes an increasingly large proportion of total revenue then this trend will usually require that the firm moves to automate every aspect of the purchase process from information provision through to successful, on-time delivery of the ordered product. This type of e-integrated commerce system will contain an almost infinite number of interlinked, interdependent activities, none of which can be permitted to fail if all aspects of an automated purchase transaction process are to be successfully implemented. Achieving the objective of operating a complex, zero error operating system is only feasible in those organisations which for many years have been totally committed to a TQM philosophy across every area of the firm's operations.

Expertise in IT based supply chain management

E-commerce systems can only deliver their promise of an interactive, rapid response to customer demands if all elements of the supply chain have been integrated and there is a seamless flow of data interchange within the organisation and between all members of the market system. Achievement of this objective can only occur where participants have extensive prior experience of developing effective IT based data interchange and decision support systems. Hence it is no coincidence that an attribute shared by firms quoted as e-commerce exemplars is that these organisations have always led their respective market sectors in incorporating the latest advances in computing and telecommunications technology into all aspects of their operations.

Seybold and Marshak (1998) undertook the demanding task of drawing upon their firm's extensive consulting experience as the basis for formulating a set of guiding principles that must be considered in seeking to establish an effective online business operation. What drives all aspects of system design is the requirement that the entire process be driven by a determination to satisfy the articulated needs of the customer. These can include provision of pre-purchase information, product range descriptions, online design services and online order placement.

What has to be recognised is that in most markets, customer needs are rarely homogeneous. The advice of Seybold and Marshak is that the early focus should be on those customers who represent the most important source of profitable sales revenue. Only after having fulfilled the online requirements of this customer group should the small firm examine how to exploit the technology to provide coverage of other, less profitable market sectors.

EXAMPLE: AN E-COMMERCE HUB

For many small firms, once having gained some basic experience of e-commerce, it is very probable that their next move will be to examine ways of enhancing service delivery (Schwarz 2000). It is very probable that this will be achieved by the small firm moving to create closer collaborative links with others within its supply chain. This move will permit the supply chain members to evolve new service offerings and the ability to extend their services further downstream into the supply chain. An example of this philosophy is apparent in a new e-commerce hub called NonstopRx.com. Two solution providers, Nonstop Solutions and Supply Chain Solutions have created this hub for the US pharmaceutical industry. The industry is highly fragmented, with suppliers attempting to service numerous end user sites across the country. The new website will seek to enhance supply chain operations by addressing the inefficiencies of:

- large volumes of product and price change information being faxed to wholesalers from numerous suppliers;
- highly complex pricing and distribution contracts which currently involve the time of numerous administrative staff and finance personnel;
- poor management of product flows resulting in excess inventories and a poor on-time delivery record;
- rebates and chargebacks creating another massive administrative burden for wholesalers.

The objective of the new hub service is to develop and operate e-commerce supply chain models using client data to establish systems to optimise deliveries, by determining how best to manage transportation, product handling, administrative activities and inventory carrying costs. The two solution providers are optimistic that these goals can be achieved. Evidence to support their perspective is provided by the fact that Nonstop Solutions has already managed to reduce the inventory of the retail chain Longs Drugstores by 44 per cent and freed up $60 million in capital without reducing delivery service levels.

DISCUSSION QUESTIONS

1. Discuss how the effective management of information can contribute towards optimising the effective management of business operations within a small firm.
2. Compare and contrast the various views which have been expressed about whether small firms should operate highly formalised, structured management information systems.
3. How has the advent of the Internet impacted information management practices within the small firms sector?

REFERENCES

Anon. (1998), 'No factory is an island', *The Economist*, 20 June, pp. 8–11.
Aragon, L. (1997), 'Finding middle ground', *PC Week*, 15 September, pp. 91–2.

Bergeron, F. and Raymond, L. (1992), 'Planning of information systems to gain a competitive edge', *Journal of Small Business Management*, Vol. 30, No. 1, pp. 21–36.

Bianchi, A. (1993), 'Quick-response Apparel', *Inc.*, Boston, November, pp. 35–7.

Buzzell, R.D. and Ortmeyer, G. (1995), 'Channel partnerships streamline distribution', *Sloan Management Review*, Vol. 36, No. 3, pp. 85–97.

Chabrow, E. (2000), 'Supply chains go global', *Information Week*, 3 April, pp. 50–62.

Chalmers, R.E. (1999), 'Small manufacturers seek best ERP fit', *Manufacturing Engineering*, October, pp. 42–6.

Chaston, I. (2000), *Entrepreneurial Marketing*, Macmillan Business, Basingstoke.

Chen, J. and Williams, B.C. (1998), 'The impact of EDI on SMEs', *Journal of Small Business Management*, Vol. 36, No. 4, pp. 68–72.

Cyert, R.M. and March, J.G. (1963), *A Behavioural Theory of the Firm*, Prentice-Hall, Englewood Cliffs, N.J.

Davis, S.M. (1987), *Future Perfect*, Addison-Wesley, Reading, Mass.

Dean, J.W. and Sharfman, M.P. (1996), 'Does decision process matter?' *Academy of Management Journal*, Vol. 39, No. 2, pp. 368–82.

Dodge, H.R. and Robbins, J.E. (1992), 'An empirical investigation of the organisational life cycle', *Journal of Small Business Management*, Vol. 30, No. 1, pp. 27–39.

Dyck, T. (1997), 'Match made in corporate heaven', *PC Week*, 15 September, pp. 82–3.

Fuller, T. (1996), 'Fulfilling IT needs in small business: a recursive learning model', *International Small Business Journal*, Vol. 14, No. 4, pp. 25–38.

Gilbert, A. (1999), 'ERP installations derail', Information Week, 22 November, pp. 77–8.

Goldhar, J.D. and Lei, D. (1995), 'Variety is free: manufacturing in the twenty-first century', *The Academy of Management Executive*, Vol. 9, No. 4, pp. 73–91.

Loadi, M.E. (1998), 'The relationship among organisational structure, information technology and information processing in small Canadian firms', *Revue Canadienne des Sciences de l'Administration*, Vol. 15, No. 2, pp. 180–99.

Luria, D. (1996), 'Why markets tolerate mediocre manufacturing', *Challenge*, July/August, pp. 11–16.

MacGrath, A. (1996), 'Managing distribution channels', *Business Quarterly*, Vol. 60, No. 3, pp. 56–64.

Malone, S. (1985), 'Computerising small business information systems', *Journal of Small Business Management*, Vol. 23, No. 2, pp. 10–16.

Meikle, G. (1997), 'New software supports the smaller manufacturer', *New Zealand Manufacturer*, July, pp. 14–17.

Moad, J. (1997), 'Forging Flexible links', *PC Week*, 15 September, pp. 74–8.

Nonaka, I. (1991), 'The importance of information and knowledge', *Harvard Business Review*, July–August, pp. 65–77.

Pollard, C.E. and Hayne, S. (1998), 'The changing faces of the information system issue in small firms', *International Small Business Journal*, Vol. 16, No. 3, pp. 70–87.

Rabon, L.C. (2000), 'Land's End expands B2B services', *Bobbin*, Columbia, June, pp. 8–14.

Schwarz, B. (2000), 'E-business: new distribution models coming to a site near you', *Transportation & Distribution*, Vol. 41, No. 2, pp. 3–4.

Seybold, P.B. and Marshak, R.T. (1998), *Customers.Com*, Random House, New York.

Storey, J. (1994), *New Wave Manufacturing Strategies*, P. Chapman, London.

Trunick, P.A. (1999), 'ERP: Promise or pipe dream?' *Transportation and Distribution*, January, pp. 23–6.

Tucker, R.B. (1991), *Managing the Future: Ten Driving Forces of Change for the 90s*, Putnam, New York.

Unitec (2000), *Business Information Systems Resource Book for 06.521*, Unitec Faculty of Business, Auckland, New Zealand.

Urbaczewski, A., Jessup, L.M. and Wheeler, B.C. (1998), 'A manager's primer in electronic commerce', *Business Horizons*, Vol. 41, No. 5, pp. 5–17.

Zuckerman, A. (1999), 'Part 1 ERP: pathway to the future of yesterday's buzz?' *Transportation and Distribution*, Vol. 40, No. 8, pp. 37–43.

11

SERVICE MARKETING

LEARNING OBJECTIVES

After studying this chapter you should be able to understand:

1. the unique characteristics of service markets;
2. the marketing implications of variables such as product intangibility and perishability;
3. the nature of service gap theory and the use of the SERVQUAL model to analyse service gap scenarios;
4. the problems associated with competing effectively with large firm service providers;
5. the impact of the Internet on the service marketing process;
6. strategies for avoiding price competition in online service markets;
7. how customer attitudes can influence the selection of a service provision strategy.

CHAPTER SUMMARY

Service firms tend to dominate the small firms sector in most Western nation economies. Service markets exhibit a number of characteristics. These include product intangibility, variation in customer needs and product perishability. As a result the actual quality of service provision can significantly impact customer satisfaction. One approach for determining the cause of gaps between customer expectations and perceptions is to utilise the SERVQUAL model.

In the past small firms were able to outperform large firms on service quality. This is no longer the case, with large firms now often able to offer service quality superior to that of their small firm counterparts. Small firms need to evolve strategies to resist this trend. One possible solution is to acquire scale by joining a small service firm network. The Internet offers new opportunities for the provision of services. Problems differentiating service offerings mean that online trading can encounter intense price competition. To avoid this outcome, small service firms need to identify how to add value to their service offerings. The small firm also has to understand how the attitudes of customers in terms of being transactionally or relationship orientated can influence the management of the service marketing process.

INTRODUCTION

A characteristic of 20th century Western nation economies has been the increasing importance of service industries as a proportion of gross national product (GNP) and as a source of employment. Various factors have contributed to fuelling this growth of the service sector. In consumer markets, higher levels of affluence have permitted individuals to afford more expensive holidays, participate in leisure pursuits and delegate many household functions such as cleaning and repairs to external providers. These same individuals, along with industrial sector firms, are also purchasing technologically more complex products, which has spawned a whole new sector of industry offering specialist hi-tech support services in areas such as design, installation, maintenance and training.

Within the SME sector of Western nation economies, the number of service firms is now much greater than that of small businesses engaged in manufacturing. In part this reflects the growing demand for services. An equally important reason, however, is that many owner/managers are attracted to starting a new service business because entry barriers into most service sectors are quite low. For example, many people wanting to start their own business will opt to enter market sectors such as providing house and garden maintenance services, operating a small guesthouse or hotel or opening a small retail outlet.

An additional factor influencing the high number of small service firm startups in some market sectors is that this is the conventional behaviour of professionals seeking to acquire more control over their career. Thus, for example, many accountants and lawyers start life working in large multi-office practices. Then after some years they leave and start their own practice. Similarly a significant proportion of medical professionals such as doctors and dentists opt to run their own practices in preference to working for large healthcare provider organisations.

A widely accepted definition of service marketing is that provided by Kotler (1997): 'A service is any act or performance that one party can offer to another that is essentially intangible and does not result in the ownership of anything. Its production may or may not be tied to a physical product.' The characteristic of *intangibility* specified in this definition means that services, unlike physical products, cannot be seen, tasted, felt, heard or smelled before purchase. To reduce customer uncertainty, owner/managers will thus often need to concentrate on providing tangible evidence of service quality. Some of the multitude of mechanisms available to small firms for achieving this goal include:

- *place*, which is the physical setting around which the provision of services is delivered (such as an accounting practice based in an office which communicates an image of modernity and efficiency);
- *people*, who are involved in working at the customer/organisation interface (such as well trained, uniformed employees encountered at the reception desk in a small estate agent's office);
- *equipment*, which should be of the necessary standard to rapidly and efficiently assist in the service provision process (such as the latest equipment in a dentist's surgery);
- *communication systems*, which are composed of a diversity of channel flows and associated materials which effectively promote the organisation's desired market position as a service provider (such as the newsletter produced by a legal practice highlighting the types of service which the partners are capable of providing).

A second characteristic of services is their *inseparability*, which captures the fact that many services are simultaneously produced and consumed. The implication of this situation is that for many service outcomes to occur, the provider and the customer must be able to interact with each other. Thus, for example, if a company approaches a small law firm needing urgent advice on a product liability claim and the partner with appropriate specialist knowledge is unavailable, then the potential risk is that the client may be lost and go to another practice which can provide immediate guidance.

A third characteristic of services is their *variability*, caused by both differing customer needs and the capabilities of employees within the provider organisation. Thus, for example, some customers entering a single office, estate agency business may just need information on houses available for sale in the area. Other customers may require the services of the firm to be shown some houses. A small minority may be seeking guidance on investment properties. These individuals will possibly require the services of the only individual in the estate agency who has the necessary experience concerning the range of sophisticated investment instruments which might be utilised to fund a property purchase. Hence in order to manage these types of variability, the estate agent's front line staff will need training to (a) efficiently handle simple enquiries and (b) ensure customers with more complex service needs are smoothly handed on to an appropriately qualified, senior property advisor within the firm.

Unlike manufactured goods, which can be produced and inventoried for later use, a fourth characteristic of services is that they are highly *perishable*. For example, an inability to sell all rooms in a small hotel on any one day means that a proportion of total revenue on this occasion has been lost forever. Sasser (1976) has proposed a number of marketing strategies for responding to the perishability problem which involve actions for more effectively matching supply and demand. These include:

* *differential pricing* to move demand away from peak to off-peak periods (such as a small wine bar offering 'buy one get one free' during its early evening 'happy hour');
* *alternative service provision* to meet the varying needs of customers during peak periods (such as a small retail shop hiring staff to work at weekends);
* *service modification* to ensure that during peak periods the needs of major purchasers receive priority (such as a small tavern not permitting customers to occupy tables in their restaurant area in the evenings unless these patrons are planning to order a meal);
* *demand management systems* which permit the service provider to rapidly (a) identify current available capacity and (b) propose alternative solutions (such as a holiday boat hire business which has an online reservation system to immediately identify whether a specific boat is available and where appropriate, offer alternative dates or boats);
* *temporary capacity expansion* whereby the provider can increase their ability to respond to customer needs during peak periods (such as a small tourist attraction hiring college students as temporary staff during the holiday season);
* *service sharing* where a number of organisations work together and are willing to cross refer customers (such as a group of small accountants forming a marketing network to offer a broader range of specialist services to potential clients);
* *customer participation* in which customers are encouraged to become self providers (such as a small estate agency offering an online house search facility).

SERVICE QUALITY

The unique attributes of service markets described above mean that unlike the case of many tangible goods situations, it is extremely difficult to separate the marketing activity from all of the other functions being undertaken within the small firm. Furthermore the nature of the buyer-seller interaction which occurs at the production/consumption interface can have significant impact on the customer's repeat buying decisions. For example if a customer arrives at a restaurant to discover that a mistake has been made over a reservation, the way the staff resolve this problem will have significant influence on whether the customer can be placated or is 'lost forever'.

Eigler and Langeard (1977) have proposed that there are three main categories of resource involved in the buyer-seller interaction:

* *contact personnel* who interact directly with the customer;
* *physical resources*, human and technical, used by the small firm in undertaking the production, delivery and consumption of the service offering;
* *the customer* who is the person forming a repeat purchase loyalty decision based on the quality of service received to date.

Gronroos (1984) has proposed that management of these three variables is a marketing task which differs from traditional mass marketing because it involves not just marketing staff, but instead draws employees and assets from across the entire organisation. As illustrated by the example case of a small hotel in Figure 11.1, Gronroos has proposed that in service firms there exist three marketing tasks. He describes these as external marketing (the normal formal processes associated with the management of the 4 Ps), interactive marketing (the activities which occur at the buyer-seller interface), and internal marketing. This latter variable is concerned with all of the activities associated with ensuring that (a) every employee is customer conscious and (b) employees and physical assets reflect a commitment to the philosophy that every aspect of the operation is directed towards delivering total

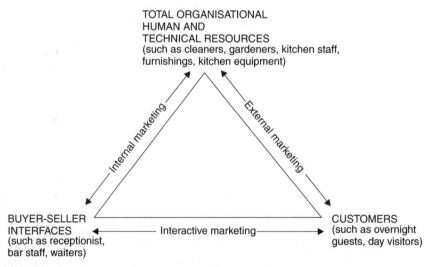

Figure 11.1 Small service firm marketing tasks in a small hotel

customer satisfaction. Internal marketing is a holistic process which integrates the multiple functions of the small firm. This is achieved by ensuring all employees understand all relevant aspects of organisational operations and are motivated to act in a service orientated manner. To achieve this goal the small firm must be able to assess the effectiveness with which the staff interact with customers.

A number of writers have posited that the objective of service satisfaction is to minimise the gap that may exist between customers' desires and their actual experiences. In the development of a feasible technique for measuring expectations and perceptions, possibly one of the most important contributions has been made by Parasuraman, Berry and Zeithmal (Parasuraman *et al.* 1985, 1988; Zeithmal *et al.* 1990). This team implemented a carefully sequenced research project to evolve an effective model for assessing the effectiveness and quality of the service provision process. The first stage of their research was to identify those variables that could be used to determine how customers form their expectations. They identified the following five variables:

- *reliability* – the ability to perform the promised service dependably and accurately;
- *tangibles* – the images created by the appearance of physical facilities, equipment, personnel and communication materials;
- *responsiveness* – the willingness to help customers and provide prompt service;
- *assurance* – the process by which the knowledge, ability and courtesy of employees engenders customer trust and confidence in the service provider;
- *empathy* – created by the caring, individualised attention which employees offer the customer.

Having identified these generic expectations, Parasuraman *et al.* created their SERVQUAL model to define the following five types of gap that can exist between expectations and perceptions:

- *gap 1* – between the customer's expectations and the organisation's perceptions of customer need;
- *gap 2* – between the organisation's perceptions and the definition of appropriate standards for the quality of service to be delivered;
- *gap 3* – between the specified standards of service and the actual performance of the service provision process undertaken by the organisation's employees;
- *gap 4* – between actual service delivered and the nature of the service promise made in any communications with the customer;
- *gap 5* – the overall gap between customer expectations and perceptions created by the combined influence of gaps 1 to 4.

The magnitude and influence of the five service gaps can be measured using these authors' SERVQUAL tool. The technique involves surveying customers to determine their expectations and perceptions by asking them to compare their perspectives of desired service with experience of actual service received. Other gap dimensions are measured by surveying employee attitudes about various aspects of operations within their organisation (such as the existence of quality standards, mechanisms established for integrating all aspects of the service delivery process across the entire organisation).

Application of the SERVQUAL tool can be illustrated by specifying possible factors influencing clients' views of the quality of services being provided by a small accountancy practice (Figure 11.2). Type 1 service gaps would occur if the clients and the practice held differing perspectives about which are the critical factors influencing customer expectations. Type 2 service gaps would occur if the senior partner(s) and clients had very differing views about which formal standards are important in terms of monitoring customer satisfaction. Avoiding the occurrence of type 3 service gaps will probably require that the practice invests in actions to optimise the service provision process. These actions could include expanding the provision of staff training programmes, increasing the number of accounting technicians to improve the speed of task execution, and exploiting electronic technology for both internal and external data interchange. Nevertheless all of these investments are of little benefit if communication between employees and between the practice and the clients results in promises over issues such as the time to complete service tasks not being reflected in actual outcomes. Where communication and actual experience differs, this will lead to the emergence of a type 4 service gap. The combined influence of service gaps 1 to 4 is reflected in a type 5 service gap: the difference between clients' expectations and their actual service experience.

SERVICE MARKETING STRATEGIES

The fundamental strategic philosophy that small firms should avoid confrontations with large companies and compete by offering a differentiated product is completely valid in the context of service sector operations. Hence success as a small service provider often occurs because a small firm identifies an unfulfilled specialist need and occupies this niche ahead of competition.

One example of this type of service market strategy is provided by the specialist clothing company, Mothers In Motion (Adler 1999). The founder, Bess Hilpert, is a marathon runner who discovered while expecting her third child that finding running shorts to accommodate her ever increasing size meant monthly trips to her local clothing store. Her solution was to become a wholesaler for a diverse range of sportswear for pregnant athletes. The product range includes unitards, yoga suits, extra-supportive sports bras and

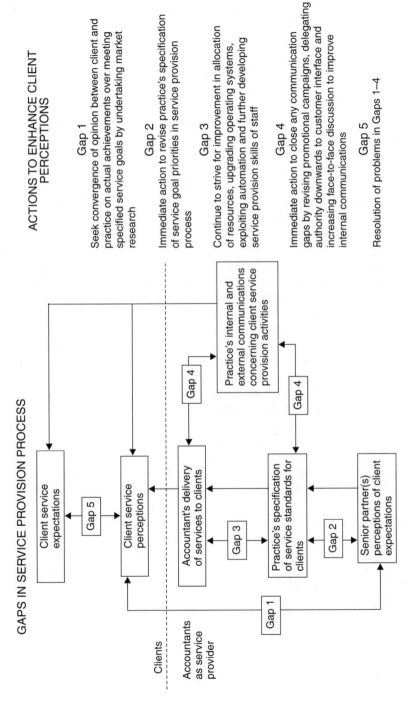

Figure 11.2 Service gap theory applied to a small accountancy practice

ACTIONS TO ENHANCE CLIENT PERCEPTIONS

Gap 1
Seek convergence of opinion between client and practice on actual achievements over meeting specified service goals by undertaking market research

Gap 2
Immediate action to revise practice's specification of service goal priorities in service provision process

Gap 3
Continue to strive for improvement in allocation of resources, upgrading operating systems, exploiting automation and further developing service provision skills of staff

Gap 4
Immediate action to close any communication gaps by revising promotional campaigns, delegating authority downwards to customer interface and increasing face-to-face discussion to improve internal communications

Gap 5
Resolution of problems in Gaps 1–4

GAPS IN SERVICE PROVISION PROCESS

Client service expectations

Gap 5

Client service perceptions

Practice's internal and external communications concerning client service provision activities

Gap 4

Gap 4

Accountant's delivery of services to clients

Gap 3

Practice's specification of service standards for clients

Gap 2

Senior partner(s) perceptions of client expectations

Clients

Accountants as service provider

Gap 1

swimming costumes. Based in Round Rock, Texas, the company has achieved distribution in maternity boutiques, athletics supplies stores and health clubs. The firm's success has attracted the attention of larger retailers and Mothers In Motion products are now stocked by the upmarket department store, Nordstroms.

Unfortunately, although occupying a premium price/premium service market niche is intuitively appealing to the small service firm owner/manager, a number of factors can create obstacles when acting to adopt this type of market positioning. One factor is the problem that customers may be extremely price conscious and hence have little interest in being offered a premium priced, superior service value proposition. This is the situation facing many small accountancy practices whose primary customer group is small firms. This client group tends to have minimal appreciation of how an accountant can assist its business operations. As a result it has a tendency only to be interested in paying the lowest possible price for those services necessary to ensure that at year end an acceptable tax filing is made to the Government.

A second factor is that as service sector products move into the maturity phase on the product life cycle curve, customers increasingly tend to seek a standardised offering and in many cases, purchase decisions are based upon lowest possible price. Concurrently any interest in the quality of service which clients may have exhibited during the introduction or growth phases of the product life cycle can be expected to be significantly less important in the maturity phase (Tordoir 1994). Lindahl and Beyers (1999) have generated empirical data to support this concept. These researchers surveyed small producer service firms across a diversity of market sectors. They found that in mature, highly competitive market sectors such as financial services and insurance, price tends to be the primary variable influencing the customer purchase decision. This situation can be contrasted with sectors such as R&D and IT consultancy, which are still in an introduction or growth stage. Consequently with clients seeking specialist, knowledge based services, factors such as established reputation, ability to provide expertise and commitment to building long term relationships are most likely to dominate customers' choice of service provider.

The other factor influencing the degree to which customers are price orientated is the behaviour of large firms. In the past, small service firms could often protect themselves from this source of competition by being able to deliver a higher level of service quality. More recently, however, large service firms, having recognised that poor service quality can damage market image, have adopted a dual strategy of offering both low prices and outstanding service. In the retail sector, large firms have recognised the benefits of adopting TQM and JIT operating philosophies to offer their customers a wide choice of very competitively priced goods. Additionally these retailers are using the wealth of data generated by checkout scanners, credit card purchases and loyalty cards to gain an in-depth understanding of how to customise their service portfolio to minimise the gap between customers' expectations and their actual shopping experience.

EXAMPLE: DRIVEN TO DESPAIR

Oswald and Boulton (1995), in their study of the US wholesale drug distribution industry, have provided a well documented example of what can happen in a service sector market when large firms decide to use both price and service excellence to destroy all potential sources of competition. Over the last 20 years the US drug industry has faced societal, legislative and technological change. With both rising healthcare costs and an ageing population, the drive is on to find the most efficient ways of delivering all aspects of medical care.

The fact that American consumers face the situation that over 50 per cent of their prescription drug requirements are not covered by healthcare insurance has created pressure to reduce product costs. At all levels within the industry from manufacturers, through wholesalers to retail outlets, major mergers and acquisitions have occurred as large companies have fought to find ways of capturing economies of scale. The first small business sector impacted by this trend was that of independent pharmacies. In the face of rising competition from national chains such as Wall-Mart, independent outlets' share of the 'prescriptions filled' market has fallen dramatically.

Historically the independent regional drug wholesalers were an important element in the US drug distribution chain. What has happened, however, is that national wholesalers have moved to achieve an even greater market share of this business. The industry leader is McKesson Corporation which has achieved market dominance through a strategy of offering the broadest product range, the lowest prices and highest level of service quality to retail customers. This has been achieved through a mix of exploiting its buying power to drive down procurement costs whilst concurrently investing in automated IT logistics management systems. The company has also created an online information service to provide pharmacies with access to knowledge about the medical effectiveness of the latest available drug treatments.

Another giant national wholesaler is Bergen Brunswig Corporation which through acquisition and the construction of regional mega-distribution centres is able to offer retail customers and hospitals a next day, full product line delivery service. The company's distribution centres exploit technology such as automated picking and totally computerised order entry and transaction management systems. This latter capability means that retail customers no longer have to be involved in the lengthy process of managing the volumes of paperwork that were a characteristic of a pre-electronic era.

Even regional wholesalers that previously survived by occupying a specialist market position are finding national firms developing the capability to enter these previously well protected niches. A lead protagonist in this field is Moore Medical. This company has exploited its 20 years of catalogue marketing and ten years of tele-sales marketing to enter market segments such as emergency medical services, offering both a rapid, customised response to a diverse range of customer groups.

To remain competitive in the face of national wholesalers offering lower prices and increasingly superior service quality, regional operations are struggling to survive. Some have adopted the philosophy of joining independent drug whole-saler groups as a path to offering a full range of generic drugs. These actions are usually accompanied by developing free advisory services for retail customers such as merchandising, inventory management, pre-pricing and electronic order entry systems. How long such strategies will protect these smaller oper-ations is questionable and many industry observers predict that in the 21st century there will be no way small firms can continue to survive in the US drug whole-saling business.

FIGHTING TO GROW

When owner/managers perceive that large firms pose a threat to future growth, there are a number of response options available. One way of describing these options is to assume there are two dimensions of action. Dimension 1 is to seek ways to increase the size of the small business and thereby reduce the scale gap that exists between the business and large firm competitors. The other dimension is the classic small firm strategy of adopt-ing a niche position to avoid direct confrontation with large firms. Combining these two dimensions permits the creation of the alternative position matrix shown in Figure 11.3.

Where the intensity of competition from large firms is increasing, then those small firms which decide to offer standard services and not implement any action to acquire greater scale, can usually expect to encounter difficulties sustaining their current level of sales. In Figure 11.3, this decision is described as a 'crumbs from table' strategy. In the UK, small shops in rural locations provide an example of this scenario. Most of the local inhabitants will do their weekly major shopping in large multinational outlets located in or just outside the nearby large town. Their purchases in the local shop will tend to be restricted to the occasional items they forgot to purchase during their weekly shop and frequently purchased, time perishable goods such as daily newspapers.

A growth strategy based upon deepening the niche requires the small service firm to identify an opportunity that can be exploited through the further development of the organisation's service portfolio. Lowry *et al.* (1999) describe a case example of this strategy being used by an insurance broker in

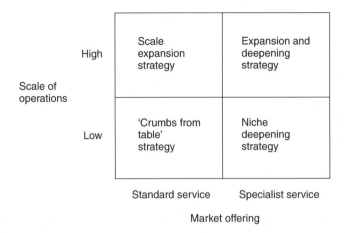

	Standard service	Specialist service
High	Scale expansion strategy	Expansion and deepening strategy
Low	'Crumbs from table' strategy	Niche deepening strategy

Scale of operations

Market offering

Figure 11.3 An alternative service positioning matrix

the USA. The six partners in a Midwest firm recognised that the large national US insurance companies had adopted a strategy of market share increase by cutting out intermediaries and selling direct to customers. Survival in the face of this trend was highly questionable. Analysis of opportunity revealed that an under served national market was meeting the insurance needs of independently owned hotels, motels and guesthouses. To acquire national recognition of their expertise in the niche, the firm developed a portfolio of customised insurance products for the US hospitality industry. Market development was achieved through a mix of direct selling, mailshots and the appointment of agents elsewhere in the country. Added momentum was achieved by the firm (a) leading the creation of a national association of small firms involved in the US hospitality industry and (b) launching a hospitality industry newsletter.

Using scale to combat large firm competition usually requires the business to rapidly increase in actual size or move to form a business relationship with other organisations. Rapid size increase involves the owner/manager having to consider the strategy of growth through acquisition. Most owner/managers do not have the financial resources to consider such an option. Hence a more usual route for increasing scale is to enter into some form of business alliance (or 'network'). Reijnders and Verhallen (1996) have researched the role of alliances within the menswear sector of the Netherlands retail industry. The sector contains national chains, small retailers who are members of a retailer cooperative alliance, and independent retailers. The share of sales by each of these three types of trading operation is 45 per cent, 35 per cent and 20 per cent respectively.

Within the retail alliance, members cooperate over activities such as combining their purchases to obtain discounts from suppliers, operating a centralised computer system, pooling promotional resources and exchanging market information. The researchers found that compared to independent retailers, the alliance members were able to offer a broader product range, higher levels of promotional activity, higher sales per outlet and higher profitability.

Small accountancy practices rarely have the staff resources to deliver the broad range of financial management and consultancy services offered by multi-office national and international accounting firms. A common solution to this problem is for the practice to enter into horizontal alliances with other small practices (Wang and Mohen 1997). These alliances can achieve greater geographic coverage either by forming alliances with other practices elsewhere in the country or by linking with other practices to gain access to specialist skills which the first practice lacks. These alliances can be extended by forming further alliances with organisations in other sectors such as the legal professions and the IT industry.

Traditionally in the UK, the estate agency industry has been the preserve of small independent practices. In the late 1980s, however, a change in the Financial Services Act caused a number of financial institutions such as banks and insurance companies to perceive the estate agency industry as an area of opportunity (Bishop 1993). The primary interest of these major firms was not in selling houses but in gaining direct access to consumers who would be in the market for mortgage and insurance services. Their market entry strategy was that of acquiring numerous small estate agents and rebranding these operations as multi-office, national entities. For the small estate agents who remained in the market, aspirations of growth were greatly frustrated because they could not compete with large national firms who were exploiting economies of scale in areas such as promotion, administration and procurement. The few small practices which attempted to sustain growth in the face of these market constraints tended to adopt the joint strategic solution of seeking scale and deepening their market niches. The market niche deepening typically focussed on specialising in upmarket property, offering clients a customised, relationship orientated marketing service. This operational philosophy demanded that these estate agents begin to exhibit a high level of market presence. This could not be achieved if the estate agent remained a single office operation. Achievement of scale under these circumstances usually involved a dual strategy of (a) forming formal alliances with like minded operations elsewhere in the country and (b) initiating merger or acquisition programmes.

EXAMPLE: GROWING PAINS

Small service businesses are often successful because the owner/manager is personally involved in both service delivery and close monitoring of the activities of all employees. Furthermore it is not unusual that many of these firms are family owned businesses in which close relatives of the owner are employed in management roles, further reinforcing the commitment to achieving service excellence. A common problem in this scenario, however, is that to sustain business growth new managers have to be hired from outside the firm and it becomes difficult to sustain the family based, hands on, personal commitment to service quality.

Umbreit (1996) documents the problems of scaling up a family business in his analysis of the San Francisco based Fairmont Hotels group. Benjamin Swig purchased the original Fairmont Hotel in 1946. Market positioning was based upon offering a premium priced, premium quality, guest customised service. This was linked to a strong focus on building long term relationships with guests to sustain a high level of repeat purchase. In 1965, the company embarked on an expansion programme, purchasing hotels in New Orleans, Dallas, Chicago and San José. The family did not have the resources to manage all these new acquisitions and hence day-to-day operations passed into the hands of professional managers.

In the 1980s, the US hotel industry faced an unprecedented period of capacity expansion by the major national chains. The outcome was the emergence of excess capacity that forced all hotels to increase promotional expenditure and reduce room rates. By 1991 Fairmont Hotels was on the brink of insolvency and the Swig family decided to hire a new CEO, Bob Small. This individual had extensive experience of running successful upmarket hospitality operations.

Upon arrival Small found the operation was still run as a family business with a highly autocratic, centralised management structure that had created a top-down model in which lower level management perceived themselves as lacking the authority to make any decisions. Small invoked a number of major changes in organisational structure and replaced director level staff whom he perceived as exhibiting inadequate managerial skills. Following numerous focus group meetings with staff around the country, he instigated a complete retraining programme for staff and created a service quality assessment system which management and employees could utilise to identify areas where service quality required improvement.

Corporate clients were the core source of company revenue. Bob Small realised that the personal relationship which the Swig family had built with these customers over the years had not been sustained by the non-family management staff. His response was to become personally heavily involved in visiting corporate customers and concurrently ensuring that all key managers across the group understood that frequent meetings with corporate customers were a vital component of their assigned job roles. A more flexible approach to managing corporate business was also introduced with the aim not of maximising price per room but adjusting prices to improve occupancy rates and thereby maximise revenue per room. For example when Apple Computers announced that because of internal financial difficulties, they could no longer afford the room rate at the Fairmont, the hotel immediately reduced the tariff on the understanding it would remain at this lower level until Apple's financial position improved. This focus on maximising occupancy and being flexible on pricing during a period when poor economic conditions were impacting corporate travel expenditure in the US was rewarded by increased corporate sector sales as the American economy began to recover. By 1994, in all its five locations, Fairmont Hotels was consistently outperforming the competition.

THE INTERNET

Potential entrepreneurs have not been slow to recognise the possible opportunities available through utilising the Internet as a new channel through which to market and deliver services. Unfortunately a significant proportion of these individuals appears to have been so dazzled by the stories of Californians becoming overnight e-millionaires that they have ignored the fundamental rule of survival for small business: that revenue must exceed costs.

In 1998, for example, Mr Bowlin in Cedar Falls, Iowa launched a virtual bookstore www.Postively-You.com from his spare bedroom (Gajilan 2000). His selected market niche was self help and motivational books. Spurred on by early success, he quit his day job, raised $90,000, rented office space and hired employees. His next move was to start undercutting Amazon.com on prices and broadening the product range. Rapid sales growth caused the bank handling the credit card sales to become worried about the firm's book distribution capabilities. The bank decided to delay forwarding monies received from credit card purchases, and within months the cash starved business went into liquidation.

Similar business failure stories are now emerging from elsewhere in the world. In New Zealand, FlyingPig tried to model its operation on Amazon. com (Hendrey and De Boni 2000). Within months of the launch, a number of the original investors pulled out. In November 2000, the company was sold to a publishing business that owns a number of offline and online magazines. Another New Zealand business, Beauty Direct, was created as a virtual shopfront selling cosmetics. The original investors have seen their shares drop from the listing price of 25c to a low of 7c. The founders commented that break even will take at least three years to achieve. They have how now sold a majority shareholding to CS Company, a privately owned New Zealand cosmetics distribution and marketing company.

EXAMPLE: SERVICE FIRMS CAN SUCCEED

One group of small service firms that has clearly benefited from the Internet is that of software developers specialising in resolving e-commerce operating problems (Tomlinson *et al.* 2000). One example is eTango based in Barcelona, Spain. The company's sole product is a database that firms can use to store answers to customers' questions and thereby streamline e-mail responses to enquiries. Once installed the database continually updates the 'frequently asked questions' section of a firm's website. It also allows customers to use keywords when searching for an answer to a question. If a question has never been asked before, the question is routed to an employee who can then place both the question and their answer back into the eTango database.

Another success story is the new technology provider, Fantastic Corporation, based in Switzerland. This company's software assists its customers to streamline the creation, transmission and viewing of broadband data. The system uses Internet protocols so it can be used on any kind of network such as satellite, cable, digital television or wireless.

Major online winners in other service sectors have been existing firms that have supplemented their terrestrial service outlets with the addition of a website transaction channel (Amire 2000). Sees Candies in San Francisco markets its confectionery products through a chain of retail outlets. In 1998, the firm launched a website and has found that over 60 per cent of online sales are coming from consumers living in areas where Sees Candies does not have a retail outlet. The website is perceived by customers as a convenient extension of the company's mail order business, permitting site visitors to view 98 per cent of the products featured in the firm's mail order catalogue.

Achieving market awareness for an online operation can require significant expenditure on promotional activity. One way round this problem is to achieve greater scale by bringing together a number of retailers on a common site. This is the philosophy underlying the creation of www.planetchocolat.com. This company's website features both upmarket, brand name chocolates and a number of family owned confectionery stores. Having attracted firms such as Chocolates by Bernard, a Canadian firm with 40 outlets, the founder of the business, Arjun Reddy, is now aiming to build a global online chocolate operation.

When considering whether the Internet represents an opportunity or a threat, the owner/manager needs to understand that services differ from tangible goods in the degree to which they possess search, experience and credence attributes. With tangible goods, the customer is able to examine the physical nature of the product during the search phase prior to purchase. In contrast, evaluation of services tends to come only from the experience of consumption and the market reputation, or credence, of the service provider. This situation, linked to the lack of physical differentiation among competing offerings, can often result in price being the key variable influencing purchase behaviour in service markets (Berry and Yadav 1996).

In an offline world, small service providers may partially or totally avoid price based competition because potential customers lack either the time or the ability to undertake a detailed price comparison search prior to purchase. The advent of e-commerce has totally changed this situation because at the touch of a button, potential customers can price compare either by visiting different websites or by accessing the growing number of online intermediaries who provide information on price variations between service suppliers. Under these circumstances the power in an online world has passed from the supplier into the hands of the customer. Online customers are in a position to influence behaviour within service supply chains. This will mean that small firms will either have to become more price competitive or alternatively, find new ways of differentiating themselves from competition.

In many markets, especially where there are minimal opportunities to differentiate services (such as home and car insurance), as price becomes the dominant purchase decision factor this will result in many services becoming commodity goods. Determining how to respond to the commoditisation of a market sector will require a careful reassessment of the online marketing strategies of many small e-business operations. In some cases the small firm may be unable to identify a mechanism by which to differentiate its offering from competition. The probable outcome in these situations is that the price war winners will be large firms which are able to exploit economies of scale to fund their survival.

For those small firms which decide to implement a strategy designed to avoid participation in price wars, there are a number of options available that have already been validated in the world of offline service provision (Berry and Yadav 1996). One approach is to recognise that sometimes, one firm's price war is an opportunity for another firm to help customers more effectively search for the best price proposition. For example, a small travel agent can now use online search engines to find for its business clients the lowest possible prices for all aspects of an overseas travel package.

Another approach to avoiding price wars is to shift the market sector away from being transactionally orientated by attempting to build a relationship with individual customers. One way of relationship building is to seek to enter into a long term contract with the customer. This approach is relatively common in the provision of professional services in business to business service markets. The aim of the supplier is to exploit the stability of the contract period as an opportunity to develop new or improved products that can enhance the content and delivery of their service provision portfolio.

Some service market customers are willing to form relationships with providers who offer convenience and time saving as core components of their service offering. To exploit this strategy, the small service firm will need to examine ways of creating 'bundles of services'. For example, an insurance broker offering online cover can develop an insurance bundle for small businesses which for a single premium provides health and safety, employee liability, theft and flood damage insurance. Given the very clear risk of price competition and commoditisation in online service markets, it is critical that the owner/manager undertake a regular assessment of their firm's price/value

	Extremely over priced service offering	Over priced service offering	Superior performance service package
High			
Average	Over priced service offering	Average value service package	Superior value OR poorly priced service package
Low	Economy service package	Superior value OR poorly priced service package	Extreme value OR very poorly priced service package

PRICE (label at left)

| Low | Average | High |

CUSTOMER PERCEPTION OF VALUE OF SERVICE
PROPOSITION

Figure 11.4   An e-commerce price/value matrix

market position. One way to achieve this objective is to consider that there are two dimensions influencing positioning. One is the pricing of the online service proposition relative to prevailing prices within a market. It is suggested that this can be classified as either low, average or high. The second dimension is customers' perceptions of the relative value of the firm's service proposition. Again this can be classified as low, average or high. Having acquired data on these two dimensions, the owner/manager can assess the firm's online positioning by creating a matrix of the type shown in Figure 11.4. If the small firm's offering falls somewhere along the three diagonal cells, then this will usually mean a correct decision has been made over the nature of the service package and price available to the customer. If a small firm's position is above the diagonal, immediate attention is necessary because it would appear customers perceive the service offering as over priced. Alternatively if actual positioning falls below the diagonal, the small firm needs to determine whether this was an intentional action to support a 'superior value' service proposition or if a pricing error has been made. Should the latter be the explanation, the owner/manager will have to assess whether a pricing move, or a revision in the nature of the service proposition, should be instigated.

CUSTOMER SATISFACTION

Errors at the buyer-seller interface or during the execution of the internal processes associated with service delivery can severely reduce customer satisfaction. This business risk has caused widespread debate on how best to manage service sector organisations. In two classic articles, Levitt (1972, 1976) eloquently argued for the adoption of a manufacturing orientation in the management of services. He believes that this approach allows for (a) simplification of tasks, (b) clear division of labour, (c) substitution of equipment and systems for employees and (d) minimal decision making being required of the employees.

Early entrepreneurs in the fast food chain industry such as Ray Croc of McDonalds very effectively demonstrated the validity of Levitt's proposals. Many small firms have learnt from McDonalds' success. They also use clearly defined procedures: assembling the order, placing it on the tray and collecting the money. In the 'back room', other operatives execute tasks designed to ensure the rapid and efficient production of food of uniform quality. This manufacturing orientation approach permits the operation of an efficient, low cost, high volume food service operation which is also able to concurrently deliver a high level of customer satisfaction.

The concept of the industrialisation of service operations has not been without its critics. Some academics argue that the approach is not only dehumanising, it also results in an inability to respond to heterogeneous customer needs because employees are forced to respond to all situations by adhering to the rigid guidelines laid down in the organisation's operating policy manual. Zemke and Schaaf (1989) believe service excellence is more likely to be achieved by 'empowerment', which involves encouraging and rewarding employees who exercise initiative and imagination. A more balanced position has been adopted by Bowen and Lawler (1997). They posit that appropriateness of a service philosophy is a contingency issue; namely an industralisation or empowerment orientation will be dependent upon the market in which the firm operates and the influence of senior management on the firm's internal culture and upon the nature of existing internal organisational processes. Accepting these proposal it is possible to construct a comparative analysis of the type shown in Table 11.1.

A transactionally orientated small service provider can reasonably assume that customers will accept an automated system for providing feedback on order entry, payment acceptance and shipment confirmation. However on the basis of the factors of influence shown in Table 11.1 it seems reasonable to suggest that as customer orientation moves from a transactional to a relationship based scenario, a small service provider will need to consider complementing automated online service provision with access to service delivery by employees. Young (1999) has suggested that in the next few years the main focus in exploiting new technologies will be on those directed at developing a seamless service by integrating automated Internet transaction systems with call centre technologies. A typical scenario would be a website providing basic information, automated transaction services and a 'call me' button. The customer facing problems or needing more detailed information would use

Table 11.1   Factors influencing the service style orientation

Factor	Range of response to factors	
Owner/manager orientation	Autocratic	Delegator
Customer orientation	Transactional	Relationship
Service product need	Standard solutions	New, innovative solutions
Business environment	Predictable, stable	Changing, unstable
Service delivery technology	Simple	Complex
Firm's closeness to customer orientation	Low	High
Firm's service solution orientation	Established, well known	Applying new approaches
Average skills of workforce	Adequate for executing standard tasks	Capable of executing complex tasks

the call button facility to be automatically routed, via the same line as the Internet connection using voice-over Internet protocol (VoIP), to an employee of the firm.

Dannenburg and Kellner (1998) believe there will a convergence of technology in the provision of online services to concurrently satisfy the needs of both transactionally and relationship orientated customers. They posit the next really important advance in this area will be picture telephony and video conferencing technology being utilised to upgrade the quality of human intervention within the online customer/supplier interaction process. The problem confronting the smaller firm is that such technology will be expensive and that large firms, by exploiting their economy of scale, are likely to be the early adopters of mixed machine and people intervention systems. The probable solution for the small service provider will be to outsource this aspect of their operations to Internet service providers who can offer both website hosting and call centre services.

The outsourcing of the online customer interface raises the question of how the small service firm can ensure that it remains capable of delivering service excellence. This is especially the case where the small firm is seeking to execute the dual strategy of simultaneously delivering lower cost outputs while concurrently maximising personalisation and customisation of services. Even before the advent of the Internet, Quinn and Paquette (1990) argued it is merely dogma that strategic conflicts exist between low cost and high flexibility in service sector scenarios. In their view, achieving both aims relies on two factors. Firstly there is need to design service systems that permit all employees to have access to data concerning their role in customer satisfaction: for example the firm's accounting staff having access to data concerning customers' online ordering and invoice payment histories. The second need is to use technology to permit inexperienced people to perform very sophisticated tasks: for example operatives in manufacturing having online access to an online procurement system that permits assessment of scheduled arrival dates for out-of-stock raw materials. In the process of achieving these goals, the organisation will probably recognise that new organisational forms are now demanded in order to optimise employee productivity.

Owner/managers traditionally prefer to remain in absolute control over all key decision making activities. However effectively exploiting the response speed and decision flexibility offered by computer based information systems means that owner/managers must be willing to delegate authority. For it is only if a significant proportion of decision making authority is delegated that the small firm can ensure that employees are empowered to make the best possible decision for immediately satisfying customer needs.

Large international organisations such as accountancy and consultancy firms offering complex client-specific services have already moved to exploit IT as a support system to ensure customers are provided with leading edge services. Technologies such as Lotus Notes and videoconferencing have permitted these organisations to reorientate themselves into networked structures which use electronic media to ensure the dispersed nodes of their service operation can continually remain in touch with each other. One of the major benefits of their system is that an individual facing a difficult client problem can now use the organisation's electronic bulletin board to discover if anybody elsewhere in the world may have already evolved an effective solution.

Clearly single location small service firms will not have to be too concerned about investing in sophisticated electronic data interchange systems to ensure employees are optimising knowledge sharing as a component in delivering service satisfaction. Once, however, small firms become involved in using networks to acquire greater scale of operation, then rapidity of information interchange can become a critical issue. This is not a subject that has yet received much consideration by small business researchers. Anecdotal evidence would tend to suggest that professional service firm networks are beginning to adopt common electronic data interchange systems using software such as Lotus Notes.

DISCUSSION QUESTIONS

1. Review the unique characteristics of service markets. How do these characteristics influence the service marketing process?
2. Discuss how the SERVQUAL model can be of assistance in understanding and managing service gaps which may confront an organisation.
3. Review how the Internet is influencing the effective management of the service marketing process.

REFERENCES

Adler, C. (1999), 'Mothers in Motion', *Fortune*, 25th October, pp. 27–8.

Amire, R. (2000), 'Confectioners harness e-commerce', *Candy Industry*, Northbrook, Illinois, May, pp. 6–8.

Berry, L.L. and Yadav, M.S. (1996), 'Capture and communicate value in the pricing of services', *Sloan Management Review*, Vol. 37, No. 4, pp. 41–52.

Bishop, P. (1993), 'The changing structure of estate agency', *The Service Industries Journal*, Vol. 13, No. 4, pp. 307–16.

Bowen, D.E. and Lawler, E.E. (1992), 'The empowerment of service workers: what, why, how and when', *Sloan Management Review*, Spring, pp. 31–9.

Dannenberg, M. and Kellner, D. (1998), 'The bank of tomorrow with today's technology', *International Journal of Bank Marketing*, Vol. 16, No. 2, pp. 8–16.

Eigler, P. and Langeard, E. (1977), 'Services as systems: Marketing implications', In Eigler, P. and Langeard, E. (eds), *Marketing Consumer Services*, Marketing Science Institute, Cambridge, Mass., pp. 89–91.

Gajilan, A.T. (2000), 'Wish I'd thought of that!' *Fortune*, 15th May, pp. 3–7.

Gronroos, C. (1984), 'A service quality model and its marketing implications', *European Journal of Marketing*, Vol. 18, No. 4, pp. 36–44.

Hendrey, S. and De Boni, D. (2000), 'Rough landing for flying e-tailer', *Business Herald*, Auckland, Section E, p. 1.

Kotler, P. (1997), *Marketing Management: Analysis, Planning, Implementation and Control*, 9th edn, Prentice-Hall, Upper Saddle River, New Jersey.

Levitt, T. (1972), 'Production-line approach to service', *Harvard Business Review*, Sept.–Oct., pp. 41–52.

Levitt, T. (1976), 'Industrialisation of services', *Harvard Business Review*, Sept.–Oct., pp. 63–74.

Lindahl, P. and Beyers, W.B. (1999), 'The creation of competitive advantage by producer service establishments', *Economic Geography*, Vol. 75, No. 1, pp. 1–20.

Lowry, J.R., Avial, S.M. and Baird, R. (1999), 'Developing a niche strategy for insurance agents', *Chartered Property and Casualty Underwriters Journal*, Vol. 52, No. 2, pp. 74–83.

Oswald, S.L. and Boulton, W.R. (1995), 'Obtaining industry control: The case of the pharmaceutical distribution industry', *California Management Review*, Vol. 38, No. 1, pp. 138–53.

Parasuraman, A., Zeithmal, V.A. and Berry, L.L. (1985), 'A conceptual model of service quality and its implications for future research', *Journal of Marketing*, Vol. 49, Fall, pp. 34–45.

Parasuraman, A., Zeithmal, V.A. and Berry, L.L. (1988), 'SERVQUAL: A multiple item scale for measuring consumer perceptions of service quality', *Journal of Retailing*, Vol. 64, No. 1, pp. 12–23.

Quinn, J.B. and Paquette, P.C. (1990), 'Technology in services: creating organisational revolutions', *Sloan Management Review*, Winter, pp. 67–78.

Reijnders, W.J.M. and Verhallen, T.M.M. (1996), 'Strategic alliances among small retailing firms: Empirical evidence from the Netherlands', *Journal of Small Business Management*, Vol. 34, No. 1, pp. 36–45.

Sasser, W.E. (1976), 'Match supply and demand in service industries', *Harvard Business Review*, Nov.–Dec., pp. 133–40.

Tomlinson, R., Fox, J., Murphy, C. and Kahn, J. (2000), 'Why is this man smiling?' *Fortune*, 24th July, pp. 8–25.

Tordoir, P. (1994), 'Transactions of professional services and spatial systems', *Tijdschrift voor Economische en Sociale Geografie*, Vol. 85, pp. 322–32.

Umbreit, W.T. (1996), 'Fairmont Hotels' turnaround strategy', *Cornell Hotel and Restaurant Quarterly*, Vol. 37, No. 4, pp. 50–61.

Wang, C.L. and Mowen, J.C. (1997), 'AIM: A new perspective on relationship marketing for professional services', *Journal of Professional Services Marketing*, Vol. 15, No. 2, pp. 55–68.

Young, K. (1999), 'Customer care centres on profit', *The Banker*, October, pp. 132–4.

Zeithmal, V.A., Parasuraman, A. and Berry, L.L. (1990), *Delivering Quality Service: Balancing Customer Perceptions and Expectations*, The Free Press, New York.

Zemke, R. and Schaaf, (1989), *'The Service Edge: 101 Companies that Profit from Customer Care*, New American Library, New York.

12

INTERNATIONAL MARKETING

LEARNING OBJECTIVES

After studying this chapter you should be able to understand:

1. the importance of international business;
2. the various theories posited to explain how firms move into international markets;
3. the chain model for guiding the overseas market entry process;
4. the business implications of the world economy becoming increasingly globalised;
5. the factors likely to influence the success of firms in overseas markets;
6. the theories associated with the importance of planning and market research to support effective overseas market entry;
7. the need to vision futures when seeking to succeed in global markets;
8. the future conditions firms can expect to encounter in global markets.

CHAPTER SUMMARY

The level of international trade can greatly impact a nation's economy. Various theories have been posited to explain success in international markets. One theory presents overseas market entry as a natural progression from having succeeded in a domestic market. The chain model proposes a series of incremental approaches associated with scaling up overseas marketing activities. Validation of the chain model has proved somewhat difficult in the case of small firms, which tend to rely on social or business networks when determining how best to become international operations. As the world economy has become globalised, even small firms need to begin to modify and adapt their products to compete in this changing world. The degree of adaptation will be influenced by factors such as the nature of the product, owner/manager attitudes and complexity of market systems.

Research on export success reveals a number of influencing variables. It is also thought that propensity to enter overseas markets is greater among larger firms. Conventional wisdom also suggests that careful planning and market research are critical performance determinants in overseas markets. Here again research on actual small firm practices suggests that many owner/managers are willing to ignore such wisdom and adopt a somewhat intuitive, entrepreneurial approach when considering overseas market entry. Longer term success in global markets requires visioning ahead of competition. A study by Tradenz has provided a template of the future market scenarios that firms can expect to encounter increasingly over time.

INTRODUCTION

The economic policies of governments across the world make the important fundamental assumption that export performance is a major determinant for sustained growth in gross national product (GNP). This is a valid assumption, no matter whether countries are developed nation economies exporting high technology goods such as telecommunications products or developing nations exporting basic commodities such as food products. The earliest theories concerning the internationalisation of firms have evolved from neoclassical economics and industrial trade theory (Coviello and McCauley 1999). Known as the foreign direct investment theory (FDI), this view of internationalisation posits that firms choose an optimal strategy for minimising transaction costs. The theory proposes, for example, that a firm might decide to enter an overseas market because it is able to offer goods or services at a lower cost than the incumbent domestic producers within this market.

A fundamental assumption in the application of FDI theory is that the decision maker within a firm exhibits bounded rationality. Such an assumption has caused questions to be posed about whether FDI theory is applicable in the context of the SME sector. This is because identification of behaviour bounded in rationality by owner/managers has proved difficult in any market, let alone in the context of an export market scenario. Furthermore researchers seeking to empirically validate FDI theory have encountered a number of problems, not least of which is the selection of appropriate measurement parameters. Hence in view of this situation, it seems probable that FDI theory has minimal applicability as a paradigm for explaining the export behaviour of SME sector firms (Andersen 1997).

A more popular model of internationalisation, which has been perceived as applicable to both large and small firms, is the establishment chain (or stage) model. Influential contributors to the development of this model were

Johanson and Vahlne (1977). They proposed that internationalisation is an incremental process, influenced by the rate at which firms acquire market knowledge. Thus over time, as the firm gains experience from operating in overseas markets, as described in Figure 12.1, this will influence managerial attitudes over both the degree of perceived risk and the willingness to invest in fixed assets in overseas locations.

The chain model shown in Figure 12.1 proposes that as the firm acquires overseas trading experience, this knowledge will permit the evolution of a willingness to become more deeply involved in creating permanent organisational infrastructures in overseas locations. Where the small firm has very limited knowledge, then the most appropriate operational approach is indirect exporting. This process involves a third party managing the distribution of goods or services into overseas markets. Once the small firm has acquired some knowledge of exporting, then it will probably decide to become directly involved in exporting through activities such as appointing overseas agents and/or distributors.

Licensing is a very simple, low risk way for small firms to become involved in overseas markets without making any significant new investments. For licensing to be effective, however, it is clearly necessary to structure the licence in a way that generates revenue for the licensor. The concurrent aim is to avoid the subsequent pitfall that the new knowledge acquired by the appointed licensee permits them, at a later date, to become a competitive threat.

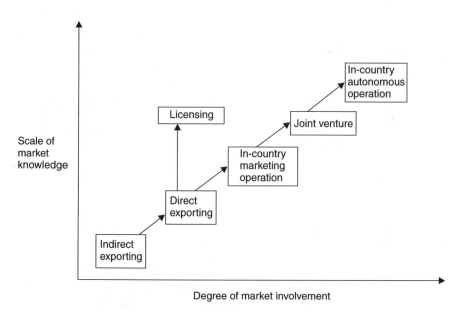

Figure 12.1   The establishment chain model of overseas market management

The next strategic step, having gained knowledge through direct exporting, is for the small firm to establish its own marketing operation within an overseas market. This usually involves investment in activities such as establishing a sales force, constructing warehouse facilities and mounting country specific advertising campaigns. If a small firm achieves major overseas sales success, it is often the case that continuing to ship product in from its domestic plant is an obstacle to profit optimisation. In this type of situation, the small firm may either enter into a joint venture with another in-country producer or invest in a new 'greenfield' production site in the overseas market.

In service markets, the inseparability of production and consumption strongly influences the marketing process. Inseparability usually necessitates that the provider and customer must be in close proximity to each other. This situation applies, for example, in the case of the delivery of services by hotels or health clubs. The implication of this situation is that many small service firms entering overseas markets are unable to consider the options of indirect or direct exporting (Ekeldo and Sivakumar 1998). Service firms' inability to engage in direct exporting means that overseas market entry will typically involve processes such as management contracts, franchising, joint ventures or investment in sole ownership assets in overseas markets.

These authors also posit that that in both service and tangible product sectors, the basic chain model often requires modification to include the impact of a number of moderating influences on the entry mode decision. One factor is the size of market. Most firms will tend to be attracted to overseas markets that offer the largest sales potential. In smaller markets, the usual entry preference of manufacturers will be exporting and that of service firms, granting franchises. Another influencing factor is the intensity of competition in overseas markets, because this is likely to impact profitability. Where profit potential appears to be limited, again manufacturers will favour exporting and service firms, franchising. A related issue is that of market entry barriers. One such barrier is the requirement that before employees can practise, they must have a qualification recognised by a national professional body inside the overseas market. Another moderating variable is political stability. Low political stability is usually assumed to increase operating risks. Here again manufacturers will probably favour exporting and service firms, granting a franchise.

EXPORT NETWORKS

Attempts to empirically validate the application of the chain model to explain actual internationalisation activities by SME sector firms have not been particularly successful. Observations of small firms reveal the existence of some fundamental, contradictory behaviour traits. None of these seem to support the view of the archetypal owner/manager being a rational, planning orientated decision maker. In the real world, owner/managers appear to approach exporting on an almost random walk basis. This is reflected by actions such as responding to an unsolicited overseas enquiry without considering the need for further market research, or selecting a market on the basis of it being somewhere the individual would like to visit. There is also the question of the timing of market entry decisions. The chain model posits that firms will not enter overseas markets until they have established a strong, secure domestic market operation. Here again exceptions emerge regarding when small firms enter overseas markets. In some cases, small firms can be found which, only a few months after business startup, initiate export activities. Alternatively some small firms, having started to export, instead of investing in consolidating the firm's position in these first markets, move to open up a whole range of new overseas opportunities.

This inability to validate rational internationalisation decision models in SME sector firms has caused researchers to revisit the issue of owner/manager market entry behaviour. Some of these researchers have drawn upon theories of social exchange and resource dependency theory to determine how inter-personal and inter-organisational relationships influence the behaviour of small firms (Johanson and Mattsson 1990). Their studies have led to the emergence of the view that internationalisation is often critically dependent upon a small firm's business and social network relationships.

These relationships can involve customers, suppliers, competitors, support agencies, families and friends. Thus, for example, in the case of a social network, a small firm's first entry into an overseas market may be because a relative living elsewhere in the world asks the owner/manager if the firm would be willing to supply a product or service that they need. A common occurrence in business networks is that the small firm is a member of a domestic network within which a major actor, such as a key customer, requests the small firm to support their international operations. An example of this situation is provided by small firms in the Nordic countries which have entered overseas markets at the request of large global customers such as ABB and Wartsila (Holmlund and Kock 1998).

EXAMPLE: CHINESE NETWORKS

In examining the behaviour of Chinese firms it is critical to recognise that cultural orientation will influence business behaviour within the SME sector (Siu 2000). Chinese owner/managers attach significant importance to traits such as doing favours for others, taking into account the view of family members when reaching a decision, and a willingness to trust those with whom the firm does business. These Confucian values, which are fundamental to the achievement of the social and business goals of being in 'harmony with others', mean that Chinese firms are naturally orientated towards operating as social and business networks.

These values, plus an orientation preference towards a cooperative business philosophy, are reflected in the behaviour of Chinese SME firms when entering overseas markets. Siu's research caused him to classify small Chinese exporting firms into three types: prospecting marketers, production marketers and partnership marketers. His study also revealed that the level of commitment to networking, although strong, varied in importance across these three types of firm.

Prospecting marketers are totally committed to networking as the basis for developing new market opportunities. Their primary orientation is towards creating and maintaining strong customer networks. Production activities are perceived as less important and in many cases, the small firm subcontracts part of the production work to other firms operated by close relatives or family.

Production marketers are firms with extensive experience in technology and engineering but often lacking the capital to fund the acquisition of raw materials or components. To overcome this problem, this type of firm will often form strong network relationships with one or more larger suppliers. Through trust built over many years between network members, the small firm is able to obtain liberal credit terms from suppliers, which permits them to fund the processes associated with fulfilling the orders placed by customers.

Partnership marketers tend to be firms that have been in business for many years and have accumulated an in-depth understanding of the product knowledge required to survive in their market sector. These firms recognise the need to continually innovate in order to respond to changing market demand. To acquire a full understanding of changing market demand, this type of firm will be a member of a network in which customers and producers work closely together in the specification and development of new products.

Another major impetus in the acceptance of networking theory as an appropriate paradigm to describe the process of internationalisation within the SME sector has been the research undertaken on market behaviour of high technology small firms. Jones (1999) notes that conventional theory of the firm proposes that in the face of internal resource constraints, small firms are unlikely to internationalise their operations except as a slow, gradual process. As this author comments, however, observation of actual practice suggests high technology firms very rapidly become involved in exporting. In some cases this occurs from the first day of business startup.

A key reason for this phenomenon is that high technology firms are operating in markets that (a) are rapidly changing and (b) where customers are willing to cross borders in their search for the best available solution. Additionally the small firm will have adopted an international orientation in order to ensure that it has access to the latest developments from around the world in the field of technology in which the firm is a participant. Cross border links established in order to access new technology may or may not then be utilised by the small firm as a path back into an overseas market.

Jones researched the nature of cross border linkage related to three types of activity: R&D, production and marketing/distribution. He concluded that it was difficult to discern any obvious pattern in the timing between company formation and the creation of overseas linkages. The data did however permit classification of small high-technology firms into the following four types:

- *Reluctant developers* have little involvement in international links and usually the primary purpose of such overseas links as they have is to import materials and new technology.
- *Conventional developers* initially formed inward procurement links and subsequently utilise this experience to sell into overseas markets.
- *Rapid developers* tend to form either inward or outward links soon after the formation of the firm and retain these same types of linkage over the longer term.
- *International entrepreneurs* form outward and inward links at the time of company formation and then sustain these multidirectional activities as the business continues to grow.

Whichever pattern of linkage is exhibited by high technology small firms, Jones found that a common pattern across many of these firms is the importance of social and business networks. The implication of this finding is that the choice of overseas markets entered during the formation of import or export links will be strongly influenced by the network with which the owner/manager has a social or business affiliation. This situation does imply, however, that there is somewhat of a fortuitous component associated with overseas activities. In some cases, links will be made with firms and countries overseas that offer access to the latest technology, whereas in other cases, membership of a network may guide the owner/manager to establish links with second rate or inappropriate import or export opportunities.

INTERNATIONAL STRATEGY

In the early 1980s, the Harvard Professor Theodore Levitt (1983) observed that world markets are converging as customers increasingly seek the same product benefits no matter in which country they are located. Factors driving convergence include the branded goods multinational operations run by major companies, world tourism, falling travel costs and access to global communications media such as satellite television and the Internet. The outcome, Levitt argued, is a convergence in customer needs and product specifications, and the adoption of common lifestyles. He proposed, therefore, that the most successful internationalisation strategy would be for the firm to seek to offer standard product propositions and marketing programmes across all markets around the world. Ohmae (1990) has expressed a similar view. He proposed that market convergence had already led to the emergence of standard customer needs across world markets. Support for this perspective is provided by the success of firms such as Microsoft, Intel, Oracle and Boeing Corporation.

Critics of the standardisation philosophy have, on the basis of their observation of real world practices, concluded that in many product categories, firms are using very different marketing strategies than those employed in their domestic operations, to sustain their position in overseas markets. A key reason for this variation in strategic behaviour is that major differences in customer needs and cultural values mandate that firms implement marketing campaigns that are reflective of variations which exist between countries around the world. Authors such as Wind (1986) have proposed, therefore, that international marketing will involve a process based upon adaptation of products and marketing strategies to reflect specific variations in market circumstance that are encountered in different markets.

In an attempt to resolve the debate over standardisation versus adaptation in international markets, Jain (1989) suggested that these two approaches are actually extremes on the same continuum. This means that firms will opt to adopt the marketing strategy most appropriate to the variations in circumstances that they encounter around the world. He posits that a more practical theory would be to assume firms adopt a contingency orientation towards strategy specification, electing to standardise or to adapt marketing programmes depending upon the circumstances encountered in an overseas market. Strategy selection will be driven by determining the most appropriate response to encountered differences in variables such as target markets, market position, the nature of the product, environmental issues and internal organisational factors.

Acceptance of Jain's contingency theory means that small firms have a number of options available to them when considering the selection of an international marketing strategy. One way of visualising these options is to assume there are two dimensions, product specification and marketing mix, either or both of which can be adapted for business operations in overseas markets. As shown in Figure 12.2, this approach generates a contingency matrix in which the firm has four alternative propositions upon which to base an international marketing strategy.

In attempting to determine the degree to which firms adapt their marketing operations in overseas markets, Cavusgil *et al.* (1993) interviewed firms in Michigan and Illinois. Although their article does not contain specific details on response in relation to the size of firm interviewed, the majority of the firms in the sample frame appear to have been drawn from the SME sector. In their study, the researchers examined product and promotional adaptation

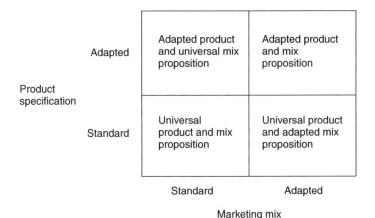

Figure 12.2   An international marketing contingency matrix

in relation to decisions made prior to market entry, and revised decisions based upon experience gained from operating in an overseas market. The interviews revealed that prior to market entry, the most important factors influencing the product adaptation decision are legal regulations, differences in culture and complexity of product technology. In the case of technology, the more complex the product, the less likely is the firm to revise its product specification from that already offered to domestic customers. Product adaptation after market entry is most influenced by the firm's acquisition of trading experience, cultural specificity of the product and intensity of competition. Promotional adaptation prior to market entry is strongly influenced by product uniqueness and the intensity of competition in overseas markets. These factors, plus acquisition of international trading experience, also influence the decision to revise promotional activity having once entered an overseas market.

The study also revealed that companies operating in consumer goods markets are more likely to modify either their product or their promotional proposition in overseas markets. Such modifications are less probable in the case of firms operating in industrial overseas markets, where greater uniformity of product and to a lesser degree, of promotional campaigns, can be expected. In those markets where the products are high technology goods, there tends to be a much higher degree of product standardisation. Hence firms in such sectors can be expected to exhibit the universal standardisation marketing strategy which Levitt posits as the future trend in the world of international marketing management.

Other researchers have undertaken subsequent studies that, in general, confirm the findings of Cavusgil *et al*. Studies that have provided empirical results on the propensity of firms to adapt distribution processes suggest that modification of this variable in response to overseas market conditions is a relatively common event. Data on adaptation of the price variable in overseas markets have produced much less conclusive results (Shoman 1999). In an attempt to examine this and other issues, Shoman undertook a study of marketing practices among manufacturing firms in Israel. The majority of firms surveyed were SME sector operations. He found that product adaptation (such as in product design, quality, supporting services and breadth of product line) enhances export performance over the longer term. This contrasts with promotional adaptation, which has both an immediate and a long term impact on export performance. In the case of price, standardisation of quoted prices, currencies used, payment security and credit terms are all likely to have a positive influence on long term performance. Shoman found, however, that contrary to the findings of other researchers, standardisation of physical distribution and channels of distribution also had a positive impact on both short and long term performance.

Lim *et al.* (1993) commented that although marketing strategy was important in the effective management of overseas markets, it is also necessary to examine strategic response in relation to the wider context of non-marketing issues such as managerial orientation, organisational flexibility, production, production technology and access to financial resources. From the results of a survey of SME manufacturing firms in Ohio, Lim *et al.* concluded that successful involvement in international operations is strongly influenced by the presence of visionary attitudes and a strong commitment to exporting among senior management. They argue that lack of vision or commitment will result in the firm being unable to overcome effectively the problems that can be encountered as an organisation moves into exporting. Other statistically significant dimensions in implementing a successful international marketing strategy are efficient production, competitive technology, and having a unique product. Another critical factor is the willingness of senior management to commit sufficient internal resources to both the formulation and implementation of the selected international marketing strategy.

One of the potential complications in researching relationships between overseas market performance and organisational strategy, however, is that the required capabilities of the firm may vary depending upon the nature of the small firm's export strategy and decisions concerning overseas market entry. To accommodate the possible interaction of variables, Julien *et al.* (1997) researched the export behaviour of small Canadian manufacturing firms in relation to the issues of:

- whether the firm is proactive or reactive;
- the complexity of the export marketing strategy (for example, whether it is based upon complex, customer specific product innovation or reliant upon a very simple action such as mounting a small scale advertising campaign);
- the degree to which the firm allocates a significant level of resources to supporting overseas marketing activities.

Respondent firms were asked to provide data on variables designed to measure the strategic and marketing dimensions of their export operations. Virtually all respondents exhibited similarities in terms of having over recent years increased production capacity, introduced technological innovation, diversified their product lines, implemented employee training programmes and invested in structured R&D activities. Analysis of the results also suggested that respondent firms could be classified into three different operational types. Type 1 firms exhibit a very strong commitment to exporting, type 2 firms an average level of commitment and type 3 firms a low level of commitment. The identified strategies and operational policies of these different types of firm were found to be as follows:

Type 1 firms have clearly defined export objectives; product attribute emphasis is on quality, design and performance; a diversified network of overseas intermediaries; adoption of a systematic overseas marketing promotional plan linked to the activities of intermediaries; pricing policy based on profit maximisation; overseas managerial operational responsibility delegated to individuals both within and outside the firm.

Type 2 firms have reasonably well defined export objectives; product attribute emphasis is on design and reliability; distribution mainly through distributors; some customisation of overseas promotional campaigns; pricing policy based on sales maximisation; some internal delegation of overseas marketing management responsibilities.

Type 3 firms have poorly defined export objectives; product attribute emphasis is on technical superiority; distribution based around selling direct to the end user customer; no specific overseas promotional campaign strategy; pricing policy based on opportunistic sales volume maximisation; owner/manager assumes responsibility for all overseas managerial activities.

Miller *et al.* (1998) have also adopted the perspective that in determining the nature of strategies utilised by successful small firm exporters, it is probable that firms can be classified into distinct groups with inter-group variance existing in terms of how export strategies are implemented. Their study focussed on the activities of small US manufacturing firms engaged in exporting products to Latin America. The rationale for focussing on one geographic market destination was that this would reduce the possible variance created by collecting data from firms operating in different overseas markets. Although this approach minimises the influence of inter-country variance, the authors note that the selection of a single geographic area might limit the degree to which their results can be generalised in terms of applicability to the export activities of small firms operating elsewhere in the world. From their study the authors were able to identify the following four types of firm:

- *Market builders* engage in a wide spectrum of activities to win business. Their strategy centres upon generating sales in an environment where foreign currency is scarce. Compensation for this constraint is achieved by relying upon political influence, creative financing, barter, countertrade, establishing an overseas manufacturing subsidiary and emphasising the sale of spare parts and repairs instead of new products. These firms are totally willing to modify any aspect of their operations such as design, manufacturing, distribution and promotion to optimise market performance.

- *Conservative order takers* focus on exploiting sales opportunities and seeking to minimise transaction costs. These firms are reactive sellers using a wide spread of activities such as promoting themselves at trade shows and appointing numerous non-exclusive distributors and agents. To protect profitability these firms tend to be somewhat inflexible when responding to requests for price discounts from customers in overseas markets.
- *Cost conscious customer accommodators* focus on accommodating customer needs whilst attempting to control operating costs. These firms endeavour to optimise both manufacturing and marketing costs and where savings are achieved, these are passed on to overseas customers in the form of lower prices. There is also a willingness to respond positively to customer requests for payment processes that find ways around the financial legislation that may exist in their respective countries.
- *Stateside marketers* who seek to maximise profitability by selling through third party export corporations based in the US. These firms utilise detailed market research activities to identify overseas market opportunities and rely upon the financial resources of the US export corporations to handle any problems caused by dealing with cash-poor customers.

EXAMPLE: B2B AN EASIER EXPORT PROPOSITION?

With the exception of consumer clothing firms such as Land's End and Eddie Bauer, few US consumer goods catalogue marketing operations have established successful, large scale export operations. This can be contrasted with the B2B sector where a much higher number of US catalogue operations have developed a significant presence in overseas markets (Dowling 2000). Examples include the office supply supplier Viking Office Products, the promotional products supplier Seton Name Plate, Henry Schen, a medical products operation, and the plumbing and electrical supplier Barnett. Entry into overseas markets is especially high in the case of B2B computer catalogue marketing operations. Examples include firms such as Systemax, Black Box and Programmer's Paradise.

The market entry strategy of B2B firms has often been to create alliances or make acquisitions. Systemax, for example, launched internationally by buying a small UK computer suppler and subsequently built a distribution centre in Scotland. Programmer's Paradise has acquired small software companies in Italy, Germany, the Netherlands and the UK. Other firms have established 'greenfield' sites in major overseas markets. Viking Office Products, for example, set up an order fulfilment operation in the UK and this approach was also adopted by Seton Name Plates.

The reason why B2B operations, when compared to consumer goods companies, face fewer problems entering overseas markets is that product demand tends to be more generic which means minimal product adaptations are required. Generic demand also makes promotional activity much easier because in most cases all that is required is to print the catalogue in different languages. Additionally in many categories, distribution is simple and more cost effective. This is because the product need tends be standardised. The outcome is that reorder frequencies are high and customers tend to order much larger quantities of product than their counterparts in consumer goods markets. Furthermore because most B2B customers know what they want, the level of product returns is relatively low.

EXPORT SUCCESS FACTORS

A number of researchers have adopted the view that to understand why some small exporting firms are more successful than others, it is necessary to identify empirically which factors are important influencers of performance in overseas markets. Katsikeas *et al.* (1997), in their study of small Canadian firms, classified organisations into the two groups 'experimental exporters' and 'active exporters'. The former group has some involvement in exporting, but activities are subservient to domestic operations with overseas sales usually being generated on a somewhat random, opportunistic basis. This contrasts with active exporters who are strongly committed to developing overseas markets and perceive exporting as an important source of future revenue. The experimental exporters believe operating overseas is a risky, uncertain activity and that ability to gain access to new markets is a critical factor influencing performance. Active exporters, presumably because of their greater experience, do not perceive exporting as an uncertain activity and think that gaining market access is not a critical issue. These latter firms place emphasis on developing internal competencies in areas such as identification of optimal opportunities, determining appropriate marketing actions and creating systems for resolving any operating problems that might arise in overseas markets.

In a very large scale research project covering both Canadian and UK small firms, Beamish *et al.* (1993) sought to determine empirically the influence on performance in overseas markets of factors such as geographic coverage, commitment to exporting, distribution selection and marketing activities. In relation to geographic coverage the study showed that small firms which operated across a number of overseas markets can be expected to outperform their counterparts which focus upon serving only one or two markets. The authors concluded that this is a reflection of an evolutionary process: as a firm gains experience in a limited number of markets, its success stimulates the owner/manager to initiate a marketing expansion programme.

In both Canada and the UK, there was a clear relationship between the level of commitment to exporting within firms and their success in overseas markets. In relation to distribution it appeared that the more successful firms are those which concentrate on developing long term relationships with members of a single channel. Analysis of marketing activities revealed that another contributor to success was the ability to offer a broad product line and, if operating across numerous markets, a willingness to modify products to suit need variation in different countries. Another important factor influencing performance is the willingness to invest in the creation of a sales force dedicated to the in-market management of overseas trading activities.

Owner/managers have an important influence over the strategic and operational decisions within most small firms. Leonidas *et al.* (1998), in a review of the literature on this subject, posit that certain characteristics of the owner/manager can be expected to be a dominant influence on achieved success in overseas markets. Included under the heading of 'general-objective' characteristics are the factors of age, educational background and work experience. The authors conclude that published studies provide inconclusive evidence about the influence of age and educational background. In relation to work experience, however, most studies have found a positive relationship between the owner/manager's having prior work experience in international business and their interest in developing overseas operations for their own firm.

Under the heading of 'specific-objective' characteristics, the authors include the factors of ethnic origin, language proficiency, time spent abroad and foreign travel. It appears that published studies on ethnic origin and foreign travel are inconclusive in terms of identifying a positive relationship between these variables and export activity. This can be contrasted with the situation with language proficiency and time spent abroad where in most studies, a positive correlation was found between both these variables and small firms' involvement in exporting. Under the heading 'general-subjective' characteristics, Leonidas *et al.* include the variables of risk tolerance, innovativeness, flexibility, commitment, and managerial dynamism. They conclude that the majority of studies have shown a positive correlation between success in export markets and the variables of a willingness to take risks, degree of innovativeness and degree of flexibility. Results concerning export success and managerial dynamism appear somewhat more inconclusive.

FIRM SIZE AND PROCESS FORMALISATION

The prevailing theory of the influence of company size on the propensity to enter overseas markets is that large firms are more likely to be involved in exporting than smaller firms. The benefits bestowed by size are assumed to include being able to exploit economies of scale to gain price based market advantage, having spare resources that can be directed towards exporting and having a greater ability to assess, manage and bear the risks of mounting international operations. In a review of the literature concerning these assumptions, Philp (1998) supports the view that possibly these large firm advantages may have been overstated. Hence in order to acquire additional understanding about this issue, this researcher studied the behaviour of both large and small firms in the Australian food and beverage processing industry.

He concluded that there were some features that distinguished small exporting enterprises from their large firm counterparts. Firstly small firm export activity is more likely to be inhibited by the lack of specific export skills and experience within the firm. Secondly some owner/managers appear to be unaware of the incremental sales and profit opportunities associated with moving into overseas markets.

Firms of any size that are major exporters exhibit a strong orientation towards being export minded. This is reflected by a strong willingness to be involved in activities such as participating in export trade shows, making overseas visits and modifying product or promotional strategies to suit the needs of overseas customers. In the specific context of export minded small firms, their owner/managers tend not to be inhibited by their firm's possible lack of exporting experience. Nor are they concerned about having to learn to cope with the complex procedures and documentation often associated with the exporting of goods.

A similar study, of how the size of firm might influence the export behaviour of firms in Norway, also concludes that the size of firm does not appear to have a major bearing on propensity to become involved in export marketing (Oysten 1999). This author's analysis of how organisations evolve their source of competitive advantage for export operations reveals variation between small and large firms. The former are more likely to focus upon exploiting advantages based upon product quality and technological superiority. Although these variables are also perceived as contributing towards market success in larger firms, these latter organisations tend to perceive that achievement of advantage should be based upon superiority of customer service and building close relationships with other members of their overseas market supply chains. Another identified difference is that larger Norwegian firms exhibit a proactive orientation towards developing overseas market opportunities. In contrast smaller firms appear to adopt a somewhat more reactive approach of not seeking out new customers. Instead they are satisfied to wait for unsolicited orders or informal contacts made by attending trade fairs.

Most marketing textbooks that contain materials on the issue of managing international operations place heavy emphasis on the need for extensive market research as an antecedent to successful entry in new overseas markets (for example, Kotler 1997). Managers are typically advised that information should be acquired on:

- *macro-environmental variables* such as economics, sociocultural conditions, politics, legislation, demographics and the physical environment;
- *market characteristics* such as size, growth rates, structure, entry conditions, customer preferences and competition;
- *marketing mix requirements* in relation to product, price, promotion and distribution.

Conventional wisdom is that small firms face a major constraint in overseas markets because they lack the resources required to fund large scale market research projects. It is also often argued that mechanisms are required to remove this constraint. Hart and Tzokas (1990), for example, support the view that 'there is a clear need to show managers that market research results in intangible benefits' and that 'this issue calls for the education of SME decision-makers on the utility of export marketing information'. Although clearly strong believers in the need for a classicist approach to international marketing, these two researchers encountered some difficulty in showing clear relationships between the commitment of SME firms to undertake form-alised, structured market research and the performance of these firms in over-seas markets. Using a positivist, survey based approach these researchers found no correlation between performance and the formal collection of data to assist market attractiveness assessment or determination of customer needs for product adaptation. Their study did show a positive correlation between company performance and acquisition of data on generic background data on economic conditions, transport and market infrastructure. These researchers also found that most SME firms adopt an informal approach to data acqui-sition. Instead of accepting the possibility that this result is indicative of a networking approach to marketing, they attribute this outcome to 'the close proximity of SMEs to their customers'.

Leonidas *et al.* (1999) used a research methodology based around in-depth interviews to gain an understanding of which types of information were perceived as important by SME exporters in Cyprus. Respondents indicated that the most important source of information was the views expressed by overseas customers on the issues of product need and terms and conditions of sale. Other information, such as sociodeomographics, political-legal issues and distribution, were all seen as relatively unimportant. The approaches used by the Cypriot exporters to acquire this information were of an unstructured, qualitative nature. The two most important information sources were meet-ing with customers in overseas markets and using contacts from within the owner/managers' social or business networks. Although these owner/managers made use of secondary information sources such as trade publications and

Government support agencies, it appeared that most firms did not feel that these types of data were of any real importance in determining their export marketing strategies.

Linked to the prescribed view that small firms must undertake formal market research studies in overseas markets is the conventional theory that the resulting data can then be used to formalise international marketing planning. Walters (1993) pointed out that within the literature there is in fact minimal empirical evidence that links success in overseas markets with the adoption of a formal marketing planning orientation by small firms. He felt that possibly planning is reflective of company size in that larger firms utilise a formalised planning approach in order to coordinate activities within multi-layered, departmentally structured organisations. To test this hypothesis he researched export planning activities in US companies. His study supported the hypothesis that large firms are more likely to adopt a classicist planning approach and that export planning in smaller firms is usually a more informal process. Interestingly, however, he could prove no correlation between the adoption of a planning orientated philosophy and the performance of firms.

Where a positive correlation did emerge was in the degree to which involvement in exporting influences the planning orientation. In those firms where exports are the predominant source of all sales revenues and the firm operates in numerous overseas markets, there was evidence to suggest that overseas market performance is enhanced by the adoption of a planning orientation. Walters feels that this is reflective of the fact that where firms are active in numerous overseas markets, these firms use the planning process to coordinate the complexity of activities associated with a multi-market operation. In view of these findings, he concludes that for many exporters 'formal planning may be primarily the result rather than the cause of high export intensity'. Furthermore the research indicated that some respondent firms which do not use marketing planning reported a high level of success in overseas markets. These data cause Walters to posit the view that 'Successful non-planners who are able to make good decisions on the basis of intuitive and informally acquired information are best placed to exploit market opportunities. Firms able to react rapidly and decisively in export markets can be expected to enjoy advantage over competing firms, and this should result in superior profit and sales performance.'

Miller *et al.* (1998) subsequently expressed very similar opinions about the debate concerning how important marketing planning is. Their conclusion from a study of highly successful SME exporters was that formalised, planned and informal, unplanned approaches to international marketing can both be effective. In their opinion the degree of planning that is undertaken is not a key issue. They believe that the what is important for the exporting firm is to adopt an approach that ensures the firm's operations are compatible with the operating environments encountered in overseas markets.

GAINING OWNERSHIP OF FUTURES

Researchers of globally successful firms, Hamel and Prahalad (1994), have concluded that market leadership can only come from 'seeing the future' and ensuring ownership of this future ahead of competition. They propose that in existing markets this is probably achieved by seeing the future and then changing the rules. The alternative is to see the future and invent new markets. Hamel and Prahalad believe successful global players tend to exhibit the characteristics of:

* having infinite curiosity and being prepared to take on apparently impossible challenges;
* never being satisfied with their achievements, and reinvesting profits in new products and/or process innovation;
* always being open minded and willing to learn from any source.

The next step in crafting the future is to recognise that that a small firm's current market vision usually only represents the 'tip of the demand iceberg'. Imagine the vast new range of opportunities available if the owner/manager does not limit thinking to merely extending known satisfaction into new markets, but is prepared to probe the issue of what forms of satisfaction have not yet even been recognised by the customer.

In some cases an examination of the 'prevailing rules of the game' may stimulate identification of a new global vision that can permit a new small firm to successfully challenge large firm incumbents. This approach has been extensively studied by Slywotzky (1996). One case he presents is that of the US steel industry which by the mid 1960s owned vertically integrated plants generating huge revenue flows. By the 1970s, these American corporates faced the threat that through massive investment, the Japanese producers had expanded output to the point where their share of the market was almost equal to that of the US producers. One individual, Kenneth Iverson of Nucor Corporation, then developed a new vision. Why not use scrap steel as a raw material instead of iron ore, build small, low cost, highly flexible factories located near to customers, and offer low cost steel using a JIT philosophy? From this vision emerged a whole new industry know as 'mini-mills'. Importantly Iverson is not an individual who believes in a single vision. He recognised that competition from other mini-mills would eventually threaten his business. So in the late 1980s, Nucor took the high risk strategy of building a 'state of the art' thin strip continuous casting plant in Indiana which permitted the firm to move into flat rolled steel for use in appliance and automobile manufacturing.

Another perspective on effective visioning is provided by Christensen's (1997) analysis of the emergence of new technologies within industrial sectors.

He posits that it is rarely the case that large firms actually miss the opportunities offered by new technologies. Instead what happens is their existing customers continue to demand that they improve current products and that consequently, new opportunities are left to be exploited by new market players. His analysis of the computer disk drive market shows how in the 1960s, mainframe computer customers demanded greater capacity from producers of 14" drives. The first generation of smaller, 8", drives lacked capacity and were ignored by the large hardware firms. New smaller firms entered the market. They recognised that the producers of minicomputers were the real source of opportunity for 8" drives. Then along came the 5.25" drive and history repeated itself. In this case the minicomputer firms were not interested. Thus a new generation of small firms marketed their smaller 5.25" drives to PC manufacturers. Having become the dominant players, they in turn were replaced by producers of 3.5" drives. This new group of small firms were successful because they targeted their marketing, not at the major PC manufacturers, but at those who were producing the first generations of laptop computers.

SMALL FIRMS AND THE BORDERLESS WORLD

Many of the managerial experiences that underpin the basic theories of international marketing were evolved during the Cold War. In those days the world was divided into two distinctly separate trading blocks, the communist and non-communist nations. The non-communist nations often sought to protect their domestic industries through policies such as tariff barriers, import taxes and public sector organisations only procuring goods and services from domestic suppliers. In view of this economic heritage, it is perhaps understandable that even to this day, some marketing literature still tends to concentrate on managing foreign customer behaviours and the environmental constraints which firms can expect to encounter as they move into new overseas markets.

By the 1970s, the European nations had already begun to realise the economic disadvantages of continuing to retain economic independence. Their solution was the creation of the European Common Market, subsequently renamed the European Union (EU). Similar actions have occurred elsewhere in the world. Examples include NAFTA, the Canada, America and Mexico North American free trade area, APEC, a forum of 18 Asia Pacific nations, and Mercosur, a regional cooperative trade agreement between Brazil, Argentina, Paraguay and Uruguay. Concurrent with these actions to create regions of free trade, the other major impact on the global economy has been the post-*perestroika* dissolution of the USSR. In turn this has been followed by other communist nations such as China opening up their borders to overseas investors.

The removal of trade barriers and convergence in demand for the same lifestyle goods mean that all firms need to recognise the validity of Ohmae's (1990) claim that we now live in a 'borderless world'. Thus it is no longer safe for smaller firms to restrict activities to serving only domestic markets, while concurrently assuming that overseas marketing can safely remain the preserve of large multinational corporations. If a 'blinkered' attitude is exhibited by small firms, they will be unable to learn first hand of changes in customer behaviour which are occurring around the world. They will then be ill equipped to respond to new sources of competition that will inevitably occur as overseas suppliers enter their domestic markets.

Some useful insights on responding to a changing world order are provided in reports issued by the New Zealand trade export support service, Tradenz. The New Zealand economy is essentially constituted of numerous small firms. Hence assisting this sector of the economy develop the capability to expand into new overseas markets has been a prime objective of this Government agency. One key phase in its programmes was the research undertaken by Val Lindsey at the University of Auckland to understand the factors influencing the success of manufacturing firms operating in markets outside of New Zealand (Tradenz 1990). This study posited a profit life cycle through which most firms will pass during their journey towards achieving dominance of global market niches. Phase 1 of the cycle is where the firm first enters world markets and, because it still lacks many of the operational features of world class firms, profits are eroded. This failure demands a period of retrenchment, rethinking and replanning of international marketing activities. The firm having invested in an organisational development programme in order to begin to acquire world class capabilities, phase 2 of the cycle is a period during which profit growth ensues. Unfortunately continued success often leads to entry into phase 3 of the cycle, where profits again downturn because the firm lacks sufficient human, financial and/or production resources to become a dominant player in world markets. At this stage, some firms are forced to retrench; whereas others acquire a new injection of equity based capital to fund the restructuring necessary to create a truly world class organisation.

Tradenz also recognised that in addition to firms needing to understand the characteristics exhibited by world class marketing operations, the management of such firms will also need to comprehend and effectively respond to the environments likely to prevail in world markets in the 21st century. Tradenz's strategic development director, David Espie, therefore crafted a guidance document in which he presents a fascinating view of a changing world (Tradenz 1997). The organisation's view is that the forces of openness which have created a borderless world mean that opportunities for growth from expanded global marketing activities are almost infinite, even for SME sector firms. It highlights, for example, the opportunities available as China moves to establish a developed nation economy and from India's recent moves to create a more outward looking economy. Linked to this scenario, it points to Akamatsu's (1990) 'flying geese' pattern of industrial development in which nations move from labour intensive production towards the creation of automated, capital intensive industries. It is argued that if the existing developed nations act to assist these flying geese, they will find major new market opportunities in developing economies for their knowledge based industries such as computing and automated manufacturing tools.

The Tradenz study also emphasises the importance of not just relying on carefully crafted plans based upon detailed research, but also of being willing to rapidly respond to non-forecastable, unexpected 'wild card' events. This philosophy is illustrated by the New Zealand Carter Hot Harvey Roofing Company. During a bush fire in California, the only home in the fire zone that survived was the one which had a roof made from the company's fire resistant Decra Tile. By exploiting the dramatic evidence provided by aerial photographs of this and other natural disasters, the firm has been able to gain global awareness of the ability of their product to protect homes during events such as forest fires and earthquakes.

Another aspect of the Tradenz study was to note that actual manufacturing of goods and/or the production of core services is increasingly becoming a smaller and smaller component of overall product costs. This is especially the case if globalisation permits the standardisation of output. Alternatively modern process technologies permit producers to experiment concurrently with adding value by customising output to suit individual customer needs. Hence small firms are advised to 'think global, but respond locally'. This can be achieved by exploiting the power of computerised databases to rapidly identify newly emerging micro-market niches and to respond with appropriately tailored products or services. The small firm will also have to be increasingly vigilant about changing power bases within its marketing channels. Traditional end user outlets may be replaced by new market entrants such an online cyberspace retail operations. Component suppliers may find their horizons about their manufacturer customer base have to widen to encompass the new manufacturers in countries such as India and Brazil.

The final issue covered in the Tradenz report is the impact of what it calls 'electronic connectedness', which demands that firms recognise the growing importance of technologies such as EDI, the Internet and videoconferencing for communicating with others in their sector's supplier-customer chain. In an electronically interlinked borderless world, only if firms desire to sink into oblivion should they resist adopting innovations such as website home pages with 'hot buttons' to be used by customers seeking more information, comparing offerings, placing orders and/or seeking post-purchase services from their suppliers.

EXAMPLE: MICRO-EXPORTING

The advent of auction websites such as www.e-Bay.com has created a whole new market opportunity for small micro-businesses, often run by a single person. Many of these micro-firms are started by amateur collectors. These individuals have realised they can translate their hobby into a business by using auction sites to sell items such as stamps, coins and baseball cards. Operating with virtually no overheads and minimal inventory, the only significant cost if they use the eBay site is a listing charge plus, if the item is sold, a percentage of the sale price (Freedman 2000).

The Internet is recognised as an effective vehicle for small firms to acquire a global presence. What is only now beginning to be recognised is that by using online auctions, even micro-enterprises can generate export sales. For example, Grandwatches is a one person business run by Omar Nuno. He is a fulltime Medicare claims processor by day, and at night spends his time trading in cyberspace. His product is brand name watches, which he sells at one to two per cent above cost. These razor thin margins are only feasible because he has virtually no operating costs. His operation attracts customers from countries as far apart as Belgium and Japan.

Another example is Ed Ciliberti, a real estate broker based in California. Three years ago, as a hobby, he opened a booth in an antiques mall. Sales and profits were somewhat low. Then in 1999 he decided to move into the global marketplace by listing his products on the eBay site. In three months he earned $30 000 on sales of $70 000. An antique peanut roaster he purchased for $250 and could not sell at the mall went for $2950 on eBay. His success in this borderless, electronic world is such that he now spends 60 hours a week running his online operation and has cut back his real estate activities to only 15 hours a week.

The access to a global world offered by online auctions has not, however, gone totally unnoticed by existing terrestrial small businesses. Veloso is a retail business opened eight years ago to sell sports cards from a retail outlet in Natick, Mass., USA. Sales were reasonable but when two years ago the founder Marcello Velos started trading through eBay, the business really took off. Marcello still runs his retail outlet, but mainly because it provides a convenient location for storing inventory and shipping product.

DISCUSSION QUESTIONS

1. Review the various theories which have been posited concerning the processes associated with firms entering overseas markets.
2. Discuss the factors likely to influence the success of firms in overseas markets.

3. Review how actual behaviour of small firms in overseas markets seems at odds with conventional international marketing management wisdom.

REFERENCES

Andersen, O. (1997), 'Internationalisation and market entry modes: A review of theories and conceptual frameworks', *Management International Review*, Vol. 37, No. 2, pp. 27–42.

Akamatsu, K. (1990), *Flock Formation of Flying Geese Patterns of Industrial Development, Economic Development and International Trade: the Japanese Model*, translated and revised by Yamazawa, I., Resource Systems Institute East-West Centre, Honolulu, Hawaii.

Beamish, P.W., Craig, R. and McLellan, K. (1993), 'The performance characteristics of Canadian versus UK exporters', *Management International Review*, Vol. 33, No. 2, pp. 121–34.

Cavusgil, S.T., Zou, S. and Naidu, G.U. (1993), 'Product and promotion adaptation in export ventures', *Journal of International Business Studies*, Vol. 24, No. 3, pp. 479–501.

Christensen, C.M. (1997), *The Innovator's Dilemma: When New Technologies Cause Great Firms to Fail*, Harvard Business School Press, Boston, Mass.

Coviello, N.E. and McCauley, A. (1999), 'Internationalisation and the smaller firm: A review of contemporary empirical research', *Management International Review*, Vol. 39, No. 3, pp. 223–56.

Dowling, M. (2000), 'Why B-to-B succeeds overseas', *Catalog Age*, May, pp. 87–90.

Ekeldo, I. And Sivakumar, K. (1998), 'Foreign market entry mode choice of service firms: A contingency perspective', *Academy of Marketing Science*, Vol. 26, Vol. 4, pp. 274–92.

Freedman, D.H. (2000), 'Can you survice the eBay economy?' *Inc*, Boston, March, pp. 88–95.

Hamel, G. and Prahalad, C.K. (1994), *Competing for the Future*, Harvard Business School Press, Boston, Mass.

Hart, S. and Tzokas, N. (1999), 'The impact of marketing research on SME export performance', *Journal of Small Business Management*, Vol. 37, No. 2, pp. 63–75.

Holmlund, M. and Kock, S. (1998), 'Relationships and the internationalisation of Finnish SME companies', *International Small Business Journal*, Vol. 16, No. 4, pp. 46–63.

Jain, S.C. (1989), 'Standardisation of international marketing strategy: Some research hypotheses', *Journal of Marketing*, Vol. 53, pp. 70–9.

Johanson, J. and Mattsson, L.G. (1990), 'Internationalisation in industrial markets: A network approach', In Ford, D. (ed.), *Understanding Business Markets: Interaction, Relationships and Networks*, Academic Press, London, pp. 468–86.

Johanson, J. and Vahlne, J.E. (1977), 'The internationalisation process of the firm: A model of knowledge development and increasing market commitment', *Journal of International Business Studies*, Vol. 8, No. 1, pp. 22–32.

Jones, M.V. (1999), 'The internationalisation of small high-technology firms', *Journal of International Marketing*, Vol. 7, No. 4, pp. 15–41.

Julien, P., Joyal, A., Deshaies, L. and Ramangalahy, C. (1997), 'A typology of behaviour among small and medium-sized exporting businesses', *International Small Business Journal*, Vol. 15, No. 2, pp. 33–50.

Katsikeas, C., Deng, S.L. and Wortzel, L.H. (1997), 'Perceived export success factors of small and medium-sized Canadian firms', *Journal of International Marketing*, Vol. 5, No. 4, pp. 53–72.

Kotler, P. (1997), *Marketing Management, Planning, Implementation and Control*, eighth edn, Prentice-Hall, London.

Leonidas, C.L., Leonidas, S.K. and Piercy, N.F. (1998), 'Identifying managerial influences on exporting: Past research and future directions', *Journal of International Marketing*, Vol. 6, No. 2, pp. 74–102.

Leonidas, C.L., Leonidas, S.K. and Adams-Florou, A.S. (1999), 'Types and sources of export information', *International Small Business Journal*, Vol. 17, No. 3, pp. 30–48.

Levitt, T. (1983), 'The globalisation of markets', *Harvard Business Review*, May–June, pp. 92–102.

Lim, J., Sharkey, T.W. and Kim, K.I. (1993), 'Determinants of international marketing strategy', *Management International Review*, Vol. 33, No. 2, pp. 103–22.

Miller, V., Becker, T. and Crespy, C. (1998), 'The strategies of excellent manufacturing exporters', *International Journal of Commerce & Management*, Vol. 8, No. 3, pp. 41–70.

Ohmae, K. (1990), *The Borderless World: Management Lessons in the New Logic of the Global Market*, Collins, London.

Oysten, M. (1999), 'The relationship between firm size, competitive advantage and export performance revisited', *International Small Business Journal*, Vol. 18, No. 1, pp. 53–72.

Philp, N. (1998), 'The export propensity of the very small enterprise', *International Small Business Journal*, Vol. 16, No. 4, pp. 79–93.

Shoman, A. (1999), 'Bounded rationaility, planning, standardisation of international strategy and export performance', *Journal of International Marketing*, Vol. 7, No. 2, pp. 24–50.

Siu, W. (2000), 'Marketing philosophies and company performance of Chinese small firms in Hong Kong', *Journal of Marketing Theory and Practice*, Vol. 8, No. 1, pp. 25–37.

Slywotzky, A.J. (1996), *Value Migration: How to Think Several Moves Ahead of the Competition*, Harvard Business School Press, Boston, Mass.

Tradenz, (1990), *Export Manufacturing – Framework for Success*, Tradenz, Wellington.

Tradenz, (1997), *Competing in the New Millennium*, Tradenz, New Zealand.

Walters, G.P. (1993), 'Patterns of formal planning and performance in US exporting', *Management International Review*, Vol. 33, No. 4, pp. 43–61.

Wind, Y. (1986), 'The myth of globalisation', *Journal of Consumer Marketing*, Vol. 3, pp. 23–6.

INDEX